Collins
BIG CAT

Guided Reading Handbook

Complete teaching and assessment support

Blue

Green

Orange

Turquoise

Series Editor: Gill Matthews

HarperCollins
P U B L I S H E R S
Since 1817

William Collins' dream of knowledge for all began with the publication of his first book in 1819.

A self-educated mill worker, he not only enriched millions of lives, but also founded a flourishing publishing house. Today, staying true to this spirit, Collins books are packed with inspiration, innovation and practical expertise. They place you at the centre of a world of possibility and give you exactly what you need to explore it.

Collins. Freedom to teach.

Published by Collins
An imprint of HarperCollins*Publishers*
The News Building
1 London Bridge Street
London
SE1 9GF

Browse the complete Collins catalogue at
www.collins.co.uk

10 9 8 7 6 5 4 3 2 1

ISBN 978-0-00-825185-7

British Library Cataloguing in Publication Data
A catalogue record for this publication is available from the British Library.

Authors: Catherine Casey, Emma Caulfield, Gill Matthews, Liz Miles

Series editor: Gill Matthews

Commissioning editor: Sarah Thomas

In-house editor: Natasha Paul

Development editor: Karen Williams

Copyeditor: Sally Byford

Proofreader: Jennifer Steele

Cover design: 2hoots Publishing Services Ltd

Cover artwork: © 2011 Charlotte Middleton

Typesetter: 2hoots Publishing Services Ltd

Artwork: Kasia Dudziuk, Ellie O'Shea and Erica Salcedo, Advocate Art

Production controller: Sarah Burke

Printed and bound by CPI Group (UK) Ltd, Croydon, CR0 4YY

Collins would like to thank the teachers and children at the following schools who took part in the development of Collins Big Cat Guided Reading Handbooks: East Oxford Primary School; Albert Pritchard Infant School, Wednesbury; Frederick Bird School, Coventry; Westrop Primary, Swindon.

Contents

Free downloads of editable lesson plans, resources and assessments are available at www.collins.co.uk/CBC_GRHB

Introduction

Guided reading has been a valuable teaching strategy in schools for over 20 years. Initially, it was introduced as a somewhat rigid practice in terms of organisation and approach but, over time, the strategy has been adapted and tailored to meet the needs of individual schools and children. However, in the light of the 2014 curriculum and associated expectations, many schools are reviewing how guided reading is used and the impact it can have on teaching and learning. *Collins Big Cat Guided Reading* supports schools in refreshing their use of guided reading, and it supports teachers in running successful, engaging guided reading sessions.

As a literacy consultant, I have worked with many schools looking at the teaching of reading and I've seen some very effective guided reading sessions. They haven't always looked like, or even sounded like, 'traditional' guided reading but the teacher has taught and the children have been engaged and, above all, have learned. As Series Editor of *Collins Big Cat Guided Reading Handbooks*, I've tried to capture what's best from all of that practice and distil it. My aim has been to create units around each Big Cat book that focus on two key elements: teaching and learning. This may sound obvious but they can be overlooked in the scramble for evidence of attainment. So, within each unit, you will find focused teaching of both decoding and specific higher order reading skills, along with opportunities for children to practise and consolidate those skills in a supportive group environment.

One issue that has really come to the fore in recent years is a concern over children's limited language and lack of understanding of vocabulary. I don't know if children's vocabulary is any poorer than it was 10 or 20 years ago but I do know that everyone's vocabulary is enriched through talking and reading. So, built into every unit, there is a vocabulary boost session, based on the approach outlined in *Bringing Words to Life* by Beck *et al.*, published by The Guilford Press 2013. Each vocabulary boost session focuses on three focus words that emerge from the Big Cat book: words that will enhance and enrich the children's understanding of what they read. The children are introduced to the words, carry out word-related activities and are encouraged to use them in other contexts. Just imagine – if we give children three new words per week, say 36 per term, around 110 per year – that's more than 200 new words across the two years of Key Stage 1! And that's just through guided reading – there's nothing to stop you carrying on boosting vocabulary at other times and in other subjects.

The elephant in the guided reading room has always been independent work. One question that I'm asked more than any other is 'What can I give my independent groups to do that they can get on with, that isn't low level, keeping them occupied kind of stuff, but that is worthwhile?' Alongside the guided reading materials, there are suggestions for independent sessions that build on the content of each book. I firmly believe that we need to give children opportunities to work independently in order for them to become independent learners, but these activities need to be purposeful.

Having read my way through the Big Cat series, I feel that the range and quality of books make it ideal for use as a guided reading programme: the lively content engages the children; the skilled writing supports the teaching of the higher order reading skills and the richness of the language lends itself to boosting children's vocabulary. Above all, the books encourage readers to revisit and enjoy the reading experience.

Bearing that in mind, I'd like to say thank you to my fellow authors: for bringing your vast experience, knowledge and enthusiasm to *Collins Big Cat Guided Reading Handbooks*. I think we've created a resource that places quality guided reading at the heart of the reading curriculum and that promotes reading in a positive light.

Gill Matthews

How to use this book

This handbook focuses on the Blue to Turquoise bands of Big Cat which, broadly speaking, equate to national expectations at Year 1. It is entirely up to you which order children experience the books within each band. You might want to spend time developing children's understanding of non-fiction and concentrate on a selection of those titles. Or, you could give children the option to choose which book they would like to read. Whatever you decide to do, you will find comprehensive notes and a bank of Resource sheets to support your teaching.

The units

Books in the Blue to Turquoise bands are an ideal length for reading in one guided reading session. In order to maximise the use of the books and to make sure that the children's reading experience is a fulfilling one, each unit offers two adult-led sessions and guidance for a series of independent sessions. The units start with a guided reading session to enable the teacher to introduce the book and the skills that the children will use in the guided session and the later independent sessions. This is then followed up with a vocabulary boost session.

The skills focus

Five of the seven key skills taught through the units are taken from the National Curriculum. The remaining two skills, fundamental to producing well-rounded readers, are: 'check reading makes sense' and 'read words accurately and fluently'.

To support focused teaching, a maximum of four skills are addressed in each unit.

- Draw on knowledge of vocabulary to understand texts
- Identify/explain key aspects of fiction & non-fiction texts, e.g. character, events, title
- Identify/explain the sequence of events in texts
- Make inferences from texts
- Predict what might happen on the basis of what has been read so far
- Check reading makes sense
- Read words accurately and fluently

The skills of collaborative working and discussion through paired and group activities are integrated into every unit and, underpinning it all, is the constant portrayal of reading in a positive light.

The guided reading sessions

Guided reading gives the opportunity to focus on a group of five or six children who have similar needs and are of a similar reading ability. In Year 1, a guided reading session could last around 20 minutes. The session starts with 'Tune in' – a whole group introduction in which the teacher focuses on, and demonstrates, the particular skills to be taught. This is followed by 'Heads together' when children are given the opportunity to put those skills into practice, either working individually, with their Reading Partner, or as a group. During this part of the guided reading session, the teacher has the opportunity to observe and listen to the children. In both the 'Tune in' and 'Heads together' sections of the lessons, specific, targeted questions are given, along with expected answers, for the teacher to ask. Finally, 'Wrap up' gives the group the chance to review the activity and reflect on their learning. Throughout the session, discussion and reflection are actively encouraged.

The vocabulary boost sessions

These sessions are also designed to last around 20 minutes. The objective of the sessions is to build children's vocabulary through discussion and exploration of specific focus words based on concepts in the books. The focus words are either taken directly from, or build on words in, the book. They are words that will develop and enhance children's understanding when they read.

In 'Tune in', the teacher introduces the focus words, giving child-friendly definitions and using the focus words in example sentences that show the words in different contexts. As the session moves into 'Heads together', the children explore the focus words to develop and embed a deeper understanding of the words' meanings and how they can be used in different sentences and contexts. This is done through engaging, interactive oral activities. The session ends with 'Wrap up', generally a group discussion in which the teacher checks understanding. Often, the children are asked to choose one or more of the focus words as their words of the week and to use them as frequently as they can – both at home and at school.

The independent sessions

The independent sessions support and encourage individual, paired and group activities based on the books. They build on the key skills taught in the guided reading and vocabulary boost sessions and involve the children in hands on, oral and, where appropriate, written responses.

The assessment units

Eight books per band have been identified as texts that can be used for assessment as well as for teaching the focus skills. These provide teachers with a set of clear assessment sheets to regularly monitor children's progress in the key skills and support them in identifying books which will give children further practice of the skills. For each assessment text, there is a photocopiable sheet with a set of five questions designed to support summative assessment of the focus skills. You might want children to answer all five questions, or you can edit the question sheet so that there is a particular skills focus to the assessment.

Once you have determined if there are particular skills which the children need to spend more time on, use the skills coverage grids on pages 8 to 11 to identify books that focus on these particular skills.

The resource sheets

Resource sheets are provided to support purposeful independent activities. All of the Resource sheets are are available as digital downloads on www.collins.co.uk and can be edited should you decide to amend them to suit a particular purpose, scenario or child.

Skills coverage grid

Blue lesson plans

	Draw on knowledge of vocabulary to understand texts	Identify/explain key aspects of fiction & non-fiction texts, e.g. character, events, title	Identify/explain the sequence of events in texts	Make inferences from texts	Predict what might happen on the basis of what has been read so far	Check reading makes sense	Read words accurately and fluently
Top Dinosaurs	x	x		x			x
Talk Talk Talk	x		x	x			x
Mojo and Weeza and the Funny Thing	x			x	x		x
Funny Fish	x	x			x		x
Bert's Band	x		x		x		x
Robots	x	x	x			x	
The Fantastic Flying Squirrel	x	x		x			x
Sounds	x	x					x
Percy and the Badger	x	x	x			x	
What's Underground?	x	x	x			x	
Colours	x			x	x		x
Harry's Garden	x	x	x			x	
The Mermaid and the Octopus	x			x	x	x	
The Steam Train	x	x			x		x
Blast Off to the Moon!	x	x		x			x
The Lonely Penguin	x			x	x		x
Tod and the Trumpet	x		x	x			x
Growing and Changing	x	x				x	
New from Old: Recycling Plastic	x	x		x			x
Super Sam	x	x			x		x
Let's Build a Rocket	x		x		x		x
Going to the Zoo	x		x				x
Wait and See!	x			x	x		x
Knock! Knock!	x	x			x		x
It's Great to Be Small!	x	x		x			
The Prince and the Parsnip	x			x	x		x
Animals in Hiding	x	x		x			x
Arctic Life	x	x				x	
Fishy Friends	x	x			x		x
Mojo and Weeza and the New Hat	x	x		x			x

Green lesson plans

	Draw on knowledge of vocabulary to understand texts	Identify/explain key aspects of fiction & non-fiction texts, e.g. character, events, title	Identify/explain the sequence of events in texts	Make inferences from texts	Predict what might happen on the basis of what has been read so far	Check reading makes sense	Read words accurately and fluently
The Magic Pen	x		x		x		x
Spines, Stings and Teeth	x	x	x				x
I Want a Pet!	x	x		x			x
Worm Looks for Lunch	x	x	x				x
A Day at the Eden Project	x	x	x			x	
Big Cat Babies	x	x	x			x	
Nick Butterworth: Making Books	x	x		x			x
Jodie the Juggler	x	x			x		x
Crunch and Munch	x	x	x				x
Ella the Superstar	x			x	x	x	x
Scary Hair	x		x	x			x
Super Sculptures	x	x				x	
Too Hot to Stop!	x	x			x		x
I've Just Had a Bright Idea!	x	x			x	x	
Olympic Heroes	x	x		x			x
Seahorses	x	x					x
Wellies	x		x		x	x	
The King of the Forest	x		x	x			x
Wild Dog in the City	x	x		x			x
How the Elephant Got His trunk	x			x		x	
One Potato	x			x	x		x
Happy New Year	x	x		x		x	

Orange lesson plans

	Draw on knowledge of vocabulary to understand texts	Identify/explain key aspects of fiction & non-fiction texts, e.g. character, events, title	Identify/explain the sequence of events in texts	Make inferences from texts	Predict what might happen on the basis of what has been read so far	Check reading makes sense	Read words accurately and fluently
Kind Emma	x		x		x		x
The Brave Baby	x			x	x	x	
Arthur's Fantastic Party	x		x	x			x
Morris Plays Hide and Seek	x			x	x	x	
How to Make Pop-up Cards	x	x	x			x	
Bounce Kick Catch Throw	x	x	x				x
Fire! Fire!	x	x		x			x
A Letter to New Zealand	x	x	x			x	
First Day	x		x		x	x	
What is CGI?	x	x	x				x
When Arthur Wouldn't Sleep	x			x	x		x
Marathon	x	x					x
Bugs!	x	x	x				x
A Day in India	x	x	x			x	
The Titanic	x	x	x				x
Pompeii The Lost City	x	x				x	
Lost Sock	x			x	x	x	
Clementine's Smile	x			x	x		x
Slumbery Stumble in the Jungle	x			x	x		x
Turtle's Party in the Clouds	x			x	x	x	
The Gardening Year	x	x	x				x
Holidays: Then and Now	x	x		x		x	

Turquoise lesson plans

	Draw on knowledge of vocabulary to understand texts	Identify/explain key aspects of fiction & non-fiction texts, e.g. character, events, title	Identify/explain the sequence of events in texts	Make inferences from texts	Predict what might happen on the basis of what has been read so far	Check reading makes sense	Read words accurately and fluently
The Bogeyman	x	x		x		x	
Castles	x	x	x			x	
Horses' Holiday	x		x	x			x
Good Fun Farm	x			x		x	
The Stone Cutter	x		x		x		x
Harry the Clever Spider	x			x	x		x
Fly Facts	x	x	x				x
How to Make Storybooks	x	x	x				x
A Visit to the Farm	x	x	x			x	
Harry the Clever Spider at School	x		x	x			x
Going Fast	x	x		x			x
Chewy Hughie	x			x	x		x
Africa's Big Three	x	x	x			x	
Going for a Drive	x	x		x			x
What's that Building?	x	x		x			x
The Journey of Humpback Whales	x	x	x			x	
The Lost Village of Skara Brae	x	x		x			x
Brown Bear and Wilbur Wolf	x		x	x			x
The Big, Bad City	x			x	x		x
Homes Sweet Homes	x			x		x	
From Tree to Book	x	x	x				x
Landmarks of the World	x	x		x			x

Glossary of strategies

These strategies are used in the units to teach and develop the key skills. Some will be familiar to you while others may be new. Rather than explaining the strategies every time they are used in the units, they are described in detail below.

Hot-seating

Use to explore and develop children's responses to, and understanding of, characters.

- Ask a volunteer to take on the role of a character, or the teacher takes on the role to model the process.
- The rest of the group ask questions of the character, exploring why they said/behaved in a certain way, or how they felt about other characters and events.
- Some children may need the support of question cards, for example, 'when', 'how' and 'why', in order to broaden the range of questions they ask.

Modelled reading

Use to demonstrate how to decode words and to build up to reading with fluency and expression.

- Teacher reads aloud, using appropriate decoding strategies.
- Model how to use punctuation to help pace the reading and how to use vocabulary meaning to add expression.

Role on the wall

Use to explore and develop children's responses to, and understanding of, characters.

- After reading, use a Role on the wall Resource sheet to record observations about a character.
- Record the character's external features around the outside of the outline, for example, appearance, appropriate speech and movement verbs.
- Record internal features inside the outline, for example, their personality, feelings, behaviour.

Story maps

Use to develop understanding of story structure and to summarise main events.

- Children draw pictures to represent the key events in a story.
- They use their story maps to support an oral retelling of the story.

Vocabulary boost activities

Use to develop and build vocabulary knowledge.

- *I say… You say…* Children are given a word and asked to repeat it or give the definition.
- *Sentence completion* Children are given sentence stems or sentences with words missing and they choose from the focus words to complete the sentences.
- *Show me* Children act out, create an image or develop a sound effect to represent or demonstrate a focus word.
- *Tell me* Children are given a series of statements, each of which starts with 'Tell me…', that invite them to say something about one of the focus words. It could be an experience, an idea or a question.
- *Word families or Word patterns* Children are given collections of words and asked to sort them into groups according to a connection between them.
- *Would you rather…?* Children are given two scenarios that use the focus words. They are then asked to identify which scenario they would choose and why.
- *Yes/no game* Children are given sentences and asked to think about a particular aspect of the sentence, for example, does it make sense? Do you agree with this? The children answer with either 'yes' or 'no'.

Lesson plans

Top Dinosaurs

Book Band: Blue

This information book looks at five different dinosaurs and explores their contrasting characteristics.

Skills focus

- Draw on knowledge of vocabulary to understand texts
- Identify/explain key aspects of fiction and non-fiction texts, e.g. character, events, title
- Make inferences from texts
- Check reading makes sense

Guided reading session

You will need
- Multiple copies of Collins Big Cat *Top Dinosaurs*
- A tub of plastic dinosaurs for sorting (different colours and sizes)

Tune in

Pour a tub of plastic dinosaurs on to the table. Can the children sort the dinosaurs in different ways (for example, by size, by colour)? Explain that there were lots of different types of dinosaurs. Tell the children that you are all going to read a book about some dinosaurs now. It is an information book.

Begin by looking at the back cover. Model reading the title. Read the blurb. Ask children to find and point to any high frequency words they know ('some', 'were', 'out'). Look at the pictures on the back cover.

Ask the following questions:
- Which dinosaur is tall?
- Which one is small?
- Which one do you think is scary?

Turn to the front cover.

Ask the following questions:
- Does anyone know what type of dinosaur this is? *(Tyrannosaurus rex)*
- Can you describe the dinosaur? What does it look like?
- What do you think its skin would feel like?

Give the children an opportunity to share any knowledge about dinosaurs. Do they know any stories about dinosaurs?

Look at the contents page. Explain that information books often have a contents page. It is a list of the headings in the book and what page they are on. A 'heading' is the title of the page. Read the contents together. Explain that they are names of dinosaurs.

Ask the following questions:
- On what page can we learn about Velociraptors? *(page 10)*
- On what page can we find out about the Brachiosaurus? *(page 6)*

Look at how to pronounce the dinosaur names at the top of each double-page spread.

Heads together

Ask children to look at pages 2 and 3 together.

Ask the following questions:
- Do you know any of the dinosaurs on these pages?
- Which dinosaur is the smallest? *(Compsognathus)*
- Which dinosaur is the tallest? *(Brachiosaurus)*
- Which dinosaur is the scariest? *(Tyrannosaurus rex)*

Point out the labels as a feature of information books. Model reading the text.

On pages 4 and 5, recap strategies they can use to help with their reading: segmenting and blending the words 'sharp' sh-ar-p, 'teeth' t-ee-th, 'long' l-o-ng, 'short' sh-or-t, high frequency words ('these', 'they', 'had', 'but', 'why'), using picture cues (ask children to point to the long, sharp teeth and the short arms) and checking for sense. Show the children the brackets on page 4 and explain that the segmented word inside the brackets tells us how to pronounce the name.

Give each pair of Reading Partners a dinosaur to find out about (Brachiosaurus, Compsognathus and Velociraptor). Can the children use the contents to find which page they need? Can they describe their dinosaur? Remind them to use the different strategies to read the text.

Ask each pair to feed back to the rest of the group what they have learned about their dinosaur.

Look at pages 8 and 9 together.

Ask the following questions:
- What do you think the Compsognathus would have been like?
- Would you have liked to meet one?

Wrap up

Explore some of the similes in the book. Explain that a simile is a way of comparing something to something else. Look at page 11: 'They could run as fast as cars'. **Ask** children to make up their own similes:

- They could run as fast as…
- They were as small as…
- They were as tall as…

Look at pages 14 and 15 together. Discuss the features of an information text. (contents page, heading, labels and bullet points) Explain that bullet points are used to list main facts as they are quick and easy to read. Ask children to point to the heading. Can they point to the labels? Can they point to the bullet points?

Recap what the children learned about each dinosaur.

Ask: What do you think it would have been like to meet a dinosaur?

Vocabulary boost session

You will need

- Multiple copies of Collins Big Cat *Top Dinosaurs*
- A selection of information books with contents pages

Vocabulary table

Focus word	Child-friendly explanation	Example sentence	Tell me…
heading	A title for the page in an information book.	I wrote the **heading** in large letters.	Tell me what headings are used in this book.
contents	A list of topics in the book.	I found 'Tyrannosaurus rex' on the **contents** page.	Tell me which page tells us about the Stegosaurus. Use the contents to find the page number.
similes	A simile is a phrase that compares an item to something else. It says a thing is like something else.	This is a **simile** about a green t-shirt: His t-shirt was as green as the grass.	Can you think of a simile? The dinosaur was as tall as...

Tune in

Explain that in this lesson the children are going to look in more detail at some words linked to the text. Write the three focus words clearly for the children to see. Read the words together. Discuss and explain the child-friendly meaning of each word.

Reread the text. Revise the contents page together.

Ask: What is a contents page for?

Find and point to the heading on each page in the book.

Look at pages 6 and 7. Reread the text. **Ask** children to find and discuss the similes: 'They were as tall as houses' and 'They were as heavy as 15 elephants'.

Heads together

Ask children to explore and look at a selection of information books. Can they find the contents pages?

Name something that you know is from the book and ask children to find out what page it is on.

Ask children to make up some similes. Write their suggestions on the board, for example:

- The teeth were as pointy as…
- The arms were as small as…
- The dinosaur was as scary as…
- The dinosaur was as tall as…
- The skin was as bumpy as…
- The claws were as sharp as…

Wrap up

Recap the three focus words by discussing the questions in the 'Tell me' column of the table, above.

Challenge the children to think of a sentence using one of the focus words.

Follow-up independent sessions

You will need

- Resource sheet: My favourite dinosaur
- Resource sheet: Dinosaur facts
- A selection of non-fiction texts about dinosaurs
- Coloured pencils

Hand out a copy of Resource sheet: My favourite dinosaur, to each child. They choose their favourite

dinosaur and draw and label a picture of it. They then write words or sentences to describe it.

Let the children explore a selection of non-fiction texts about dinosaurs. They choose one dinosaur to find out about. How many facts can they find? They record the facts on Resource sheet: Dinosaur facts and write two 'Did you know?' sentences to read to the group.

Talk Talk Talk

Book Band: Blue

In this traditional story, Bill wants someone to talk to. When a giant bottom turns up, followed by giant legs, tummy, chest, arms and head, Bill finally gets a big new friend.

Skills focus

- Draw on knowledge of vocabulary to understand texts
- Identify/explain the sequence of events in texts
- Make inferences from texts
- Read words accurately and fluently

Guided reading session

You will need

- Multiple copies of Collins Big Cat *Talk Talk Talk*
- Flashcards of the high frequency words: 'I', 'had', 'to', 'said', 'came', 'in', 'and', 'down', 'two', 'on', 'it', 'then', 'a', 'which', 'of', 'lot', 'the', 'there', 'after', 'that', 'was', 'all', 'day'

Tune in

Begin the lesson by relating to the children's own experiences.

Ask the following questions:

- Who likes talking?
- What do you like talking about?
- Who do you like talking to?
- When do you like talking?
- Do you like talking to people on the phone, on the computer or in person?
- When can you not talk?

Introduce the book by exploring the front cover.

Ask the following questions:

- Who do you think this character could be?
- Who might be coming through the door?

Look at the title page and discuss who the illustrator is and what they do. Consider what 'retold' the story means.

Turn over the book and read the blurb. Recap that a blurb tells us more about the book.

Ask the following questions:

- Can you predict who might be coming in to talk to him?
- Why do you think the words 'wish' and 'him' are in capital letters? *(to emphasise these words)*
- Look closely at the picture on the back – how do you think Bill is feeling? *(bored, lonely)*

Play a matching game with two sets of the high frequency word flashcards ('Snap!' or pelmanism).

Discuss strategies the children can use to help with their reading: picture cues, high frequency words, segmenting and blending, checking it makes sense.

Heads together

Begin by reading pages 2 and 3 together. Model reading fluently.

Ask the following questions:

- How do you think Bill is feeling? *(fed up, bored, lonely)*
- Why does he want someone to talk to? *(to play with him, cheer him up)*

Show the children how to split the compound word 'some/one' to make it easier to read.

Explore pages 4 and 5 together.

Ask: How do you think Bill felt when he saw the giant bottom?

Can the children predict what will come through the door next? Discuss body parts and write the words 'legs', 'tummy', 'chest', 'arms' and 'head' on the board for children to practise reading.

Ask children to continue reading the text to page 13. Can they find out what happens next? How does Bill react? Listen to each child read and support where needed.

Wrap up

Discuss what Bill and the giant might talk about. Ask children to imagine a conversation between Bill and the giant: what would they say?

Ask the following questions:

- Do you think the giant is real?
- Where do you think he came from?

Consider the fact that he could be imaginary – can the children think of other books or TV characters that have imaginary friends?

Look closely at the flow chart on pages 14 and 15 to identify how the giant evolved, piece by piece.

Vocabulary boost session

You will need

- Multiple copies of Collins Big Cat *Talk Talk Talk*
- Resource sheet: The giant

Vocabulary table

Focus word	Child-friendly explanation	Example sentence	Tell me...
giant	If something is giant, it is very big.	I had a **giant** ice-cream for pudding.	Tell me some words that mean 'giant'.
discuss	If you discuss something, you talk about it.	We **discussed** the book.	Tell me some words that mean 'discussed'.
body parts	Parts of your body, for example, legs, arms, tummy, chest, head and neck.	Can you label the **body parts**?	Tell me what animal has the following body parts: four legs, a tail, a head, ears and an extra-long neck.

Tune in

Explain that in this lesson the children are going to look in more detail at some words linked to the text. Write the three focus words clearly for the children to see. Read the words together. Discuss and explain the child-friendly meaning of each word.

Reread the text.

Ask: What body parts are listed in the book? *(bottom, legs, tummy, chest, arms, head)*

Challenge the children to find the word 'giant'. *(page 5)*

Look at the front cover. Ask children to read the title.

Ask: Can they think of any words that mean 'talk'? *(discuss, chat, dialogue, speak, have a conversation)*

Heads together

Hand out copies of Resource sheet: The giant. Can the children name and label the body parts?

Wrap up

Recap the three focus words by discussing the questions in the 'Tell me' column of the table, above.

Challenge children to think of a sentence using one of the focus words.

Follow-up independent sessions

You will need

- Resource sheet: Flow chart
- Coloured pencils

Ask children to create their own giant/friend/creature/character to talk to using Resource sheet: Flow chart.

Hot-seating: The children interview the giant or Bill. Encourage the children to think of interesting questions using 'How?', 'What?', 'Why?', 'Where?', 'When?'.

Mojo and Weeza and the Funny Thing

Book Band: Blue

In this fantasy story, two monkeys find a funny thing and try to work out what it is.

Skills focus

- Draw on knowledge of vocabulary to understand texts
- Make inferences from texts
- Predict what might happen on the basis of what has been read so far
- Read words accurately and fluently

Guided reading session

You will need

- Multiple copies of Collins Big Cat *Mojo and Weeza and the Funny Thing*

Tune in

Ask children to pick up their books so that they are ready to look at the front cover. Introduce the book by reading the title aloud. Ask children to look closely at the front cover.

Ask the following questions:

- Who do you think Mojo and Weeza are?
- What type of characters are they?
- Where do you think they are from?

In the title, it says 'funny thing'.

Ask: What do you think the funny thing is?

Encourage the children to point to the title of the book; then read it aloud again, asking them to follow and join in with you. Check that they are following the text from left to right.

Turn to the back cover and draw the children's attention to the blurb. Explain that this usually tells us what happens in the story or it tries to encourage us to read the book.

Read the blurb aloud, encouraging the children to follow and join in with you.

Ask the following questions:

- What do you think now – who are Mojo and Weeza? (*monkeys*)
- What was the funny thing?

Turn to the title page and ask children to point to where it tells us the names of the author and illustrator. Read their names to the children.

Heads together

Read pages 2 and 3 aloud to the children, asking them to follow as you read and join in. Model strategies for reading longer words, for example, using phonic knowledge to blend phonemes (f-un-ny, th-ing), recognition of tricky words ('said', 'what').

Focus on the word 'it's'. Demonstrate how to pronounce it and draw attention to the apostrophe, used to show a missing letter. Check the children's understanding of the word.

Encourage the children to look at the illustrations on page 3. Check whether they can see the small picture of Mojo using the umbrella as a boat.

Read pages 4 to 7 together. As well as modelling strategies for reading, model reading with expression, reading slowly where there are ellipses (…) and loudly when the font is in capital letters or the sentence ends with an exclamation mark.

Point to the word 'didn't' on page 7.

Ask: What do you know about this word? (*It has an apostrophe showing that a letter is missing.*)

Check the children's understanding of the word.

Ask: What else do you think Mojo and Weeza might think the umbrella is for?

Wrap up

Read the rest of the story aloud, modelling reading strategies and expression and encouraging the children to follow and join in.

Ask the following questions:

- What kind of characters are Mojo and Weeza?
- What makes you think that?
- Do you think they are clever? Why? Why not?
- Would you like to be their friend? Why? Why not?
- Do you think Mojo and Weeza ever found out what an umbrella is for?

Vocabulary boost session

You will need

- Multiple copies of Collins Big Cat *Mojo and Weeza and the Funny Thing*

Vocabulary table

Focus word	Child-friendly explanation	Example sentence	Tell me...
float	If something floats, it lies on the top of water and doesn't go under.	When I am on holiday, I **float** on the sea.	Tell me about a time when you have seen something or someone float.
take off	When a rocket or aeroplane takes off, it leaves the ground and starts flying.	I can see the plane **take off**.	Tell me about something that takes off.
fill	If you fill something, you put a lot in, nearly to the top.	My teacher tells me to **fill** up my water bottle.	Tell me what you might fill.

Tune in

Explain to the children that in this lesson they are going to look closely at some of the words the author has used and what those words mean.

Read the book aloud to the children, modelling how to use the punctuation and dialogue to read aloud with expression.

Refer back to each of the focus words within the context of the story, writing up the word, giving a child-friendly explanation and asking the children to say the focus word with you. For example: In the story, the boat doesn't float. That means it doesn't stay on top of the water. Now, say the word with me – 'float'.

You may wish to use the examples in the table, above.

Refer to each of the focus words that you have written up and give the children the example sentences. Then ask them to interact with the word meanings by asking the questions in the 'Tell me' column. You may wish to demonstrate by giving some examples of your own.

Ask children to say the words with you once more.

Heads together

Explore and develop the children's understanding of the focus words.

Ask the following questions:

- When a boat goes on water, we say that it floats. What else can float?
- When a rocket leaves the ground and starts to fly, we say that it takes off. What else takes off?
- When we put lots of water into a bottle, we say we have filled it. Apart from water, what else can we fill something with?

Encourage the children to make links to their own lives and experiences and make sure that they come up with lots of different ideas for each question.

Wrap up

Review the word meanings by doing the following activity. Tell the children that you have some sentences that make sense and some that don't make sense. It's up to them to decide! If it makes sense, they say 'yes'; if it doesn't make sense, they say 'no'. Listen carefully!

- When a plane takes off, it floats on water. *(no)*
- When I am painting, I like to fill the pots with paint first. *(yes)*
- The bird takes off from the tree. *(yes)*
- I filled the pencil pot but there was nothing in it. *(no)*
- Boats can float. *(yes)*

Ask children to choose one of the focus words as their word of the week. Challenge them to use the word as often as they can, both at school and at home.

Follow-up independent sessions

You will need

- Multiple copies of Collins Big Cat *Mojo and Weeza and the Funny Thing*
- Resource sheet: Umbrella uses
- Coloured pencils
- Resource sheet: What is it? *Mojo and Weeza and the Funny Thing*

Ask children to work with their Reading Partners and to read the book aloud. They then turn to the storyboard on pages 14 and 15 and use it to help them to retell the story. They can look back in the book to help them to remember events if they need to. Once they have retold it together, see if they can retell it one at a time, using the storyboard to help. Their partner should listen carefully.

Ask children to think about what else Mojo and Weeza might have tried to use the umbrella for and then draw or write the new event on Resource sheet: Umbrella uses.

Give each child a copy of Resource sheet: What is it? *Mojo and Weeza and the Funny Thing* and ask them to match the pictures to the words.

Funny Fish

Book Band: Blue

In this story with patterned and predictable rhyming language, one funny fish is dull and brown, but it has the perfect camouflage to hide from a hungry shark.

Skills focus

- Draw on knowledge of vocabulary to understand texts
- Identify/explain key aspects of fiction and non-fiction texts, e.g. character, events, title
- Predict what might happen on the basis of what has been read so far
- Read words accurately and fluently

Guided reading session

You will need

- Multiple copies of Collins Big Cat *Funny Fish*

Tune in

Prompt children to talk about or recite any number rhymes or songs they know, especially those with reducing numbers such as 'Five Little Ducks'.

Introduce the book by explaining that this story has numbers in it too.

Read the title together and **ask** the following questions:

- Why do you think they are called 'funny' fish?
- Do they look funny in the picture?

Encourage the children to explain why the fish might be 'funny'.

Focus the children on the back cover blurb. Elicit that the 'blurb' usually gives a big clue as to what might happen in a book. Read the blurb.

Ask: What do you think happened next?

Return to the cover and ask children to find the two names. Point to each name in turn.

Ask the following questions:

- What did Michaela Morgan do? *(write the story)*
- What did Jon Stuart do? *(draw the pictures)*

Help the children to check their suggestions by pointing to, reading and explaining page 1.

Heads together

Challenge the children to follow the words as you read pages 2 and 3 aloud and to join in the last word when you stop. Pause before 'me!' to see if the children can predict the rhyming word.

Ask the children to read the text with you.

Ask: Did you hear two words that rhyme? *(sea, me)*

Write the rhyming words on the board: 'sea' and 'me'. Point out how the rhyming 'ee' sound is spelled differently but still has the same sound.

Repeat the challenge with pages 4 and 5, asking the

children to join in with the last word on page 5 when you pause – 'said'. Reread the pages with the children.

Ask: Can you identify the rhyming words. *(red, said)*

Turn to page 6 and read the first two lines with the children.

Ask: What do you think happens next?

Together read the next two lines to find out.

Ask the following questions:

- Do you feel sorry for the red fish? Why?
- What do you think happens to the yellow and brown fish?

Challenge the children to read the rest of the book. Ask them to find out what happens to each fish.

Move around the group while they read. Ask children if they have spotted any more rhyming words. If necessary, support them in reading unfamiliar words.

Wrap up

Ask children to work in groups to discuss the answers to:

- What happened to the red fish? *(It was eaten by the shark.)*
- What happened to the yellow fish? *(It was eaten by the shark.)*
- What happened to the brown fish? *(It hid among the stones.)*

Write the questions on the board.

Encourage the groups to share their ideas as a group and to back up their answers by pointing to text or pictures.

Discuss as a group why the red and yellow fish were seen and eaten.

Ask: Why was the brown fish safe? *(The shark didn't see it because it looked like a stone.)*

Focus the children on the words 'look like a stone' and the picture on page 13, to ensure their understanding.

Ask: Which was your favourite fish and why?

Reread pages 8 to 10 and ask children to listen out for rhyming words.

Ask the following questions:
- Which are the words that rhyme? *(sea/me)*
- Did you find any other words in the book that rhyme?

If necessary, focus on more pages, such as pages 11 and 13, emphasising the rhyming words.

Ask the following questions:
- How many fish were there at the beginning of the story and how many at the end? *(three, one)*
- Did you like or not like this rhyming number story about three fish? Why?

Vocabulary boost session

You will need
- Multiple copies of Collins Big Cat *Funny Fish*

Vocabulary table

Focus word	Child-friendly explanation	Example sentence	Tell me...
swish	If something goes 'swish', it moves quickly, making a soft sound.	I wore a cloak that **swished** about as I walked in the wind.	Tell me about something that might swish.
bright	If something is bright, it is very light and easy to see.	The car's headlights were so **bright** they dazzled me.	Tell me about something you think is bright.
alone	If you are alone, you are not with anyone else at all.	If you are **alone**, you can't play games that need more than one person.	Tell me about when you have been alone.

Tune in

Ask children if they found any words especially difficult. Write each word on the board and then offer a child-friendly explanation. For example, 'stone': a stone is rock, like the small stones you see in a pebbly drive and the big stones you see on a mountainside.

Read the book aloud to the children, emphasising the rhyming words, the words in bold font and those with exclamation marks.

This time refer back to each of the focus words, discussing their meaning in the context of the story. For example, point to 'bright' on page 9 and tell the children: If something is bright, it is very light and easy to see. This fish is yellow – and as bright as the sun!

Ask children to read the word with you. Give them an example sentence for the word (see the table above, or use your own example). Next, encourage them to link the focus word to their own lives by asking them to tell you about a bright thing they have seen.

Finally, ask children to say the words with you again.

Heads together

Explore and develop children's own understanding of the focus words by setting these challenges:
- Make a noise like something swishing along.
- Point to something in the room that is bright.
- Tell me where you would go if you wanted to be alone.

Encourage the group to discuss their answers.

Wrap up

Review the word meanings by asking the children to clap when they hear a word or phrase that goes well with the focus word:
- 'swish': table, mountain, swing, pencil
- 'bright': black, cloud, night, lamp
- 'alone': a crowd, one cat, three cats, school

Add the focus words to a word wall. Ask children to tick a word every time they have used it at school or at home. Challenge them to use at least one word each day.

Follow-up independent sessions

You will need
- Resource sheet: The fourth fish
- Resource sheet: Rhyming pairs
- Coloured pencils

Ask children to work in small groups and practise doing a dramatic reading of pages 2 to 6, 8 to 10 or 11 to 13. Ask children to take it in turns to read a page but they must all join in for words that are in bold type.

Give pairs of children a copy of Resource sheet: The fourth fish. Tell them to imagine there were four fish and not three at the beginning. Is it a bright fish or a fish that could hide? Encourage them to choose a colour and to draw the fourth fish being chased by the big fish, or hiding.

Give pairs of children a copy of Resource sheet: Rhyming pairs. They colour in the pairs of words that rhyme, using a different colour for each rhyming pair.

Bert's Band

Book Band: Blue

Bert's Band wins the Band Cup in this humorous story and returns home at night in triumph.

Skills focus

- Draw on knowledge of vocabulary to understand texts
- Identify/explain the sequence of events in texts
- Predict what might happen on the basis of what has been read so far
- Read words accurately and fluently

Guided reading session

You will need

- Multiple copies of Collins Big Cat *Bert's Band*

Tune in

Introduce the book by looking at the front cover. Ask children to draw the letter 'B' in the air using their finger. Read the title and model segmenting and blending the words 'Bert's' B-er-t-s, 'band' b-a-n-d.

Ask: What do you notice about the initial letters of the words in the title? *(they are the same)*

Explain that this is called 'alliteration'. Can the children think of a book title for their own name using alliteration, for example, 'Paul's Picture', 'Amelia's Art', 'Freddie's Football', 'Grace's Gardening'.

Discuss what a band is – a group of people who play music. Look at the front cover.

Ask the following questions:

- What instruments can you see? *(trumpets, trombone, drum, tuba, clarinet)*

Relate to children's own experiences.

Ask the following questions:

- Has anyone ever seen a band play?
- Does anyone play an instrument or know someone who does?

Turn to the back cover to read the blurb together. Model reading the blurb using fluency and accuracy.

Ask: When do you think people wouldn't like to hear the band? *(while they were sleeping, watching a film, in an exam, doing something quiet)*

Explain that this is a 'humorous' story, which means it is a funny story. Can the children predict what might happen in the story? Where do they think the band is going to on the bus?

Heads together

Look at pages 2 and 3 together. Ask children to look for any high frequency words they know in the text and point to them ('had', 'a', 'and', 'they', 'play').

Read the text together, encouraging children to point at the words and join in.

Ask the following questions:

- Why is 'Oompah-bang-bang-ting-a-ling' in capitals? *(because it is loud)*
- Do you think people are enjoying listening to Bert's band? *(yes, they are smiling, following the band)*

Move on to pages 4 and 5. Can the children segment and blend the words 'won' w-o-n and 'cup' c-u-p? Read the text together, encouraging the children to point at the words and join in.

Ask the following questions:

- What do you think the 'Band Cup' is? *(a trophy/a prize)*
- Can you find the cup in the picture?

Turn to pages 6 and 7. Read the text together, encouraging the children to point at the words and join in.

Ask the following questions:

- What time is it? *(night-time)*
- Why might they have arrived home so late? *(the competition was a long way away)*
- What will most people in the town be doing? *(sleeping)*

Point out the inverted commas on page 7; explain that this shows that Bert was talking.

Ask the following questions:

- Why do you think Bert asked them to take their boots off? *(to be quiet)*
- Can you predict what will happen next?

Read pages 8 to 11 together. Now can the children predict what will happen next?

Turn to pages 12 and 13.

Ask the following questions:

- What happened? *(the band crept into town quietly and then played loudly)*
- Was the band quiet? *(no)*
- What made the noise? *(they played their instruments)*

- What did the people think? *(They were angry because the band woke them up.)*

Wrap up

Discuss why the story is funny. Ask children to retell the story in their own words to their Reading Partner.

Ask the following questions:
- Where had Bert's Band been on the bus? *(to a competition)*
- What did they win? *(the Band Cup)*

Vocabulary boost session

You will need

- Multiple copies of Collins Big Cat *Bert's Band*
- Something made from brass for the children to look at

Vocabulary table

Focus word	Child-friendly explanation	Example sentence	Tell me...
humorous	If something is humorous, it is funny.	I read a **humorous** story.	Tell me a humorous joke.
brass	Brass is a type of metal used to make trumpets and trombones.	The **brass** band marched through the town.	Tell me what instruments were in the brass band.
tippy-toe	To walk on tippy-toe means to creep quietly on the tips of your toes.	The ballerina danced on her **tippy-toes**.	Can you walk on your tippy-toes?

Tune in

Explain that in this lesson the children are going to look in more detail at some words linked to the text. Write the three focus words clearly for the children to see. Read the words together. Discuss and explain the child-friendly meaning of each word.

Reread the text. Explain that this is a 'humorous' story.

Ask the following questions:
- What was humorous about it?
- Can you find the words 'brass' and 'tippy-toes' in the text? *(page 2, page 11)*

Heads together

Look at an object made from brass. Can the children describe it? What does it feel like? What does it look like?

In a safe space, ask children to practise walking on their tippy-toes. Can they walk slowly? Can they walk quickly? Then see if they can stomp and stamp their feet loudly to compare the ways of walking.

Discuss the word 'humorous'.

Ask: What do we do if something is humorous? *(laugh)*

Wrap up

Recap the three focus words by discussing the questions in the 'Tell me' column of the table, above.

Challenge the children to think of a sentence using one of the focus words.

Follow-up independent sessions

You will need

- Resource sheet: Role on the wall: Bert
- A selection of musical instruments
- A selection of non-fiction texts about musical instruments
- Magazines, catalogues, leaflets with pictures of musical instruments, paper, coloured paper, glue, scissors
- Resource sheet: Bert's words

Hand out copies of Resource sheet: Role on the wall: Bert. The children label the picture of Bert with

adjectives to describe his character on the inside and his appearance on the outside.

Let the children explore a selection of musical instruments. What sounds do they make? What do they use to make the sound? Do they know what the instruments are called?

The children explore a range of non-fiction texts about musical instruments. What facts can they find out?

Ask children to create a collage of musical instruments by cutting out pictures from magazines, catalogues, leaflets and adding labels.

The children play a game of 'Snap!' using two sets of cards cut from Resource Sheet: Bert's words.

Robots

Book Band: Blue

This non-chronological report looks at different types of robots and the jobs they do.

Skills focus

- Draw on knowledge of vocabulary to understand texts
- Identify/explain the sequence of events in texts
- Identify/explain key aspects of fiction and non-fiction texts, e.g. character, events, title
- Check reading makes sense

Guided reading session

You will need

- Multiple copies of Collins Big Cat *Robots*
- Paper and pencils
- Pictures of different robots (toy robots, car manufacturing robots, construction kit robots and so on)

Tune in

Ask children what they think of when you mention robots. What do they know about robots? Provide them with pencils and a piece of paper – can they draw a robot? Discuss each other's robots: do they all look the same? What is different about them? What do the robots do? What shape are they?

Display the pictures of different robots and discuss what is the same and what is different about them.

Introduce the book by looking at the front cover. Read the title to the children and explain that this is a non-fiction book about robots.

Turn the book over to explore the back cover and model reading the blurb using fluency. Recap that a blurb tells us more about the book. Ask children to point out and share the high frequency words they recognise ('for', 'people', 'they', 'do', 'that', 'can't', 'like', 'on', 'or', 'are', 'also', 'of').

Challenge children to find the contents page. Can they remember that a contents page lists the headings and the pages they are on? Can they remember that the contents is at the front of the book? Explore the contents together and ask children to point to the high frequency words: 'what', 'is', 'a', 'and', 'look', 'like', 'do'. Model reading the contents.

Ask the following questions to practise using the contents:

- On what page can I find out about what robots do? *(page 8)*
- What is page 14 about? *(inside a robot)*

Explain that this book is a non-chronological report. It has the same features as an information text – headings, photographs, captions, diagrams, labels – and it does not have to be read in order. Look through the book together and challenge the children to find examples of each feature.

Heads together

Turn to pages 2 and 3 together. Ask children to point to the heading.

Ask: How is the heading different to the rest of the writing? *(it's in bold)*

Read the heading together and then read the text together, encouraging the children to point to the words and join in where they can. Discuss the photographs.

Ask: What jobs are the robots doing? *(picking up and moving things, making cars)*

Return to the contents page. Explain that we don't have to read a non-chronological report in order. Give each pair a heading to find out about, for example: 'Tiny robots and big robots', 'What robots look like' and 'What robots do'. In pairs, ask children to use the contents to find the correct page and read the text together. Support them where needed. Let the pairs share what they have found out.

Wrap up

Ask children to share something they have learned about robots with the group.

Look at pages 14 and 15 together. Discuss the features of a non-fiction text: headings, diagrams, labels. Model reading the text and use a range of strategies, such as segmenting and blending, for example the word 'brain' b-r-ai-n and high frequency word recognition (the, 'see', 'this', 'to', 'can', 'up', 'what', 'do').

Ask the following questions to encourage children to share their opinion of the book:

- Did they enjoy the book?
- What did they find interesting?
- Which was their favourite page?

Vocabulary boost session

You will need

- Multiple copies of Collins Big Cat *Robots*
- Poster paper, scissors, glue
- A selection of home catalogues and magazines

Vocabulary table

Focus word	Child-friendly explanation	Example sentence	Tell me...
machine	A mechanism with many parts that work together to complete a task.	I put my clothes in the washing **machine**.	Tell me about some machines used in school.
dangerous	If something is dangerous, it is unsafe.	The farmer used **dangerous** machinery.	Tell me about some jobs that are dangerous.
camera	A camera is a machine that takes photographs.	I took my **camera** on holiday.	Tell me about when you have had your photograph taken.

Tune in

Explain that in this lesson the children are going to look in more detail at some words linked to the text. Write the three focus words clearly for the children to see. Read the words together. Discuss and explain the child-friendly meaning of each word.

Reread the text.

Challenge the children to find the words 'machine' and 'camera' in the text. (*page 2 and page 14*)

Look at pages 10 and 11 and discuss why robots do these jobs. (*They are dangerous jobs.*)

Heads together

Discuss what machines the children might have at home, for example, washing machine, dishwasher, microwave, TV, computer, printer, vacuum cleaner.

Write 'machines in the home' in the middle of a large piece of poster paper. Provide the children with a selection of home catalogues and magazines and ask them to cut out photographs/pictures of machines and stick them on to the poster to create a group collage.

Wrap up

Recap the three focus words by discussing the questions in the 'Tell me' column of the table, above.

Challenge the children to think of a sentence using one of the focus words.

Follow up-independent sessions

You will need

- Resource sheet: Design a robot
- Paper, felt-tipped pens
- A selection of non-fiction texts about robots
- cardboard boxes, cardboard tubes, foil, glue, paints and so on
- Resource sheet: Robot parts

Give each child a copy of Resource sheet: Design a robot. The children draw and label their own robot.

What will it look like? What will it be made from? What will it do?

Ask children to investigate robots using a range of non-fiction texts. What can they find out about robots? Can they find different types of robots? What jobs do the robots have? How big are the robots?

Ask children to build a robot model from cardboard boxes and junk modelling.

In pairs, the children match the definitions to the correct robot part on Resource sheet: Robot parts

The Fantastic Flying Squirrel

Book Band: Blue

This information book follows a flying squirrel as she wakes up at night and goes in search of food.

Skills focus

- Draw on knowledge of vocabulary to understand texts
- Identify/explain key aspects of fiction and non-fiction texts, e.g. character, events, title
- Make inferences from texts
- Read words accurately and fluently

Guided reading session

You will need

- Multiple copies of Collins Big Cat *The Fantastic Flying Squirrel*

Tune in

Ask children to pick up their books so that they are ready to look at the front cover. Introduce the book by asking the children to look closely at the front cover.

Ask: What is the animal? *(squirrel, flying squirrel)*

Encourage the children to point to the title of the book and then read it aloud to them. Ask them to read it aloud with you.

Turn to the title page and look at the picture.

Ask: Why do you think the title is 'The Fantastic Flying Squirrel'?

Ask children to point to the author's name on the title page. Elicit that Nic Bishop has taken the photographs in the book as well as written the words.

Ask the following questions:

- What kind of book do you think this is: information or story? *(information)*
- What makes you think that? *(photographs)*

Heads together

Read pages 2 and 3 aloud to the children, asking them to follow as you read and to join in. Model strategies for reading longer words, for example, recognition of tricky words ('the', 'some'), breaking words down (fly-ing).

Continue to read in this way, up to page 13.

Ask: What have we found out about the flying squirrel? *(she comes out at night, she lives in a tree den, she likes to eat acorns and grasshoppers, she is hungry at night, she can climb and jump as well as fly)*

For each answer, encourage the children to find and show the group where it is in the book.

Ask the following questions:

- Do you think that the flying squirrel has good eyesight? Why? *(Yes, because she can see acorns from a distance.)*
- Do you think the flying squirrel has good hearing? Why? *(Yes, because she can hear a grasshopper crunching on a leaf.)*

Wrap up

Turn to pages 14 and 15 and read them aloud, with the children joining in.

Turn back to page 9.

Ask: Why do you think the owl didn't eat the grasshopper? *(The flying squirrel ate it first.)*

Ask the following questions about the whole book:

- When does the flying squirrel try to find food? *(night-time)*
- The flying squirrel can glide. What else can she do? *(jump, climb, look, listen, eat)*
- How do we know that this is an information book, not a story book? *(real pictures, factual – about real things, not made up)*

Vocabulary boost session

You will need

- Multiple copies of Collins Big Cat *The Fantastic Flying Squirrel*

Vocabulary table

Focus word	Child-friendly explanation	Example sentence	Tell me...
forest	A forest is a place where there are lots of trees close together.	The owl lived in a tree in the **forest**.	Tell me about a time you have seen a forest.
den	A den is the name of the small house that animals like lions or foxes live in.	The foxes' **den** was under the large tree.	Tell me about the kind of den you have played in.
glide	If you glide, you move quietly and smoothly through the air.	I saw an eagle **gliding** across the sky.	Tell me about a time you have glided.

Tune in

Explain to the children that in this lesson they are going to look closely at some of the words the author has used and what those words mean.

Read the book aloud to the children, asking them to follow and join in as you read.

Refer back to each of the focus words in the book, writing up the word, giving a child-friendly explanation and asking the children to say the focus word with you. For example: The book is about a squirrel that lives in a forest. A forest is a place where there are lots of trees close together. Now, say the word with me – 'forest'.

You may wish to use the examples in the table, above.

Refer to each of the focus words that you have written up and give the children the example sentences. Then ask them to interact with the word meanings by asking the questions in the 'Tell me' column. You may wish to demonstrate by giving some examples of your own.

Ask children to say the words with you once more.

Heads together

Explore and develop the children's understanding of the focus words. Tell the children that you will say a sentence that is missing a word and that they have to say one of the new words that fits into the sentence. Tell them that either 'forest', 'den' or 'glide' will fit into the blank.

- When we throw paper plans, they… across the classroom.
- The… was full of tall, dark trees.
- The baby foxes left their… to find food.

Wrap up

Ask the following questions to review the focus word meanings:

- What's the word that means you move quietly and smoothly through the air?
- What's the word that means a place where there are lots of trees close together?
- What's the word that means the small house that animals like lions or foxes live in?

Follow-up independent session

You will need

- Multiple copies of Collins Big Cat *The Fantastic Flying Squirrel*
- Resource sheet: What does squirrel do?
- Resource sheet: Forest facts

Ask children to work with their Reading Partners and to read the book aloud together.

Hand out copies of Resource sheet: What does squirrel do? The children put the pictures in the right order and write some captions for them.

Give each child a copy of Resource sheet: Forest facts. Ask children to write three more facts about the forest in the night-time.

Sounds

This information book explores many of the sounds we hear and how they are made.

Skills focus

- Draw on knowledge of vocabulary to understand texts

- Identify/explain key aspects of fiction and non-fiction texts, e.g. character, events, title
- Read words accurately and fluently

Guided reading session

You will need

- Multiple copies of Collins Big Cat *Sounds*
- Resource sheet: Word cards for *Sounds*

Tune in

Introduce the book by focusing on the cover picture.

Ask: What is the boy doing? *(He is listening for sounds.)*

Encourage the children to quietly listen in the same way for a minute. Ask them what they can hear.

Quiz the children on the cover features. Encourage them to point to the book title and then read it together. Point to the author's name and then read it together.

Ask: Where do we find the blurb? *(on the back cover)*

Encourage the children to find it on the back cover. Elicit that it will tell them more about the book. Read the blurb aloud, dramatically sounding out the first line. Ask children to join you in reading the blurb again. Repeat the first question in the blurb: 'Which sounds do you like?' and then turn to pages 2 and 3.

Read the pages aloud to the children, dramatising the sound words (whistle for the musical notes).

Ask: Which sound did you like best?

Encourage them to find the relevant words on the pages. Point out how the sound words are in different fonts.

Focus on the index on pages 14 and 15. Demonstrate how to use it by looking up 'ears' on page 11.

Ask: Do you think this is a book that gives us information, or is a story book? Why?

Heads together

Read the index with the children, asking them to follow as you read. On page 14, point out the smaller words in the bigger words. Write 'clapper' and 'drumstick' on the board, underlining the smaller words ('clap', 'drum', 'stick'). Explain how looking for smaller words helps to read longer words.

Reread page 15 of the index with the children, emphasising the /ow/ sounds.

Ask: Which words have the /ow/ sounds. *(loud, sounds)*

Write them on the board, highlighting the spellings. Elicit how more than one letter is making the /ow/ sound.

Ask: Can you find the two letters that make the /ee/ sound in 'ears' on page 15?

Tell the children you are going to look up 'recorder' in the book. Demonstrate looking up page 9 using the index.

Read page 9, pointing out the smaller word 'too' in 'toot' and the two letters that make the /oo/ sound.

Give out the word cards from Resource sheet: Word cards for *Sounds*, to pairs of children. Challenge them to use the index to look up the words on their card and read the information. Ask children to think about whether they like the sounds they read about. Move around the pairs of children, helping them find the page number from the index.

Wrap up

Work through the index entries (bell, drum, recorder, strings) as a group, asking the relevant pairs of children to describe the sounds on the pages they read. Encourage them to explain why they liked/did not like the sounds. Encourage the children to identify the sound words ('ring' on page 4, 'bang-bang-a-boom' on page 6, 'toot' on page 9, 'twang' on page 8).

Discuss the labels and explain that information books use lines and labels to name parts of pictures.

Focus on page 5 and read it with the children.

Ask: Why are these words in a different font?

Explain that they are in 'italics' and elicit that they are captions (which explain the pictures). Explain that information books often have captions.

Ask: How do we know this is an information book?

Write the children's ideas on the board.

Encourage children to work in pairs to read the rest of the book from page 10 to 13.

Afterwards ask if they had problems with any words and encourage the rest of the group to help by identifying groups of letters that make one sound or spotting smaller words within longer words.

Vocabulary boost session

You will need

- Multiple copies of Collins Big Cat *Sounds*

Vocabulary table

Focus word	Child-friendly explanation	Example sentence	Tell me...
around	When something is all around, it is in lots of places all about, not just in one place.	There were flags all **around** the circus tent.	Tell me about anything you have seen or heard all around you.
some	Some means a few and not all, so some people climb mountains, but not all people do it.	**Some** children go to school on a bus.	Tell me what some children like to play, but you don't.
whisper	When you whisper, you speak in a very quiet voice.	I **whispered** to my friend during the school play.	Tell me when you have whispered to a friend.

Tune in

Read the book aloud to the children. Tell them to join in with the sound words when you raise your hand, encouraging them to sound out the words expressively and loudly, or softly as appropriate.

Explain to the children that you are going to look closely at what some of the words mean in the book. Refer to the focus words in the table one by one. For example, focus on 'around' on page 2. Reread page 2 to the children and give a child-friendly explanation for the focus word. Here the author says we hear sounds all around us.

Ask children to say the word again with you. Then give an example sentence using the word and finally check their understanding by asking a 'Tell me' question, using the examples in the table or your own.

Before moving on to the next focus word, ask children to say the word once more.

Repeat this with another word from the book that children are unsure of the meaning.

Heads together

Explore and develop the children's understanding of the focus words.

Ask the following questions:

- What might you see all around you?
- What do some people do on holiday but not everyone?
- Where might you whisper to a friend?

Encourage the group to discuss their answers.

Wrap up

Ask the children to complete these challenges:

- If I say something that might be all 'around' my living room, put your hand up: the fireplace, my pet rabbit, the wallpaper.
- If I say something that only 'some' people might do, clap your hands: eat, swim, drink.
- If I say somewhere I might 'whisper', make a shush noise: the playground, the car, the library.

Display the words on a word board and every day ask for a word to add to one of the lists for: something that might be all around us; something that only some people do; somewhere they might whisper.

Follow-up independent sessions

You will need

- Multiple copies of Collins Big Cat *Sounds*
- Resource sheet: What sound do I make?

Ask children to work in pairs. One child chooses an entry in the index and the other has to look it up and read the page/s. Next, they swap.

Remind the children of the sounds on pages 3 and 13 of the book. Give each child a copy of Resource sheet: What sound do I make? Explain that children need to think of what sound each thing on the sheet makes. Ask them to tick whether it is loud or soft. Can they have a go at writing the sound word for each too?

Percy and the Badger

Book Band: Blue

In this story with a familiar setting, Percy the Park Keeper tries to persuade the reluctant Badger to take a bath.

Skills focus

- Draw on knowledge of vocabulary to understand texts
- Identify/explain key aspects of fiction and non-fiction texts, e.g. character, events, title
- Identify/explain the sequence of events in texts
- Check reading makes sense

Guided reading session

You will need

- Multiple copies of Collins Big Cat *Percy and the Badger*
- Resource sheet: High frequency words

Tune in

Begin the lesson by playing a matching game with two sets of cards cut from Resource sheet: High frequency words. Turn all the cards face down. The first player picks two cards; if they match, the player keeps them. The player with the most pairs wins.

Ask the following questions:

- Who likes going to the park?
- What do you like doing at the park?
- What animals might you see at the park? *(birds, rabbits, squirrels, ducks, bees, butterflies)*

Explain that the children are going to read a story about a park keeper.

Ask: What do you think a park keeper's job is? *(to look after the park)*

Introduce the book by looking at the front cover. Explain that this is Percy the Park Keeper.

Ask the following questions:

- Have you read any other books about Percy the Park Keeper?
- What animal is this next to Percy? *(a badger)*
- Where do badgers live? *(underground)*
- What do you think Percy is doing in the picture?

Model reading the title. Look at the title page.

Ask the following questions:

- What has Percy got on his head? *(shower cap)*
- Why might he be wearing that? *(to have a shower or a bath)*

Reread the title and ask children to point to the word 'badger' and 'Percy'. Explain that Nick Butterworth wrote and illustrated the book.

Turn the book over and model reading the blurb. Demonstrate a range of strategies as you read:

recognising high frequency words, segmenting and blending the words 'old' o-l-d, 'tin' t-i-n, 'bath' b-a-th.

Ask the following questions:

- Who got out the bath? *(Percy)*
- Who didn't want a bath? *(the badger)*

Look at the apostrophe and explain it shows a missing letter: 'didn't' = 'did not'. Look at other words with apostrophes in the text: 'where's' = 'where is' (on page 6), 'couldn't' = 'could not' (on page 7), 'doesn't' = 'does not' (on page 8).

Heads together

Look at pages 2 and 3 together.

Ask the following questions:

- What characters can you see in the picture? *(Percy and the badger)*
- Where is the story set? *(in the park)*

Read the text together, encouraging the children to point at the text and join in. Can the children point to the inverted commas? What other punctuation can they spot? *(exclamation mark)*

Practise reading the last sentence, using expression. "Hello. You *do* look muddy!"

Ask: When you look at the picture on page 3, what is Percy is thinking? *(The badger needs a bath.)*

Ask children to read on in pairs to page 13, taking turns to read. Can they find out if the badger has a bath? Move around the group and listen to the children reading, supporting where needed.

Wrap up

Turn to pages 14 and 15. Ask children to work in pairs to retell the story using the storyboard.

Discuss the main events of the story.

Ask the following questions:

- Why did Percy think the badger needed a bath? *(he was muddy)*
- Did the badger want a bath? *(no)*
- Where had the badger been hiding? *(in a tree)*

- How did the badger end up having a bath after all? *(He fell out of the tree into the bath.)*

Look at pages 12 and 13.

Ask the following questions:
- What did Percy think when the badger fell in the bath? *(it was funny)*
- Did you enjoy this book?
- What was your favourite part?

Vocabulary boost session

You will need
- Multiple copies of Collins Big Cat *Percy and the Badger*
- Selection of musical instruments
- A Water tray or bowl of water

Vocabulary table

Focus word	Child-friendly explanation	Example sentence	Tell me...
crack	A loud noise made when something breaks, snaps or hits something else.	**Crack** went the tree branch beneath my foot.	Tell me some other words that describe noises.
splash	A loud noise made when something hits water.	I made a huge **splash** when I landed in the swimming pool.	Tell me what other words describe sounds that water makes.
park keeper	Someone whose job it is to look after the park. He keeps the park clean and safe.	The **park keeper** swept up the leaves.	Tell me what jobs might a park keeper do to look after the park.

Tune in

Explain that in this lesson the children are going to look in more detail at some of the words the author has used. Write the three focus words clearly for the children to see. Read the words together. Discuss and explain the child-friendly meaning of each word.

Reread the text. Look at page 2 and read the first sentence. Recap that Percy is a park keeper.

Ask: What jobs do you think he might do? *(sweep leaves, pick up rubbish, gardening, looking after the animals, locking and unlocking the park gates)*

Turn to pages 10 and 11.

Ask the following questions:
- What went CRACK? *(the tree branch)*
- What went SPLASH? *(the badger falling in the bath)*

Heads together

Let the children explore a range of musical instruments. What words can they think of to describe the sounds? Create a list on the board. For example: bang, crash, hit, scratch, scrape, tap, ting, jingle.

Allow the children to play with the water tray. What words can they use to describe the sounds? For example: splash, splosh, splat, swish, swash.

Wrap up

Recap the three focus words by discussing the questions in the 'Tell me' column of the table, above.

Challenge children to think of a sentence using one of the focus words.

Follow-up independent sessions

You will need
- Resource sheet: Story sequence
- Paper, coloured pencils
- Other books by Nick Butterworth

Using Resource sheet: Story sequence, the children order the pictures from the story and label or write a sentence to match each picture.

Ask children to draw a picture of Percy the Park Keeper doing a job to look after the park and write a sentence to go with the picture.

Look at a selection of other 'Percy the Park Keeper' books or books written by Nick Butterworth. Can the children find any similarities and differences?

What's Underground?

Book Band: Blue

This non-chronological report explores some of the things that can be found underground, both natural and man-made.

Skills focus

- Draw on knowledge of vocabulary to understand texts
- Identify/explain key aspects of fiction and non-fiction texts, e.g. character, events, title
- Identify/explain the sequence of events in texts
- Check reading makes sense

Guided reading session

You will need

- Multiple copies of Collins Big Cat *What's Underground?*
- Large piece of paper (A2) and felt-tipped pens
- Optional props: soft toys of a mole, badger, fox, rabbit, a plant in a clear cup so you can see the roots

Tune in

Ask children to pick up their books so that they are ready to look at the front cover. Introduce the book by exploring the front cover. Read the title: 'What's Underground?' Talk about the punctuation: look at the apostrophe in the word 'what's' and check if the children know that 'what's' = 'what is'. Ask children to point to the question mark. Show children that the word 'under/ground' is a compound word that can be split into two.

Ask the following questions:

- What is this a photograph of? *(a mole)*
- Where do moles live? *(underground)*
- Can you think of any other animals that live underground? *(badger, fox, rabbits, worms, ants)*
- What else is underground?

Write the word 'underground' in the centre of a large piece of paper. Ask children to suggest what might be underground and write their ideas on the paper. The children could draw pictures or look at any props you may have, such as plants or soft toys of animals that live underground.

Look at the back cover of the book. Model reading the blurb and recap that a blurb tells us more about the book. Explain that this is a non-fiction book – a non-chronological report about what we find underground.

Turn to the contents page. Explain that a contents page lists the headings in the book and what page number they are on. Read the contents page.

Compare the list to the ideas the children recorded earlier – is there anything they weren't expecting? Add to the children's ideas on the large piece of paper.

Heads together

Recap the different strategies we can use when reading, such as segmenting and blending, using picture clues, checking it makes sense, recognising high frequency words.

Look at pages 2 and 3 together. Ask children to point out the features: heading, photograph, diagram, labels.

Discuss the pictures including the burrows and tree roots.

Ask: What animals can you see? *(foxes, rabbits, worms, moles)*

Model reading the text. Can the children identify any high frequency words? (what, is, going, on, come and, see, some, like, me, a, this, is, my) Point out the split digraph in the word 'home' and the vowel digraph in w-or-m.

Turn back to the contents page and ask children to choose a page to look at. The children then read their chosen pages individually. Listen to each child read and support where necessary.

Wrap up

Ask each child to share something they found out. Discuss the pages each child looked at. Point out the features of non-fiction texts: headings, photographs, captions, labels, contents.

Turn to pages 14 and 15 and recap what's underground. Give the children time to discuss the picture in pairs.

Point out the digraphs: 'ai', 'oo' and 'er'. Model reading the words 'pipe' and 'wire' and look at the split digraph 'i-e'.

Vocabulary boost session

You will need

- Multiple copies of Collins Big Cat *What's Underground?*
- Large sheet of paper
- Coloured pencils
- Timer (optional)
- Resource sheet: Treasure!

Vocabulary table

Focus word	Child-friendly explanation	Example sentence	Tell me...
amazing	If something is amazing, it is brilliant and wonderful.	My sister's painting was **amazing**!	Tell me something that you are amazing at.
archaeologist	An archaeologist is someone who digs up old items to learn about the past.	The **archaeologist** discovered some old coins.	Tell me if you would like to be an archaeologist. Why?/Why not?
treasure	Treasure is items that are special or worth a lot of money.	The pirate was searching for **treasure**.	Tell me what might be in the pirate's treasure chest.

Tune in

Explain that in this lesson the children are going to look in more detail at some words linked to the text. Write the three focus words clearly for the children to see. Read the words together. Discuss and explain the child-friendly meaning of each word.

Reread the text.

Look at the blurb together and find the word 'amazing'.

Turn to page 13. Find the word 'treasure' and talk about what the archaeologists are doing.

Heads together

Write the word 'amazing' in the middle of a piece of paper. Ask children to work in pairs to think of some other words that mean amazing. (You could set a timer.) They then share their ideas and you can record words the children have thought of.

Discuss what the children think 'treasure' is. Give each child a copy of Resource sheet: Treasure! and ask them to draw and label pictures of the treasure they would like to find in the chest.

Wrap up

Recap the three focus words by discussing the questions in the 'Tell me' column of the table, above.

Challenge children to think of a sentence using one of the focus words.

Follow-up independent sessions

You will need

- Trays of sand/soil, items to use as buried treasure, trowels, spoons, brushes, magnifying glasses
- Maps of the London Underground
- Paper, ruler, felt-tipped pens
- Non-fiction books about animals that live underground
- Paper, collage materials, scissors, glue
- Resource sheet: Underground labels

Let the children role-play being an archaeologist! Provide children with trays full of soil or sand, buried treasure, trowels, spoons, brushes, magnifying glasses and so on.

The children look at maps of the London Underground. They then draw their own map/artwork using a ruler to create straight lines with coloured felt-tipped pens.

Ask children to choose an animal that lives underground and use the internet or non-fiction books to research it in more detail.

The children create an underground/overground collage by drawing a line horizontally across the page. Create a collage of the town or the countryside.

Hand out copies of Resource sheet: Underground labels. The children fill in the missing labels.

Colours

Book Band: Blue

In this simple non-fiction text, a visit to an art gallery inspires a girl to imagine the world in different colours and to create her own rainbow-coloured artwork.

Skills focus

- Draw on knowledge of vocabulary to understand texts
- Make inferences from texts
- Predict what might happen on the basis of what has been read so far
- Read words accurately and fluently

Guided reading session

You will need

- Multiple copies of Collins Big Cat *Colours*

Tune in

Ask children to pick up their books so that they are ready to look at the front cover. Introduce the book by encouraging the children to look closely at the front cover.

Ask: What do you think the book is about?

Ask children to point to the title of the book and then read it aloud to them. Ask them to read it aloud with you.

Turn to the back cover and draw the children's attention to the blurb. Explain that this usually tells us what happens in the book or it tries to encourage us to read it. Read the blurb aloud, encouraging the children to follow and join in with you.

Ask: Can you imagine if the world was just one colour? What would it look like?

Turn to the title page and ask children to point to where it tells us the name of the author and illustrator. Read it to the children. (Satoshi Kitamura)

Heads together

Read pages 2 to 5 aloud to the children, asking them to follow as you read and to join in. Model strategies for reading longer words, for example, recognition of tricky words ('what', 'look'), using phonic strategies and breaking the words down (paint-ing). Focus on pages 4 and 5.

Ask the following questions:

- Can you imagine a world like this?
- What colour are the animals normally?
- Do you think you would like to live in a world that is all one colour?

Read pages 6 to 11 aloud to the children, modelling strategies for reading and asking the children to follow as you read and to join in.

Ask: What do you think the girl is going to do next?

Wrap up

Read page 12 aloud to the children, asking them to follow as you read and to join in.

Ask the following questions:

- What painting might she draw on that empty piece of paper?
- What would you draw?
- What colours could you use?
- Would you use lots of colours?

Look at pages 14 and 15 together.

Ask: Can you use the pictures to help you to say what the book is about?

Vocabulary boost session

You will need
- Multiple copies of Collins Big Cat *Colours*

Vocabulary table

Focus word	Child-friendly explanation	Example sentence	Tell me...
imagine	If I imagine, I make a picture in my head.	When I read the story, I **imagined** what the giant looked like.	Tell me about something that you have imagined.
everything	Everything means all of the things.	In my bedroom, **everything** is pink.	Tell me everything that you need when you get ready for school.
try out	If you try something out, you see what it is like.	She **tried out** her new bike.	Tell me about something that you have tried out.

Tune in

Explain to the children that in this lesson they are going to look closely at some of the words the author has used and what those words mean.

Read the book aloud to the children, asking them to follow and to join in as you read.

Refer back to each of the focus words in the book, writing up the word, giving a child-friendly explanation and asking the children to say the focus word with you. For example: In the book, the girl imagines a different world. If I imagine, I make a picture in my head. Now, say the word with me – 'imagine'.

You may wish to use the examples in the table, above.

Refer to each of the focus words that you have written up and give the children the example sentences. Then ask them to interact with the word meanings by asking the questions in the 'Tell me' column. You may wish to demonstrate by giving some examples of your own.

Ask children to say the words with you once more.

Heads together

Explore and develop the children's understanding of the focus words by playing the 'yes/no' game. Tell the children you have some sentences that make sense and some that don't make sense. If the sentence makes sense, they say 'yes'; if it doesn't make sense, they say 'no'.

- When I imagine, I watch TV.
- When I am drawing a picture, I imagine what it will look like first.
- Every morning I put everything I need for the day in my bag.
- Everything in this room is blue.
- I asked my friend if I could try out her scooter.
- I'll try out the slide before I go down it.

Wrap up

Ask the following questions to review the word meanings:

- If I try something out, what do I do with it?
- How many things does 'everything' mean?
- When I imagine something, what do I do?

Ask children to choose one of the focus words as their word of the week. Challenge them to use the word as often as they can, both at school and at home.

Follow-up independent session

You will need
- Multiple copies of Collins Big Cat *Colours*
- Resource sheet: Mixing colours
- Paper, paints (blue, yellow, red, green, white), brushes
- Resource sheet: One colour classroom

Ask children to work with their Reading Partners and to read the book aloud together. Ask them to think about the book and to talk about what they liked about the book and what they didn't like. They should write down their ideas in their reading journal, using the following headings: 'What I liked about the book' and 'What I didn't like about the book'.

Give each child a copy of Resource sheet: Mixing colours. The children follow the instructions to mix different colour paints and to label the colours.

Ask children to imagine if the classroom was all one colour. What would it look like? Ask them to draw, then paint, a picture of it on Resource sheet: One colour classroom.

Harry's Garden

Book Band: Blue

This instruction text demonstrates how to make a garden, step-by-step, in an old wheelbarrow.

Skills focus

- Draw on knowledge of vocabulary to understand texts
- Identify/explain key aspects of fiction and non-fiction texts, e.g. character, events, title
- Identify/explain the sequence of events in texts
- Check reading makes sense

Guided reading session

You will need

- Multiple copies of Collins Big Cat *Harry's Garden*
- Other 'how to' books, such as recipe or craft books

Tune in

Ask children to pick up their books so that they are ready to look at the front cover. Read the title with the children and ask them to look at the photo.

Ask the following questions:

- What do you notice about Harry?
- What do you think he has been doing?

Turn to the back cover and read the blurb aloud.

Ask: What does Harry tell us is in this book?

Look together at the back cover photo and then the front cover photo, focusing on evidence that Harry made a garden.

Draw attention to page 14 and read the heading. Explain that a list of things you need is often in books that tell you how to do something. Read pages 14 and 15 aloud to the children but misread 'some small stones' as 'some small bones'.

Ask: 'Bones' – is that correct?

Ask children to check the photo. Elicit how the word should be 'stones' and reread the text correctly.

Read pages 2 and 3 with the children.

Ask: What is the first step to making a garden like Harry's? *(find something to make it in)*

Reread page 2, emphasising the word 'Find'. Explain to the children that this book has instructions and how instructions tell us to do things, like 'Find'.

Ask: Have you read any other instruction books on how to do something?

Heads together

Read pages 2 to 4 aloud to the children, asking them to listen out for the four steps of instructions.

Ask: Which words tell us to do something?

Focus the children on the words 'Find', 'Check', 'Check' and 'Put'. Then ask them to explain each of the four steps. Encourage them to look at the photos and reread the text to check that they have understood each step correctly. For example, go to page 4.

Ask: 'Put some little stones' – is 'little stones' correct?

Encourage the children to check the photo to elicit that there are some little stones.

Ask children to read the rest of the book to find out the next steps on how to make a garden like Harry's. Move around, listening to each child and prompting them to look at the pictures if they are unsure of what they have just read. Encourage them to reread a sentence if necessary.

Ask: Have you found out what the next step is?

Wrap up

Ask children if they think they could use this book to make a garden like Harry's.

Ask the following questions:

- Were the instructions on each step clear?

Check the children have understood the steps in the instructions by asking them to explain the steps, using the photos as prompts. Begin on page 2.

Ask: What did we have to do first? *(find something to make the garden in)*

Move on to page 3.

Ask: What did we have to do next? *(check that it is deep enough)*

Continue in this way. If necessary, prompt them by saying, for example, on page 9: I can see the word 'Fill' – what do we fill?

Encourage the children to use the photos to make sure their explanations make sense.

Return with the children to any pages they have had difficulties with. Ensure that they understand the meaning of any new words by giving a simple child-friendly definition.

Vocabulary boost session

You will need

- Multiple copies of Collins Big Cat *Harry's Garden* · Poster paper

Vocabulary table

Focus word	Child-friendly explanation	Example sentence	Tell me...
check	If you check something, you look carefully to make sure that something is there, or that it is okay.	I **check** that I have put the right things in my bag every morning.	Tell me about something you have to check each day.
need	If you need something, it is very important to have it.	I **need** to sleep or I'm tired.	Tell me about something you need, rather than just want.
gentle	Gentle means being very careful how you handle something and not being at all rough.	I am very **gentle** when I pick up my kitten.	Tell me about when you have been gentle with something.

Tune in

Read the book aloud to the children, asking them to put their hand up if there is a word they don't understand. Briefly pause and give a child-friendly explanation. For example: 'soil' means the brown stuff you get in the garden, which makes your hands dirty. Harry is putting some soil in the wheelbarrow so that the plants can grow in it.

Then ask children to reread the sentence with you, emphasising the relevant word.

After rereading the book, find the focus words from the table, one by one. Write the word on the board, then give a child-friendly explanation, for example: if you check something, you make sure it is there. Then explain it in the context of the book, for example: Harry tells us to check there are small holes in the bottom of the wheelbarrow.

Ask children to say the word again. Give them an example sentence using the focus word. You may wish to use the examples in the table, above.

Then encourage them to think of the word in the context of their own lives by challenging them with the 'Tell me' questions.

Heads together

Develop the children's understanding of the focus words by asking the following:

- Which would you probably check – that you'd got your pencil case or that you'd had your breakfast?
- What do you really need to do before going to school – get dressed or play a game?
- Would you be gentle with a baby bird or with a football?

Encourage them to elaborate on their answers by asking 'Why?' and 'Why not?'

Wrap up

Review the word meanings by asking the following:

- What might a cook who is baking a cake check?
- What might a tennis player need before a match?
- Why should a vet be gentle with animals?

Ask the group to choose one of the focus words and write it in the centre of a piece of large paper. Each day, ask for a suggested word that links with it.

Follow-up independent sessions

You will need

- Resource sheet: Bossy words
- Resource sheet: What comes next?

Ask children to work in groups. The children take it in turns to explain how to do something, such as tie a shoelace, pack their school bag or get to a local shop. Ask children to feed back on the instructions. Were they clear? Swap so another child takes a turn at explaining how to do something.

Give pairs of children a copy of Resource sheet: Bossy words. Ask them to think about the instruction words that told them to do things in the book and to circle them in the picture. Encourage them to think up their own instruction words to add or to look for instruction words in some other 'how to' books such as recipe books.

Hand out copies of Resource sheet: What comes next? The children sequence the order in which to make the wheelbarrow garden.

The Mermaid and the Octopus

Book Band: Blue

A mermaid plays a clever trick on a greedy octopus in this fantasy story.

Skills focus

- Draw on knowledge of vocabulary to understand texts
- Make inferences from texts
- Predict what might happen on the basis of what has been read so far
- Check reading makes sense

Guided reading session

You will need

- Multiple copies of Collins Big Cat *The Mermaid and the Octopus*
- Photograph of an octopus

Tune in

Display a photograph of an octopus.

Ask the following questions:

- What do you know about octopuses?
- How many arms do they have? *(eight)*
- Where do they live? *(in the sea)*

Introduce the book by looking at the front cover together.

Ask: What characters do you think are in this story? *(an octopus and a mermaid)*

Model reading the title using fluency and accuracy. Write the word 'Mermaid' on the board for the children to see. Model segmenting and blending the word 'mermaid' m-er-m-ai-d. Point out the 'er' and 'ai' sounds.

Explain that this is a fantasy story, about an imaginary character – the mermaid (a creature that doesn't really exist in real life). Ask children to describe a mermaid.

Look at the title page. Reread the title. Read 'Written by Julia Donaldson'.

Ask the following questions:

- Does anyone know of any other stories written by Julia Donaldson?
- Who has heard of the Gruffalo?

Turn the book over and read the blurb. Recap that a blurb tells us more about the book. Can the children predict what will happen?

Discuss different strategies for reading the book, for example: segmenting and blending the words 'get' g-e-t, 'lot' l-o-t, 'cup' c-u-p, 'bun' b-u-n, using picture clues, checking for sense and high frequency words.

Recap the sounds 'ea', 'ar', 'oo', by looking at the words 'eat', 'sea', 'tea', 'beads', 'arms', 'spoon'. Practise reading the words together.

Heads together

Look at page 2 together. Discuss the picture on page 2 and ask children to find the following items: a tea cup, two buns, a teapot, a spoon, chair, a necklace and a crown. Read the text on page 2 together as a group, with the children pointing at each word and joining in where they can.

Ask the following questions:

- What was the mermaid doing? *(having tea)*
- Who saw the mermaid? *(the octopus)*

Read page 3 together.

Ask: How do you think the mermaid is feeling? *(scared, shocked)*

Ask: What did the octopus say? *(I'm going to get you!)*

Point out the exclamation mark and model reading with expression. Ask children to practise reading page 3 in pairs using expression. Can the children predict what will happen next?

Ask children to read on in pairs. Recap the strategies for reading. Move around the group, listening and supporting where needed.

Wrap up

Look at page 7 together. Can the children find the word 'teapot'? Show children this is a compound word and how to split it: 'tea/pot'.

Turn to page 13.

Ask the following questions:

- How is the octopus feeling? *(cross)*
- Why is the octopus angry? *(the mermaid has gone, she tricked him)*
- How did the mermaid trick the octopus? *(She gave him eight things to hold so he couldn't get her.)*

Explore pages 14 and 15. Ask children to name all the items the octopus is holding.

Split the children into two groups. Ask one group to think of words to describe the octopus and the other group to think of words to describe the mermaid. Share the children's ideas.

Vocabulary boost session

You will need

- Multiple copies of Collins Big Cat *The Mermaid and the Octopus*
- A selection of fantasy stories

Vocabulary table

Focus word	Child-friendly explanation	Example sentence	Tell me...
mermaid	An imaginary creature that is half-girl and half-fish.	The **mermaid** swam in the sea.	Tell me what a mermaid looks like.
fantasy	If something is a fantasy, it is make-believe.	I read a **fantasy** story about a dragon.	Tell me what other fantasy creatures you know of.
imaginary	If something is imaginary, it is not real.	My little brother has an **imaginary** pet.	If you had an imaginary pet, what would it be?

Tune in

Explain that in this lesson the children are going to look in more detail at some words linked to the text. Write the three focus words clearly for the children to see. Read the words together. Discuss and explain the child-friendly meaning of each word.

Reread the text.

Ask the following questions:

- What type of text is this? *(fantasy story)*
- Which creature is imaginary in this story? *(mermaid)*

Ask children if they know of any other stories about mermaids.

Heads together

Explore a selection of fantasy stories.

Ask: What fantasy creatures are in the stories?

Make a list of imaginary creatures found in fantasy stories. For example: unicorns, dragons, monsters, mermaids, fairies.

Ask children to work in pairs and discuss their own make-believe creature. Could it be half-human and half-animal? Share ideas.

Wrap up

Recap the three focus words by discussing the questions in the 'Tell me' column of the table, above.

Challenge children to think of a sentence using one of the focus words.

Follow-up independent sessions

You will need

- Non-fiction books about octopuses
- A collection of fantasy books
- Collage materials
- Resource sheet: Role on the wall: Octopus
- Resource sheet: Role on the wall: Mermaid
- Magnetic letters and boards
- Paper and coloured pencils
- A collection of Julia Donaldson books

Explore a selection of non-fiction texts about octopuses. What can the children find out? Can they find one fact they didn't know before?

Ask children to look at a selection of fantasy stories. What creatures are in the stories? Can the children make a list of the creatures in the fantasy stories?

Let the children create a collage of the setting 'under the sea'.

Role on the wall for either the character of the octopus (Resource sheet: Role on the wall: Octopus) or the mermaid (Resource sheet: Role on the wall: Mermaid). The children label the picture with adjectives to describe their character on the inside and their appearance on the outside.

Ask children to create the high frequency words from the book using magnetic letters and boards: 'the', 'and', 'was', 'an', 'had', 'said', 'you', 'he', 'going', 'do', 'want', 'took', 'them', 'ask', 'my', 'gone'. Can the children find the words in the book?

Ask children to design, draw and label their own fantasy creature: part-human and part-animal.

Ask children to look at other stories written by the author, Julia Donaldson. Which is their favourite character? Which is their favourite book? Can they choose a character and describe them?

The Steam Train

Book Band: Blue

This poem follows the rhythms and sounds of a steam train as it travels to the seaside.

Skills focus

- Draw on knowledge of vocabulary to understand texts
- Identify/explain key aspects of fiction and non-fiction texts, e.g. character, events, title
- Predict what might happen on the basis of what has been read so far
- Read words accurately and fluently

Guided reading session

You will need

- Multiple copies of Collins Big Cat *The Steam Train*
- Photographs of steam trains
- A range of percussion instruments

Tune in

Begin by recapping some digraphs the children will come across in the text; write them on the board and ask children to say the sounds: 'sh', 'ss', 'ee', 'ai', 'oi', 'ar', 'ow', 'ea'. Then practise reading the words: g-o-sh, f-u-ss, p-ai-n, p-oi-n-t, d-ow-n, s-t-ea-m.

Look at some photographs of steam trains. Discuss the pictures and ask children what they know about steam trains.

Ask the following questions to relate to their own experiences:

- Has anyone ever been on a steam train?
- Where did you go?
- What was it like?

Explain that in the past all trains would have been run on steam; most trains have been replaced by diesel or electric engines now but some steam trains still run for tourists/leisure.

Introduce the book by looking at the front cover. Model reading the title: The, S-t-ea-m, T-r-ai-n. Discuss the picture and ask children to describe the train.

Ask the following questions:

- What does it look like?
- What would it sound like?
- What would it smell like?
- What would it feel like on a train?
- Where do you think the train is going?

Ask children if they can make noises like a train. Use a range of percussion instruments to explore making the sound of a train.

Turn to the back cover. Recap that a blurb tells us more about the book. Model reading the blurb using accuracy and fluency. Point out that this book is a poem.

Ask: Can you identify the rhyming words in the blurb? *(along, song; joints, points)*

Reread the blurb emphasising rhythm and invite the children to join in.

Heads together

Read through the poem aloud together; emphasise the rhythm and invite the children to join in. Practise rereading parts together.

Discuss the pictures on each page.

Ask the following questions:

- What is happening?
- Where is the train?
- Who can you see?
- What is the weather like?
- Do you think the people are enjoying the train?
- Are the people pleased to see the train?

On pages 6 and 7, discuss what 'the points' are (the levers and rails at a place where two tracks join or separate) and point out the road crossing.

Explore the made-up words that describe the sound of the train: de-deedle-dee, de-diddle-dum, tickerty-tack, diddly-dee, tickerty WHAAAH, GOSSSSSSSSSSHHHHHHHHHHHH.

Ask: Where do you think the train is going? *(to a seaside town)*

On page 6, discuss why the train has back pain and aching joints. *(it's old)*

Challenge the children to pick out all the rhyming words throughout the poem: bus/fuss, dum/come, joints/points, down/town, sea/tea.

Wrap up

Explore the train's journey through the countryside to the town.

Ask the following questions:

- What did the train pass on the way? *(bus, tractor, animals, cars, houses, fields, trees)*

- What animals did the train see? *(cows, sheep, horse, seagulls)*

Look at the map on pages 14 and 15 and recap the train's journey.

Ask children to choose their favourite page in the book and share it with their Reading Partner. What do they like about it?

Reread the poem in one go for the children to listen to.

Vocabulary boost session

You will need
- Multiple copies of Collins Big Cat *The Steam Train*
- Resource sheet: The human body

Vocabulary table

Focus word	Child-friendly explanation	Example sentence	Tell me...
gosh	Gosh means you are shocked by something or something is hard work.	**Gosh**, you ate your tea quickly!	Tell me something you have been shocked by.
joints	Where body parts join together; your elbow is a joint that joins your arm bones.	My knee **joints** are aching after that run.	Tell me where the joints are on your body.
points	Railway points are where the track splits into two and can change direction.	The railway guard switched the **points**.	Tell me why the railway guard switched the points.

Tune in

Explain that in this lesson the children are going to look in more detail at some of the words the author has used in the text. Write the three focus words clearly for the children to see. Read the words together. Discuss and explain the child-friendly meaning of each word.

Reread the text.

Challenge children to find the focus words in the text (page 2 and page 6).

Heads together

Use an enlarged copy of Resource sheet: The human body, to discuss the joints on your body. Can the children label these joints: finger joints, knuckles, wrists, elbows, shoulder joints, hips, knees, ankles?

Ask children to think of and create a list of words that mean 'gosh'. Write them on the board. For example: wow, gracious, goodness, golly.

Wrap up

Recap the three focus words by discussing the questions in the 'Tell me' column of the table, above.

Challenge children to think of a sentence using one of the focus words.

Follow-up independent sessions

You will need
- Resource sheet: Train story
- A selection of non-fiction books about trains
- A wooden train set
- Digital camera
- A selection of collage materials including cotton wool
- Old train tickets, a hole punch, a train driver's hat, green and red flags, suitcases, chairs

Ask children to research trains using a selection of non-fiction books.

The children build a wooden train track and act out stories, such as catching a train and going on a journey. Take photos using a digital camera and stick the images on Resource sheet: Train story. The children label or write captions to tell their story.

Ask children to create a collage of a steam train on a railway using a range of textures. The train could be travelling through a town, the country or the coast.

Role-play: trains. Provide the children with chairs to arrange as a train, have old train tickets, a hole punch, a train driver's hat, green and red flags and so on. Children act out different roles, such as the engine driver, ticket collector and station master.

Blast Off to the Moon!

Book Band: Blue

This simple non-fiction report explores the history of space travel and the Moon landings.

Skills focus

- Draw on knowledge of vocabulary to understand texts
- Identify/explain key aspects of fiction and non-fiction texts, e.g. character, events, title
- Make inferences from texts
- Read words accurately and fluently

Guided reading session

You will need

- Multiple copies of Collins Big Cat *Blast Off to the Moon!*

Tune in

Ask children to pick up their books so that they are ready to look at the front cover. Introduce the book by asking the children to look closely at the front cover.

Ask: What is happening? *(a rocket is taking off)*

Encourage the children to point to the title of the book and then read it aloud to them. Ask them to read it aloud with you.

Turn to the title page, read the title together and look at the picture.

Ask: What is this a picture of? *(Earth and the Moon; clarify which one is the Moon)*

Ask them to point to the author's name. Read it aloud to the children. (Michaela Morgan)

Turn to the back cover.

Ask the following questions:

- What is this part of the book called? *(blurb)*
- What is it for? *(It tells us what the book is about).*

Read the blurb aloud, encouraging the children to follow and join in with you.

Ask the following questions:

- What kind of book do you think this is, information or story? *(information)*
- What makes you think that?

Heads together

Read pages 2 to 5 aloud to the children, asking them to follow as you read and to join in. Model strategies for reading fluently, for example, looking ahead at each word, blending phonemes in your head, recognising tricky words.

Point to the caption on page 5 and tell the children that it is called a 'caption'. Ask them to say the word with you: 'caption'. Explain that it tells the reader what is in the picture.

Point out that the words 'rocket' and 'satellite' are in bold font.

Ask: Can you think why these words are in bold? *(special words)*

Read up to page 7 (including the captions) in this way. Encourage the children to look back over what you have read so far.

Ask the following questions:

- What has the book been about so far? *(trying to go to the Moon)*
- Why do you think people wanted to go to the Moon?
- Choose a caption and read it aloud to a partner.

Wrap up

Read up to page 13 aloud, modelling reading strategies and encouraging the children to follow and to join in. As you read, see if the children can find any more words that are in bold. *(astronauts, spacesuit)*

Ask the following questions:

- In space, what do the astronauts have to do that is special? *(wear special clothes, eat special food, drink from special cups)*
- Why do you think they have to do that? *(for protection, because things float away)*

For each answer, encourage the children to find and show the group where it is in the book.

Read pages 14 and 15 together. Explain that a 'glossary' is something that we only find in information books and that it tells us what some of the special words mean. Have a race to see who can find the glossary words the fastest (you may need to remind the children that they are the words in bold font).

Ask the following questions:

- What kind of book do you think this is, information or story? *(information)*
- How do you know? *(about real things, photographs, captions, glossary)*

Vocabulary boost session

You will need
- Multiple copies of Collins Big Cat *Blast Off to the Moon!*

Vocabulary table

Focus word	Child-friendly explanation	Example sentence	Tell me...
protect	Protect means to stop someone from being hurt.	When I ride my bike, I wear a helmet to **protect** my head.	Tell me about a time when you have worn something to protect you.
special	If something is special, it is different from what we always have.	We ate a **special** lunch at Christmas.	Tell me about something that is special.
explore	If you explore a place, you look around it to find out what it's like.	The boys **explored** the new park.	Tell me about a place you have explored.

Tune in

Explain to the children that in this lesson they are going to look closely at some of the words the author has used and what those words mean.

Read the book aloud to the children, asking them to follow and to join in as you read.

Refer back to each of the focus words within the context of the story, writing up the word, giving a child-friendly explanation and asking the children to say the focus word with you. For example: The book tells us that the helmet protects the astronaut's face. That means that it stops his face from being hurt. Now, say the word with me – 'protect'.

You may wish to use the examples in the table, above.

Refer to each of the focus words that you have written up and give the children the example sentences. Then ask them to interact with the word meanings by asking the questions in the 'Tell me' column. You may wish to demonstrate by giving some examples of your own.

Ask children to say the words with you once more.

Heads together

Explore and develop the children's understanding of the focus words by doing the following activity. Tell the children that if you say something that is about protecting, they say 'protect'. If it's not about protecting, they don't say anything.

- Wearing pads on my knees when I am on my scooter.
- Brushing my hair.
- Putting on sun-cream when it is very sunny.

If you say something that is about being special, they say 'special'. If it's not, they don't say anything.

- Eating breakfast every day.
- Wearing something new for a party.
- A famous person coming into school for a visit.

If you say something that is about exploring, they say 'explore'. If it's not, they don't say anything.

- Looking around a new playground.
- Going to school.
- Finding new places to hide in the park.

For each, ask children why they responded as they did.

Wrap up

Ask the following questions to review the word meanings:

- What's the word that means something that is different from what we always have?
- What's the word that means to look around a place to find out what it's like?
- What's the word that means to stop someone from being hurt?

Ask children to choose one of the focus words as their word of the week. Challenge them to use the word as often as they can, both at school and at home.

Follow-up independent sessions

You will need
- Multiple copies of Collins Big Cat *Blast Off to the Moon!*
- Resource sheet: Space gap fill
- Resource sheet: Space unscramble

Ask children to work with their Reading Partners and to read the book aloud.

Give each child a copy of Resource sheet: Space gap fill. The children use the book to find the missing words.

Give pairs of children a copy of Resource sheet: Space unscramble. Ask them to unscramble the letters to find the space words.

The Lonely Penguin

Book Band: Blue

A lonely penguin goes on a journey across Antarctica to find his friends, in this story with a predictable structure and patterned language,

Skills focus

- Draw on knowledge of vocabulary to understand texts
- Make inferences from texts
- Predict what might happen on the basis of what has been read so far
- Read words accurately and fluently

Guided reading session

You will need

- Multiple copies of Collins Big Cat *The Lonely Penguin*
- Pictures of empty Antarctic icy landscapes

Tune in

Tell the children that they are going to read a story that is set in a very cold place, called Antarctica, where there is lots of snow and ice. If possible, show them images of empty, icy Antarctic landscapes.

Ask: How would you feel if you lived here?

Encourage the children to point to the title of the book as you read it aloud. Explain that 'lonely' is the unhappy feeling we can sometimes have if we are all alone.

Ask: Why do you think the penguin is lonely?

Turn to page 2 and encourage the children to jump into the picture and imagine that they are walking in the vast icy landscape.

Ask the following questions:

- What can you hear? *(for example, wind, feet on snow)*
- How do you feel? *(for example, cold, scared, lonely)*

Read the text aloud on pages 2 and 3.

Ask the following questions:

- What is making the crunching noise? *(the penguin stepping on snow)*
- How is the penguin feeling and why? *(lonely because there is no one else there)*
- What might Penguin do?

Read pages 4 and 5 aloud to the children.

Ask: What do you think he will do next?

Turn to page 6 and ask volunteers to read or guess the first two words. Point out the repetition of 'Crunch crunch' here and on the previous pages.

Ask: Do you think they are good words for a penguin walking on snow? Why?

Heads together

Read pages 2 to 7, encouraging the children to join in chorally, especially with the words 'Crunch crunch'. Write them on the board and highlight the single sound made by the two letters 'ch'. Remind the children how more than one letter often makes only one sound.

Write 'penguin' on the board. Tell the children that some words have unusual spellings – sound out and blend the word 'penguin' pen-g-u-in. Point out how the 'u' sounds like /w/.

Suggest that for difficult words like this it is a good idea to look for smaller words, sound these out and then other parts will be easier to work out. Underline 'pen' and 'in' in 'penguin' and read the syllables: 'pen-gu-in'.

Refocus on pages 6 and 7 and ask:

- What is Penguin doing here?
- Where is he going? Why is he running?

Ask the following questions:

- Do you think this story will have a happy ending? Why?
- Do stories usually have a happy ending?

Encourage the children to talk about books they have read and what sort of ending they had. Encourage the children to work with their Reading Partner to read the rest of the story to find out if there is a happy ending.

Wrap up

Ask children if they found out what happened at the end. Was it a happy ending?

Turn back to page 11 and focus the children on the picture.

Ask: Were you worried when Penguin jumped in the water? Why?

Encourage the children to imagine how the water feels.

Ask: What did the lonely penguin do about being lonely?

Elicit how he went on a journey to find his friends.

Reread the text, asking the children to join in with you. Encourage them to read the repeated words expressively.

Vocabulary boost session

You will need

- Multiple copies of Collins Big Cat *The Lonely Penguin* • Old comics and pictures

Vocabulary table

Focus word	Child-friendly explanation	Example sentence	Tell me...
friends	Friends are people you like, such as the other children you play with.	I go on holiday with **friends** and family.	Tell me about your friends.
sliding	Sliding means slipping, such as when you are sliding on a slippery surface, like ice.	On one icy day in winter, my car started **sliding** down a hill!	Tell me about when you've seen something or someone sliding.
everywhere	Everywhere means all places and not just in one place.	I've looked **everywhere** for my lost key.	Tell me about a time when you have looked everywhere for something.

Tune in

Read the book aloud to the children, encouraging them to join in the repeated words 'Crunch crunch!'

Ask: Who was Penguin looking for? *(friends)*

Write 'friends' on the board and explain that you are going to look closely at this and other words from the book.

Read the word 'friends' on the board and explain its meaning in a child-friendly way. For example: Friends are people you like and often spend more time with.

Talk about the word in the context of the story, for example: Penguin had lost his friends but he found them and they probably missed him – Penguin was their friend too!

Ask children to read the word with you again.

Encourage the children to use the word 'friends', with a 'Tell me' challenge, such as those in the table, above. This will allow you to check their understanding.

Ask children to say the word with you – 'friends' – before moving on to the next focus word.

Heads together

Ask the following questions to help develop the children's understanding of the focus words:

- What might you do with friends at the weekend?
- Where might you see people or things sliding around?
- What kind of things do you see everywhere?

Encourage the children to discuss their answers as a group.

Wrap up

Ask the following questions to review the word meanings:

- If I said I had no friends, what would that mean?
- If I said I saw a skier sliding down a hill, what would that mean?
- If I said I'd been everywhere in the world, what would that mean?

Write the focus words on a wall and provide lots of old comics and pictures. Every day, ask children to agree on some pictures that link with one of the focus words. Discuss the children's choices, then cut the pictures out and put them alongside the word.

Follow-up independent sessions

You will need

- Multiple copies of Collins Big Cat *The Lonely Penguin*
- Resource sheet: Penguin's map
- Resource sheet: Role on the wall: the lonely penguin

Ask groups of children to choose and practise reading four pages of the book expressively. Encourage them to work out who reads which page and who joins in with the repeated lines.

Give individual children a copy of Resource sheet: Penguin's map. Ask children to find words in the book that go with each picture. Ask them to choose the one that best suits the picture and copy it underneath. Alternatively, they could discuss the best words with their Reading Partner.

Use Resource sheet: Role on the wall: the lonely penguin. The children label the picture of Penguin with adjectives to describe his character on the inside and his appearance on the outside.

Tod and the Trumpet

Book Band: Blue

In this story with a familiar setting, a passion for playing the trumpet persuades a shy tortoise to come out of his shell.

Skills focus

- Draw on knowledge of vocabulary to understand texts
- Make inferences from texts
- Identify/explain the sequence of events in texts
- Read words accurately and fluently

Guided reading session

You will need

- Multiple copies of Collins Big Cat *Tod and the Trumpet*
- Photo of a tortoise

Tune in

Show the children a photograph of a tortoise. Discuss how tortoises hide inside their shell to protect themselves from predators. Do the children know any stories about tortoises? *(The Hare and the Tortoise)*

Introduce the book by looking at the front cover. Model reading the title using segmenting and blending the words 'tod' t-o-d and 'trumpet' t-r-u-m-p-e-t and then reread using fluency.

Ask the following questions:

- Who is the main character in this story? *(Tod, the tortoise)*
- Do you think Tod likes playing the trumpet? *(yes, he is smiling)*

Discuss what an author and illustrator do (an author writes the words and an illustrator draws the pictures).

Ask: Who is the author and illustrator of this book? *(Charlotte Middleton)*

Turn the book over to look at the back cover. Recap that a blurb tells us more about the book. Read the blurb. Ask children to point out any high frequency words they know: 'is', 'so', 'he', 'in', 'his', 'but', 'no', 'one', 'can', 'the', 'come', 'out'.

Can the children predict what might make Tod come out of his shell?

Ask the following questions:

- Has anyone felt shy before?
- What does 'shy' mean?
- Can you think of a time when you would like to hide in your shell?

Explain that the setting of this story is school/nursery.

Ask: Will Tod be able to play with the other children if he is hiding in his shell?

Recap strategies the children can use when reading: decoding, high frequency words, picture clues and checking it makes sense.

Heads together

Look at pages 2 and 3 together. Discuss the pictures.

Ask the following questions:

- What are the characters doing on page 2? *(playing on the swings, see-saw and with a ball)*
- Who is missing out on all the fun? *(Tod because he is in his shell)*
- Why do you think he is in his shell? *(He is feeling shy.)*
- Where are the children? *(playground/school)*
- What is everyone doing on page 3? *(tidying up)*
- Do you like tidying up?

Model reading the text using accuracy and fluency. Reread the text together, asking the children to point to the words and to join in.

Ask the following questions:

- Can you name two occasions when Tod hides in his shell. *(When he is feeling shy and at tidy-up time.)*
- Why do you think Tod hides at tidy-up time?

Ask children to work with their Reading Partners and to continue reading the story. Can they find out what Tod does inside his shell? What makes him come out of his shell? How does he feel when he comes out of his shell? Move around the group, listening to the children read and supporting where needed.

Wrap up

Reread the text together. Ask children to point at each word and to join in.

Turn to pages 14 and 15 and ask children to retell the story in their own words using the story map.

Discuss the text to check the children's understanding.

Ask the following questions:

- What does Tod do inside his shell? *(read, draws, plays the trumpet)*
- How do you think Tod felt on page 7? *(lonely, sad)*

- What made him come out of his shell? *(He wanted to play the big trumpet and it didn't fit in his shell.)*

Look at pages 12 and 13.

Ask: How does Tod feel out of his shell? *(not scared, happy)*

Look at page 9. Discuss the words in capital letters.

Ask: Why are these words in capitals? *(for emphasis, important words)*

Ask children to practise reading page 9 using expression.

Turn to page 10. Point out the word 'slowly'.

Ask: Why do you think Tod stretches his head out 'slowly'? *(because he is nervous)*

Vocabulary boost session

You will need

- Multiple copies of Collins Big Cat *Tod and the Trumpet*

Vocabulary table

Focus word	Child-friendly explanation	Example sentence	Tell me...
shy	If you are feeling shy, you are scared, not sure and a bit nervous.	I felt **shy** when I started a new school.	Tell me a time when you have felt shy.
instrument	An instrument is a tool or mechanism.	A trumpet is a musical **instrument**.	Tell me what musical instruments you have played.
slowly	If you do something slowly, it takes a long time. You do it bit by bit.	**Slowly**, I walked on to the stage.	Can you think of any other adverbs?

Tune in

Explain that in this lesson the children are going to look in detail at some of the words the author has used. Write the three focus words clearly for the children to see. Read the words together. Discuss and explain the child-friendly meaning of each word.

Reread the text.

Ask children to find the focus words in the text (pages 2, 8 and 10). Discuss what type of instruments were on the children's desks: musical instruments – tools used to play music.

Ask the following questions:

- Who was feeling shy? *(Tod)*
- What did he do slowly? *(stick his head out of his shell)*

Heads together

Create an adverb word wall. List as many different adverbs as the children can think of.

Ask children to choose an adverb to replace 'slowly' on page 10.

Ask: How many different musical instruments do you know?

Children think of as many as they can with their Reading Partner and then share ideas.

Wrap up

Recap the three focus words by discussing the questions in the 'Tell me' column of the table, above.

Challenge the children to think of a sentence using one of the focus words.

Follow-up independent sessions

You will need

- Resource sheet: Role on the wall: Tod
- A selection of musical instruments
- A selection of non-fiction texts about tortoises
- Resource sheet: Tortoise facts
- Magazines, catalogues, leaflets with pictures of musical instruments, paper, glue, scissors

Use Resource sheet: Role on the wall: Tod. The children label the picture of Tod with adjectives to describe his character on the inside and his appearance on the outside.

Children explore a selection of musical instruments. What sounds do they make? What do they use to make the sound? Do they know what the instruments are called?

Ask children to explore a range of non-fiction texts about tortoises. What facts can the children find out? They record them on Resource sheet: Tortoise facts.

The children create and label a collage of musical instruments (find pictures in magazines, catalogues, leaflets and cut out).

Growing and Changing

Book Band: Blue

This information book shows how our bodies change as we grow from baby to child.

Skills focus

- Draw on knowledge of vocabulary to understand texts
- Identify/explain key aspects of fiction and non-fiction texts, e.g. character, events, title
- Check reading makes sense

Guided reading session

You will need

- Multiple copies of Collins Big Cat *Growing and Changing*

Tune in

Ask children to pick up their books. Look closely at the front cover.

Ask: What do you think the two girls are doing? *(one is measuring the height of the other)*

Explore the children's experiences of being measured.

Ask: What does being measured show you? *(that you are growing/getting taller)*

Ask children to point to and read the title of the book. If appropriate, identify the '–ing' endings and the root words 'grow' and 'change'.

Turn to the back cover and ask children to read the blurb.

Ask: What do you think you'll find in the book?

Establish that this is a non-fiction book – it gives information and helps us to find out things.

Turn to the contents page. If the children are not familiar with the purpose and organisation of a contents page, explain this. Establish that a contents page is organised in numerical order. Focus on a section heading, for example, 'Growing taller' and the page number (page 6). Demonstrate how to turn to page 6 to find the section and that the heading on page 6 is the same as in the contents.

Explain that a contents page helps a reader to find information rather than just looking through the book hoping to find something.

Look at the section heading 'Growing and changing' and ask children which page they should look for (page 2). Ask them to turn to page 2 and find the heading 'Growing and changing'. Explain that a heading tells you what the information on the page is about.

Read the text on pages 2 and 3 aloud to the children. Ask them to look at the two timelines on these pages and to explain to their Reading Partner what they show.

Take feedback from the discussion and establish that the timelines show how the two children change – starting from when they are babies.

Summarise that on these pages information is given through words and pictures.

Heads together

Return to the contents page and allocate a section heading to each child in the group. Don't allocate 'Timeline' on page 14 at this point.

Ask them each to find the section heading and the page number in the contents page and then to find their section in the book.

Once they have found their section, they can read the information. Remind them that the information will be given in both words and pictures.

Wrap up

Ask children to feed back on their reading to the rest of the group.

Ask the following questions:

- What information have you found out?
- Were there pictures on your pages?
- What information did the pictures give you?

Revisit some of the pages and look at the pictures and how they give information.

Turn to pages 10 and 11. Ask children to identify the labels on the photographs.

Establish that the labels are linked to certain parts of the picture and so explain what those parts are.

Challenge the children to skim through the book and find another page with labels. (pages 4 and 5)

Remind the children that on pages 2 and 3 they looked at a timeline and they now know about labelled photographs. Emphasise that these are two different ways of giving information through pictures.

Vocabulary boost session

You will need

- Multiple copies of Collins Big Cat *Growing and Changing*
- Flipboard
- Mini-whiteboards and pens

Vocabulary table

Focus word	Child-friendly explanation	Example sentence	Tell me...
walk	To move along using both feet. Slower than running.	I like to **walk** along the road when it is sunny.	Tell me about a time you have walked somewhere.
jump	To leap into the air.	The loud noise made me **jump** into the air.	Tell me about a time when you have jumped off something high.
move	To get from one place to another, you have to move.	I saw a mouse **move** across the floor.	Tell me how many different ways you can move across the classroom.

Tune in

Ask children to tell you what information they have found out from the book.

Ask the following questions:

- What do you know about the contents page in an information book? (*organised in page order, gives section headings*)
- How is information given to you in the book? (*through words and pictures*)

Explain to the children that in this lesson they are going to look closely at some of the words the author has used, what those words mean and how they can make a reader think about other words.

Turn to pages 12 and 13. Read the text at the top and then the timeline captions at the bottom of these pages.

Ask: What is the information about on these pages? Involve the children in rereading the text and identifying the movement verbs: walk, jump, move, crawl. List these verbs on a flipchart or the board.

Challenge the children to demonstrate each of the verbs and establish that 'move' is a general word, whereas the others are specific types of movement.

Focus on the word 'walk' and challenge the children to work with their Reading Partners to develop a list

on their whiteboards of other verbs that have a similar meaning to 'walk'.

Take feedback from the activity, listing the children's suggestions. Say that you'd like to add an idea to the list and write up 'stroll'.

Repeat this activity, focusing on 'jump'. List the children's suggested alternatives plus your own suggestion of 'leap'.

Finally, focus on the word 'move' and ask children to develop a list of general movement verbs. Add your own idea of 'scurry'.

Heads together

Give children the example sentences from the table, above, to let them hear the focus words in different contexts.

Explore the suggestions in the 'Tell me' column. If possible, take the children to an open area where they can demonstrate the suggested movements. Support them in exploring what it feels like to stroll, leap and scurry.

Wrap up

Ask children to choose one of the focus words as their word of the week. Challenge them to try and to use the word as often as they can – both at home and at school.

Follow-up independent sessions

You will need

- Multiple copies of Collins Big Cat *Growing and Changing*
- Resource sheet: Timeline for *Growing and Changing*
- Resource sheet: Quiz

Ask children to work with their Reading Partners and to look at the timeline on pages 14 and 15. They can look at each picture and identify the changes in

appearance and movement as the child gets older. Give each pair a copy of Resource sheet: Timeline for *Growing and Changing* and ask them to note down the changes next to each picture. Ask each pair to use their Resource sheet to explain to the rest of the group the changes they have noticed.

Give each child a copy of Resource sheet: Quiz. Ask them to use the book to answer the quiz questions on the sheet. When they have answered the questions, they can swap their sheet with their Reading Partner and check each other's answers.

New from Old: Recycling Plastic

Book Band: Blue

This information book explores how plastic is recycled, what it can be used for and why recycling is important for the planet.

Skills focus

- Draw on knowledge of vocabulary to understand texts
- Identify/explain key aspects of fiction and non-fiction texts, e.g. character, events, title
- Make inferences from texts
- Read words accurately and fluently

Guided reading session

You will need

- Multiple copies of Collins Big Cat *New from Old: Recycling Plastic*

Tune in

Ask children to pick up their books so that they are ready to look at the front cover. Introduce the book by reading the title to the children.

Ask: Do you know what recycling is? *(making something new from something that has already been used)*

Encourage the children to point to the title of the book and then read it aloud again, asking them to read it aloud with you.

Ask: What do you think 'new from old' means? *(making something new from something that is old)*

Turn to the title page, read the title of the book and the name of the author together.

Ask children to point to the word 'contents'. Explain that the 'contents' tells us what is in the book and where to find it. Read the contents aloud to the children, asking them to follow. As you read, insert the word 'page' before each number so that the children understand that is what the numbers are for.

Ask the following questions:

- What kind of book do you think this is: information or story? *(information)*
- What makes you think that? *(about real things, photographs, contents)*

Heads together

Read pages 2 to 5 aloud to the children, asking them to follow as you read and to join in where they are able. Model strategies for reading longer words, for example, recognition of tricky words ('new', 'some'), breaking words down ('some/thing'). Make sure that you read the captions.

Point to the captions on pages 4 and 5 and tell the children that they are called 'captions'. Ask them to say the word with you – 'caption'. Explain that they tell the reader what is in the picture.

Turn back to the title page. Tell the children that you are about to read page 6.

Ask: Can you use the contents to find out what page 6 is about? *(how we recycle plastic)*

Read pages 6 to 11 aloud, modelling reading strategies and encouraging the children to follow and to join in.

Wrap up

Read page 12 together.

Ask: Why do you think that too much rubbish is bad for the planet? *(nowhere to put it, looks ugly, stops new things from growing)*

Read page 13 together.

Ask: What do you think the word 'reduce' means? *(make smaller)*

Read pages 14 and 15 together.

Ask: Can you show and tell me what clues there are to show this is an information book? *(about real things, photographs, captions, contents)*

Vocabulary boost session

You will need

- Multiple copies of Collins Big Cat *New from Old: Recycling Plastic*

Vocabulary table

Focus word	Child-friendly explanation	Example sentence	Tell me...
use	If you use something, you do something with it.	I **used** the cloth to clean the window.	Tell me about something that you might use to clean with.
collect	Collect means to bring things and put them in one place.	When I was on the beach, I **collected** shells.	Tell me about something that you have collected.
sort	If you sort objects, you put them into groups.	I **sorted** the beads by their colours.	Tell me how you might sort objects like beads.

Tune in

Explain to the children that in this lesson they are going to look closely at some of the words the author has used and what those words mean.

Read the book aloud to the children, asking them to follow and join in as you read.

Refer back to each of the focus words within the context of the story, writing up the word, giving a child-friendly explanation and asking the children to say the focus word with you. For example: The book tells us about making something new from something that is used. If you use something, you do something with it. Now, say the word with me – 'use'.

You may wish to use the examples in the table, above.

Refer to each of the focus words that you have written up and give the children the example sentences. Then ask them to interact with the word meanings by asking the questions in the 'Tell me' column. You may wish to demonstrate by giving some examples of your own.

Ask children to say the words with you once more.

Heads together

Explore and develop the children's understanding of the focus words.

Tell the children that you will say a sentence that is missing a word and that they have to say one of the new words that fits into the sentence. Tell them that either 'use', 'collect' or 'sort' will fit into the blank. Say:

- The teacher asked the children to… newspapers for the art area.
- Sarah has to… a brush to sweep up the mess.
- They… the bottles into three sizes: large, medium and small.

Wrap up

Ask the following questions to review the word meanings:

- What's the word that means putting objects into groups?
- What's the word that means doing something with an object?
- What's the word that means to bring things and put them in one place?

Ask children to choose one of the focus words as their word of the week. Challenge them to use the word as often as they can, both at school and at home.

Follow-up independent sessions

You will need

- Multiple copies of Collins Big Cat *New from Old: Recycling Plastic*
- Resource sheet: Recycling questions
- Resource sheet: Recycling order

Ask children to work with their Reading Partners and to read the book aloud.

Hand out copies of Resource sheet: Recycling questions. The children use the book to help them to find the answers to the questions.

Give the children the cards cut from Resource sheet: Recycling order. They sort the cards into the correct order to show how plastic is recycled and add captions.

Super Sam

Book Band: Blue

Sam the dog has a secret: he turns into Super Sam when his owners aren't around. In this simple story with a familiar setting, Super Sam performs a heroic deed, but his secret stays safe.

Skills focus

- Draw on knowledge of vocabulary to understand texts
- Identify/explain key aspects of fiction and non-fiction texts, e.g. character, events, title
- Predict what might happen on the basis of what has been read so far
- Read words accurately and fluently

Guided reading session

You will need

- Multiple copies of Collins Big Cat *Super Sam*

Tune in

Ask children to pick up their books so that they are ready to look at the front cover. Focus the children on the illustration and read the title.

Ask: Do you think this is Super Sam? Why?

Encourage the children to describe what is 'super' or unusual about the dog.

Turn to the back cover and read the title and blurb.

Ask: The main character in this story is a dog called Super Sam – what do you think he does that is 'super'?

Return to the front cover and encourage them to find evidence in the picture and elicit how Sam is flying and wearing socks and a cape. Encourage the children to tell the group about other 'super' characters they know, for example, Superman.

Read pages 2 to 4 aloud to the children. Point out the exclamation mark on page 4 and remind them that this means the sentence should be read with excitement. Demonstrate by rereading the sentence.

Point to the word 'rescue' and briefly explain its meaning in child-friendly language. For example: rescue means to help or save someone who is in trouble. In this story, Super Sam is searching for someone to rescue or help.

Challenge the children to predict what might happen in the story.

Heads together

Read the story aloud to the children up to page 13, dramatising the spoken words to the children and reading exclamatory sentences with emphasis.

Pause at 'don't' on page 8 and point to the apostrophe and elicit that this means a letter is missing. Explain that the missing letter is 'o' and 'Don't' is short for 'Do not'.

Ask the following questions:

- What do you think of the Super Sam character now?
- Can you describe him to me?

Encourage them to give reasons for their answers.

Turn to page 13 and ask children to imagine that they are one of the owners.

Ask: How would you feel if you found out that Sam was the 'super dog' in the newspaper?

Tell the children that they are going to read the story again and that you want them to imagine how it would feel to be Sam as they read.

Encourage the children to join in with as many words as they can. Listen out for any words the whole group has difficulties with and pause to help them by reading the word as syllables or by identifying letter sounds.

Wrap up

Remind the children that they were imagining what it would be like to be Sam.

Encourage children to take turns to role-play Sam, while others ask him questions (hot-seating).

Ask your own questions to prompt the children, for example:

- Do you like flying?
- What do you think of your owners?

Ask other children to take turns to role-play Sam.

Reread pages 12 and 13.

Ask: What do you think the newspaper story says?

After encouraging the children's ideas, read pages 14 and 15 to them.

Ask: What do we know that the newspaper doesn't? *(for example, his name, where he lives, that he dreams of bones)*

Vocabulary boost session

You will need

- Multiple copies of Collins Big Cat *Super Sam*

Vocabulary table

Focus word	Child-friendly explanation	Example sentence	Tell me...
super	If someone or something is super, then it is extra special, just like Sam is an extra special dog.	I saw a weight-lifter who was **super**-strong.	Tell me about something or someone that you think is super.
worry	If you worry about something, then you feel bothered about it and you keep wondering about it. Super Sam told the puppy not to worry because he will be safe soon.	I **worry** that I will be late.	Tell me about something that you worry about.
save	If you save someone, then you take them out of danger and you make them safe.	The fireman went up a ladder to **save** a kitten that was trapped on a roof.	Tell me about an animal that might be in trouble and how you would save it.

Tune in

Explain to the children that they are going to look carefully at some of the words in the book and learn more about their meaning.

Read the book aloud to the children, stopping at the focus words or another word or two that the group will be unfamiliar with.

Reread the sentence in which the word appears. Write the word on the board, explaining its meaning in a child-friendly way. For example: Super means extra special. Sam isn't an ordinary dog – he is super because he can fly and save things!

Ask children to say the focus word with you.

When you have covered the focus words in this way, point to each in turn and give other sentences that include the words, such as those in the table, above.

Challenge children to use the words themselves by asking the questions in the 'Tell me' column. You could demonstrate by giving some examples of your own.

Ask children to say the words with you again.

Heads together

Explore and develop the children's understanding of the focus words.

Ask the following questions:

- Do you think I would be super if I could pick up a lorry?
- If I said 'I worry', would I be happy or troubled?
- If I wanted to save a baby bird that fell out of a nest, what might I do?

Encourage them to discuss their ideas as a group.

Wrap up

Challenge the children to clap once, each time they hear a word that links with the focus word. Say:

- 'super': special, dull, fantastic, boring
- 'worry': excited, unhappy, jolly, troubled
- 'save': run, laugh, help, danger

Ask children to pick one focus word as their word of the week. Challenge them to use the word as often as they can, both at school and at home.

Follow-up independent sessions

You will need

- Resource sheet: Newspaper report
- Paper, coloured pencils
- Resource sheet: Do you agree?

Ask children to work with a partner to think of another story about Sam in which he saves someone. On a copy of Resource sheet: Newspaper report, the children draw 'photos' to show the animal or person in danger and write a caption to say how Sam saves him or her. Can they think of a headline for their report?

Give pairs of children a copy of Resource sheet: Do you agree? Ask them to tick one of the columns to say whether they agree or disagree with each sentence. They then write the reason why they do or don't like Sam.

Let's Build a Rocket

In this story with patterned and predictable language, the rhyming text follows a girl as she builds her own rocket and imagines taking her friends on trips to the Sun and the Moon.

Skills focus

- Draw on knowledge of vocabulary to understand texts
- Identify/explain the sequences of events in texts
- Predict what might happen on the basis of what has been read so far
- Read words accurately and fluently

Guided reading session

You will need

- Multiple copies of Collins Big Cat *Let's Build a Rocket*
- Photographs of space rockets/spacecraft
- Resource sheet: Word cards for *Let's Build a Rocket*
- Resource sheet: Rhyming words for *Let's Build a Rocket*

Tune in

Display some photographs of space rockets and spacecraft.

Ask the following questions:

- What is this? *(rocket)*
- What is it for? *(travelling into space)*
- What parts does the rocket have? *(wings, windows, door)*
- Who travels in a rocket? *(astronauts)*
- How do you think rockets are made?
- Has anyone made a rocket before?
- If you had a rocket, where would you like to go? *(space, planets, Moon, Sun)*

Ask children to complete the sentence stem: 'If I had a rocket, I would go…'

Introduce the book by looking at the front cover together.

Ask the following questions:

- What is the child doing? *(painting a rocket)*
- What do you think the rocket is made from? *(cardboard, wood, plastic)*

Model reading the title. Use segmenting and blending to read the words 'let's' l-e-t-s and 'rocket' r-o-ck-e-t.

Turn the book over to look at the back cover. Model reading the blurb using fluency and accuracy. Point out the apostrophe and discuss that it shows a missing letter: the letter 'a' in 'I'm' = 'I am' and the letter 'u' in 'let's' = 'let us'.

Explain that this book is a poem.

Ask the following questions:

- Can you spot the rhyming words in the blurb? *(done, Sun)*

- Can you think of any other words that rhyme with Sun?

Reread the blurb.

Ask the following questions:

- Do you think they will be able to visit the Sun?
- Is it a good idea to visit the Sun? *(no, it's too hot)*

Can the children predict where the friends might go?

Play a game of 'Snap!' with two sets of the high frequency word cards cut from Resource sheet: Word cards for *Let's Build a Rocket*.

Give the children copies of the words 'done', 'sun', 'soon', 'moon', 'hot', 'spot', 'fly', 'high', 'land' and 'planned' cut from Resource sheet: Rhyming words for *Let's Build a Rocket* and ask them to work together to find the matching pairs.

Heads together

Look at pages 2 and 3 together. Model reading the text, using fluency and rhythm. Which high frequency words do the children recognise?

Ask: Can you spot the rhyming words? *(done, sun)*

Ask children to practise reading aloud in pairs. Discuss that on page 3, the child is imagining their trip to the Sun. Can the children predict what will happen next? Will the friends get to the Sun?

Recap different strategies the children can use: segmenting and blending the words 'trip' t-r-i-p, 'sun' s-u-n, 'mean' m-ea-n, 'hot' h-o-t, 'just' j-u-s-t and 'pick' p-i-ck, picture clues, checking for sense and high frequency words.

Ask children to read on in pairs. Encourage them to point to each word and remind each other of strategies to tackle unknown words. Move around the group and support where needed. Can they find out where the child imagines going in the rocket next?

Wrap up

Ask the following questions:

- Where did the child imagine going? *(the Sun, the Moon, up high)*

- Why didn't they go to the Sun? *(too hot)*
- Why couldn't they go to the Moon? *(no air)*
- Does the child know how the rocket will land? *(no)*

Go back through the book and find all the rhyming pairs.

Look at pages 6 and 7 and discuss the '–ing' ending on the words 'building', 'finishing' and 'taking'.

Finally, turn to pages 14 and 15 and ask children to discuss the picture in pairs. What can they see?

Ask: What equipment has the child got? *(paint, paintbrush, a stool, instructions, a telescope)*

Complete the sentence stem 'If I had a rocket, I would go…'

Vocabulary boost session

You will need

- Multiple copies of Collins Big Cat *Let's Build a Rocket*
- Set of cards cut from Resource sheet: Rhyming words for *Let's Build a Rocket*

Vocabulary table

Focus word	Child-friendly explanation	Example sentence	Tell me…
astronaut	An astronaut is a person who goes into space.	The **astronaut** went to the Moon in a spaceship.	Tell me which planet you would like to visit as an astronaut.
rhyme	Words that have the same sound at the end.	The words 'sun' and 'done' **rhyme**.	Tell me what words rhyme with 'cat'.
imagine	If you imagine something, you picture it in your head.	I **imagined** going on holiday to a desert island.	Can you imagine going on holiday? Tell me where you would go.

Tune in

Explain that in this lesson the children are going to look in more detail at some words linked to the text. Write the three focus words clearly for the children to see. Read the words together. Discuss and explain the child-friendly meaning of each word.

Reread the text.

Ask: Can you find the rhyming pairs?

Look at page 9.

Ask the following questions:

- What are the astronauts wearing? Why? *(spacesuits, for protection)*
- Where did the child imagine going? *(Sun, Moon, up high)*

Heads together

Ask children to discuss in pairs the following statements:

- Imagine you are on the Moon; what would it be like? What do you think you would hear? See? Smell? Feel?
- Imagine you are inside a space rocket; what would it be like? What do you think you would hear? See? Smell? Feel?

Give the children a set of the cards cut from Resource sheet: Rhyming words for *Let's Build a Rocket*, to sort and match the rhyming words. Can they add any of their own words?

Wrap up

Recap the three focus words by discussing the questions in the 'Tell me' column of the table, above.

Challenge the children to think of a sentence using one of the focus words.

Follow-up independent sessions

You will need

- Junk (empty bottles, cardboard boxes and tubes, foil, plastic containers, foil)
- Paper, coloured pencils
- A selection of non-fiction books about space

Junk modelling: let the children use a range of empty bottles, cardboard boxes and tubes, foil, plastic containers and bottle tops to make their very own rocket.

Ask children to design and label a picture/diagram of a rocket. What would they like it to look like? What will it need? What shape will it be? What colour will it be? What would it be made from? Does it have windows/a door/wings?

Ask children to explore a range of non-fiction books about space, astronauts and planets. What facts can they find out?

Let the children draw a picture of where they would go in their rocket. Can they add adjectives?

Going to the Zoo

Book Band: Blue

In this poem, a boy and his family visit a zoo where all the animals behave in the most unexpected ways.

Skills focus

- Draw on knowledge of vocabulary to understand texts
- Identify/explain key aspects of fiction and non-fiction texts, e.g. character, events, title
- Identify/explain the sequence of events in texts
- Read words accurately and fluently

Guided reading session

You will need

- Multiple copies of Collins Big Cat *Going to the Zoo*
- Timer
- Flipchart

Tune in

Ask children to pick up their books and look at the front cover, point to, and read, the title.

Challenge them to name as many zoo animals as they can in 30 seconds. List the animals they call out on the board or flipchart.

Ask children to read the blurb on the back cover.

Ask: What do you notice about the blurb? *(it rhymes)*

Check that all of the children can hear and identify the rhyming words.

Look at the front cover again.

Ask: Can you spot any animals? *(giraffes)*

Do the children notice the tail disappearing through the entrance?

Ask: Who do you think is going to the zoo? *(It looks like a family.)*

Heads together

Model how to read page 2 aloud, reading with expression and emphasising the rhyme and rhythm of the poem.

Read page 4 aloud together, as a group.

Ask: What animals are mentioned on this page? *(parrots, monkeys, giraffes, chimpanzees)*

Support the children in finding the animals in the illustration.

Ask the following questions:

- How do you think the family are feeling? *(They look as if they think the animals are funny.)*
- Why do you think this is? *(The animals are doing funny things.)*

Explain to the children that they are going to read the rest of the book with their Reading Partners.

Ask: What will you do if you come across any tricky or new words?

Explore the strategies that the children can draw on, for example, using initial sounds and other phonic strategies, breaking longer words down into syllables, using contextual and picture clues.

Give the children the chance to read pages 6 to 13 with their Reading Partner. Remind them to think about using the rhyme and rhythm of the text to help them to read with expression.

As they read, work around the group listening to each child. Support them in reading longer words and, if necessary, remind them of why they are reading.

Wrap up

Ask children to tell you which animals were mentioned in the book.

Check them against the list you made earlier on the flipchart, adding any if necessary.

Ask the following questions:

- Were the animals doing anything unusual or strange?
- Who do you think is telling the story? *(the boy on the front cover)*

Prompt the children to explain why they think this.

Vocabulary boost session

You will need

- Multiple copies of Collins Big Cat *Going to the Zoo* • Sticky notes

Vocabulary table

Focus word	Child-friendly explanation	Example sentence	Tell me...
eating	To put food in your mouth, chew it up and swallow.	I am **eating** all of the red sweets before my brother finds them.	Tell me about something that you like to eat.
laugh	You make this noise when you find something funny.	When my friend told a joke, it made me **laugh**.	Tell me about something that would make you laugh.
sing	A musical sound you make with your voice.	I like to **sing** in the shower.	Tell me about a song that you have sung.

Tune in

Ask children to remind you about the book *Going to the Zoo*. Refer to the list of animals made during the Guided reading session.

Ask the following questions:

- What were the animals doing?
- What did you notice about the words in the book? *(It's a rhyming text.)*

Challenge the children to find the first page where the animals are mentioned. *(page 4)* Read the text on this page aloud using plenty of expression. Say that you think these are very unusual animals and that they need some very unusual words to tell us what they are doing.

Ask: What are the parrots doing? *(eating carrots)*

Say that isn't a very exciting word to use. We can do better than that! Can you tell me another word that we could use instead of 'eating'?' Encourage the children to respond with alternatives.

On the board, write up the word 'eating' and underneath list the synonyms that the children give you, for example, chewing, guzzling, chomping. If the children can't offer any alternatives or haven't suggested 'crunching', add this to the list, saying: I'll give you a word – 'crunching'. That means the same as 'eating'.

If appropriate, draw the children's attention to the alliteration in 'crunching carrots'.

Repeat for 'laugh' and 'sing'.

Heads together

Work around the group, asking the children the 'Tell me' questions from the table, above.

As the children are doing this activity, quickly place sticky notes over the original words on page 4.

Wrap up

Reread page 4 aloud together, encouraging the children to replace the now covered-up words with the synonyms.

Ask children to choose one of the words as their word of the week. Challenge them to try to use the word as often as they can – both at home and at school.

Follow-up independent sessions

You will need

- Resource sheet: Zoo animals
- Resource sheet: More animals
- Multiple copies of Collins Big Cat *Going to the Zoo*

Hand out copies of Resource sheet: Zoo animals. The children write the name of each animal and what they were doing in the story in the boxes. They can then work with their Reading Partner and retell the story using the map as the prompt.

Children work with their Reading Partners to prepare a performance reading of the book *Going to the Zoo*, with actions and sound effects.

Give pairs of children a copy of Resource sheet: More animals. The children think of four more animals who might live in the zoo. They draw them and write about what they do.

Wait and See!

Book Band: Blue

When Mr Cat runs past carrying a big bag, his friends all follow to find out what's inside, in this story with patterned and predictable language.

Skills focus

- Draw on knowledge of vocabulary to understand texts
- Make inferences from texts
- Predict what might happen on the basis of what has been read so far
- Read words accurately and fluently

Guided reading session

You will need

- Multiple copies of Collins Big Cat *Wait and See!*

Tune in

Ask children to pick up their books so that they are ready to look at the front cover. Introduce the book by reading the title aloud and ask children to join in.

Ask: Have you ever been told to 'wait and see'? When?

Draw out the children's understanding of the phrase 'wait and see', suggesting that there is a surprise coming. You may have to give an example.

Encourage the children to look closely at the front cover.

Ask the following questions:

- What is happening in the picture? *(a cat is carrying a bag, a bear and mouse are watching)*
- What do you think the story is about?

Turn to the back cover and read the blurb aloud; encourage the children to follow and join in with you.

Ask: Now that you've read the blurb, what do you think the story is about?

Heads together

Read pages 2 to 5 aloud to the children, asking them to follow as you read and to join in. Model strategies for reading longer words, for example, using phonic knowledge to blend phonemes ('day', 'went'), recognition of tricky words (past, 'said').

Ask the following questions:

- What is the weather like in the story? *(sunny)*
- What do you think Mr Cat has in the bag?
- What do you think happens next?

Read pages 6 and 7 aloud to the children, asking them to follow as you read and to join in. As well as modelling strategies for reading, model reading with expression – using your voice to indicate a question or exclamation.

Ask: When we are reading, how do we know to change our voice? *(punctuation)*

Point out a question mark.

Ask the following questions:

- What job do you think this is doing? *(telling the reader that it is asking something)*
- What is it called? *(question mark)*

Point out the exclamation mark.

Ask the following questions:

- What job do you think this is doing? *(telling the reader to read loudly or with expression)*
- What is it called? *(exclamation mark)*

Tell the children that as you read the rest of the story, you want them to look out for the question and exclamation marks and change their voices when they are reading those parts.

Read pages 8 to 11 in this way.

Wrap up

Ask: Do you have any other ideas what might be in Mr Cat's bag?

Encourage the children to look back over the story so far.

Ask the following questions:

- Why do you think the animals are so interested in what is in the bag?
- What might you be carrying in a bag that a dog might be interested in? *(food)*

Read pages 12 and 13 together.

Ask the following questions:

- Why do you think the words are written in capital letters? *(Mr Cat is speaking loudly, he wants all his friends to hear)*
- Why do you think Mr Cat waited until he'd seen all of his friends before he showed them what was in the bag? *(he wanted to surprise them/he was teasing them/he wanted to have all of the friends together)*
- Do you like surprises? Why?
- Do you think the animals in the story liked the surprise? Why? *(yes, they are all smiling, looking pleased)*

Vocabulary boost session

You will need

- Multiple copies of Collins Big Cat *Wait and See!*

Vocabulary table

Focus word	Child-friendly explanation	Example sentence	Tell me...
wait	If you wait, you don't do anything right now, you do it later.	When we cross the road, we **wait** until there are no cars coming.	Tell me about a time when you have had to wait for someone or something.
follow	If you follow someone, you move along behind them.	Clare **followed** John down the path.	Tell me about a game you play when you follow someone.
ask	Ask means to say a question because you want to know the answer.	Dad **asked** me what I wanted to eat for lunch.	Tell me some questions that you asked last week.

Tune in

Explain to the children that in this lesson they are going to look closely at some of the words the author has used and what those words mean.

Read the book aloud to the children, modelling how to use the punctuation and dialogue to read aloud with expression.

Refer back to each of the focus words within the context of the story, writing up the word, giving a child-friendly explanation and asking the children to say the focus word with you. For example: The title of the story is *Wait and See!*. If you wait, you don't do anything right now, you do it later. Now, say the word with me – 'wait'.

You may wish to use the examples in the table, above.

Refer to each of the focus words that you have written up and give the children the example sentences. Then ask them to interact with the word meanings by asking the questions in the 'Tell me' column. You may wish to demonstrate by giving some examples of your own.

Ask children to say the words with you once more.

Heads together

Explore and develop the children's understanding of the focus words.

Ask the following questions:

- Before crossing a road, you need to wait. Why? When else might you need to wait?
- If I follow someone, I am moving along behind them. Working with a partner, can you show me how you follow someone?
- Which of these is someone asking something? Say 'ask' to show you think it is. Wait and see! / Please can I have a drink? / What is the time?

Encourage the children to make links to their own lives and experiences to help them.

Wrap up

Tell the children that you will say a word (or phrase) and they are to tell you which of the three new words it (or they) make/s them think of: 'wait', 'follow' or 'ask'.

- Question *(ask)*
- Don't move *(wait)*
- Walk behind *(follow)*
- Why? *(ask)*
- Stay *(wait)*

Ask children to choose one of the focus words as their word of the week. Challenge them to use the word as often as they can, both at school and at home.

Follow-up independent sessions

You will need

- Multiple copies of Collins Big Cat *Wait and See!*
- Resource sheet: Who lives here?
- Resource sheet: Mr Cat's picnic

Ask children to work with their Reading Partners and to read the book aloud.

Hand out copies of Resource sheet: Who lives here? The children use the book to help find out where the animals live. They write in the box next to each animal.

Give each child a copy of Resource sheet: Mr Cat's picnic. The children write a list of what is in Mr Cat's picnic beneath the picture of the picnic. What else could they have had at the picnic?

Knock! Knock!

Book Band: Blue

In this patterned story with a predictable structure, Joe is waiting for his friend to come and play, when three unexpected visitors knock at the door, each with a problem for Joe to solve.

Skills focus

- Draw on knowledge of vocabulary to understand texts
- Identify/explain key aspects of fiction and non-fiction texts, e.g. character, events, title
- Predict what might happen on the basis of what has been read so far
- Read words accurately and fluently

Guided reading session

You will need

- Multiple copies of Collins Big Cat *Knock! Knock!*

Tune in

Ask children to pick up their books so that they are ready to look at the front cover. Introduce the book by reading the title.

Ask: Who do you think is knocking?

Point out the exclamation marks and explain that these mean we have to read the words with excitement or dramatically. Demonstrate and then ask volunteers to read the title expressively again.

Write the word 'knock' on the board. Remind the children how some words have silent letters.

Ask: Where is the silent letter in this word? *(identify 'k' if necessary)*

Ensure that they understand how 'ck' are not silent letters because together they make a sound.

Encourage the children to describe any other stories they have read or jokes that begin with someone knocking on a door. Elicit how a knock makes you want to know who is there. It creates curiosity and suspense.

Turn to the back cover and read the blurb. Ask children whether they think this story will be exciting. Why?

Ask: Do you think this story will be exciting? Why?

Heads together

Read pages 2 and 3 aloud to the children, asking them to follow as you read.

Focus on page 3 and point to the ellipsis. Explain that this means the sentence continues on.

Reread page 3 and then read pages 4 and 5. Point out how the page ends with an ellipsis again.

Ask: Do you think this is a good way to end a page?

Elicit how it is exciting to have to turn the page to find out who is knocking.

Focus on the words 'POLAR BEAR!' on page 4. Explain how the capital letters and exclamation mark make us read the words with emphasis.

Encourage the children to join in as you read pages 2 to 5 with expression, building the suspense with the ellipses.

Ask the following questions:

- Who do you think was knocking this time?
- Do you think Harry will arrive in the end?

Ask children to predict what happens and to give reasons for their predictions.

Ask children to read the rest of the book with their Reading Partner to see how exciting they can make the story sound each time the door knocks. Ensure that the children take turns to read a double page.

As they read, move around, listening to each child. If necessary, help with difficult words, pointing out single sounds made by more than one letter. Check that they read words in capitals with emphasis and notice the exclamation marks. Check that they notice the ellipses, too.

Wrap up

Ask: How exciting did you make the story sound as you read it?

Ask volunteer pairs to read some pages to the group. Encourage other volunteers to suggest how it can be made even more exciting.

Ask children to close their books and try to remember who came to the door and in which order. Write the children's ideas on the board. Next, ask children to look through the pictures in order, to check that each item in the list is correct and in the correct order.

Turn to page 12.

Ask: Why was Joe too tired to play?

Refer back to pages 3, 5, 7 and 10, writing the phrases down that tell us how Joe went to the door. Elicit how Joe gets more tired, pointing out how, at first, he 'shot up' and lastly 'crawled'.

Encourage the children to join in with a final dramatic reading of the story.

Vocabulary boost session

You will need

- Multiple copies of Collins Big Cat *Knock! Knock!*

Vocabulary table

Focus word	Child-friendly explanation	Example sentence	Tell me...
expecting	When you are expecting something to happen, you think that it is going to happen and you are waiting for it.	I am **expecting** the bus to arrive at the bus stop soon.	Tell me about a time when you have been expecting a visitor.
melted	When something has melted it means it has changed from a solid thing to liquid.	My lolly **melted** and dribbled down my shirt.	Tell me about something you have seen that melted.
fuel	Fuel is the stuff that cars and lorries burn to make them go.	I drove the car to fill the tank with more **fuel** for the journey.	Tell me about anything that needs fuel to work.

Tune in

Read the book aloud to the children, modelling how to read longer words by sounding out the smaller words, for example, in 'jumped' ('jump') and 'opened' ('open'). Check that they are familiar with letters that commonly make one sound, such as 'ck' in 'knock', 'ai' in 'wait' and 'ay' in 'way'.

Explain to the children that they are going to look closely at some of the words the author has used and what those words mean.

Look at each focus word in turn, returning to where they appear in the story, such as 'expecting' on page 2. Write the word on the board, asking the children to say it out loud. Explain it in a child-friendly way and with reference to the story. For example: 'Expecting' is when you think something is going to happen. In this story, Joe thinks that Harry is coming – he is expecting him and waiting for him to come.

When you have looked at each word and written them on the board, go through the focus words, giving another sentence that uses each word. You can use the example sentences in the table above or make up your own.

Next, challenge the children with the 'Tell me' questions.

If necessary, demonstrate with your own answers.

Finally, ask children to say the focus words with you once more.

Heads together

Ask the following questions to explore and develop the children's understanding of the focus words:

- When might you be expecting school to start?
- What might you expect to have melted in the hot sunshine?
- What do you think needs fuel to work?

Wrap up

Ask the following questions to review the word meanings:

- What is the word that means changing from a solid thing to a liquid thing?
- What is the word that means you think that something is going to happen?
- What is the word that means the same as petrol?

Once a day, challenge the children to think of a sentence containing one of the focus words, prompting with the beginning of a sentence if necessary.

Follow-up independent sessions

You will need

- Multiple copies of Collins Big Cat *Knock! Knock!*
- Resource sheet: Knock! Knock!
- Resource sheet: Sentences for *Knock! Knock!*

Ask children to work with their Reading Partners to take turns to read a double-page spread while their partner has to remember what happens next without looking. Encourage them to swap so the other child then reads while their partner tries to remember what happens next.

Give each child a copy of Resource sheet: Knock! Knock! Explain that they have to find the words for who came to Joe's door. They must draw a line from the correct words to the door. Ask them to draw a picture of a new thing that might come through the door, too. Can they explain to their partner why each person or animal came to see Joe?

Give pairs of children a copy of Resource sheet: Sentences for *Knock! Knock!*. They have to choose the correct ending and then check it is the right one by looking in the book.

It's Great to Be Small!

Book Band: Blue

In this story with a familiar setting, Tiny the mouse shows Ebba the baby elephant that size doesn't matter as long as you are big on the inside.

Skills focus

- Draw on knowledge of vocabulary to understand texts

- Identify/explain key aspects of fiction and non-fiction texts, e.g. character, events, title
- Make inferences from texts

Guided reading session

You will need

- Multiple copies of Collins Big Cat *It's Great to Be Small!*

Tune in

Ask children to pick up their books. Introduce the book by asking the children to look closely at the front cover.

Ask: What animals can you see on the front cover? *(elephants)*

Are the children able to spot the adult elephant as well as the baby?

Encourage the children to point to the title of the book; then read it aloud to them. Ask them to read it aloud with you.

Challenge the children to identify the punctuation mark at the end of the title (exclamation mark). Demonstrate how this helps you to read the title with expression.

Draw attention to and read the author's name (Jane Simmons). If necessary, turn to the title page and show the children where it tells us that Jane Simmons has both written the story and drawn the pictures.

Turn to the back cover and draw the children's attention to the blurb. Explain that this usually tells us what happens in the book. Read the blurb aloud.

Ask the following questions:

- Who do you think Ebba is? *(the small elephant)*
- Who do you think her new friend is? *(the mouse)*

Heads together

Read pages 2 and 3 aloud to the children, asking them to follow as you read. Model strategies for reading longer words, for example, looking for familiar chunks ('small'; 'small-est'), breaking words down ('some-times').

Focus on the word 'wasn't'. Demonstrate how to pronounce it and draw attention to the apostrophe, used to show a missing letter. Check the children's understanding of the word.

Ask the following questions:

- What do you think might be best about being the smallest elephant?
- What might Ebba not like about being the smallest elephant?

Ask children to read the rest of the book to find out what happened when Ebba made a new friend. As they read, move around the group, listening to each child. Support them in reading longer words and, if necessary, reminding them of why they are reading.

Wrap up

Remind the children of why they were reading the book (to find out what happened when Ebba made a new friend).

Ask the following questions:

- What sort of animal is Ebba's new friend? *(a mouse)*
- What is he called? *(Tiny)*

Ask children to feed back on what happened when the two animals met.

Ask the following questions:

- Why do you think Tiny is happy to be small? *(because even though he's small, he is brave)*
- What does Tiny say that tells us he is brave? *(I'm big inside.)*

Challenge children to find this speech in the book (on page 9).

Ask the following questions:

- Have you ever done anything that was brave?
- How did you feel?

Check that the children understand that although Tiny is physically small, he is very confident.

Vocabulary boost session

You will need

- Multiple copies of Collins Big Cat *It's Great to Be Small!*

Vocabulary table

Focus word	Child-friendly explanation	Example sentence	Tell me...
great	If something is great, it is really good.	It's **great** to be your teacher because you're all fantastic children.	Tell me about a time when you thought something was really great.
sometimes	If something happens sometimes, it only happens every now and then – not all of the time.	**Sometimes** it rains at playtime and sometimes it's sunny.	Tell me something that you do sometimes.
hate	If someone hates something, they really don't like it.	I **hate** swimming in really cold water.	Tell me about something that you really hate.

Tune in

Explain to the children that in this lesson they are going to look closely at some of the words the author has used and what those words mean.

Read the book aloud to the children, modelling how to use the punctuation and dialogue to read aloud with expression.

Refer back to each of the focus words within the context of the story, writing up the word, giving a child-friendly explanation and asking the children to say the focus word with you. For example: In the story, Tiny says it's great to be small. That means he thinks it's a really good thing to be small. Now, say the word with me – 'great'.

You may wish to use the examples in the table, above.

Refer to each of the focus words that you have written up and give the children the example sentences. Then ask them to interact with the word meanings by asking the questions in the 'Tell me' column. You may wish to demonstrate by giving some examples of your own.

Ask children to say the words with you once more.

Heads together

Ask the following questions to explore and develop the children's understanding of the focus words:

- Do you think it would be great to be able to fly through the air or to breathe underwater?
- Do you sometimes have a bath and sometimes have a shower?
- Would you hate to eat a pickled onion or an apple?

Encourage children to elaborate on their answers by following up their responses with the question 'Why?'

Wrap up

Ask the following questions to review the word meanings:

- If we say that something is great, does it mean that it's fantastic or horrible?
- If something happens sometimes, does it mean that it happens all of the time or just some of the time?
- If you hate something, does it mean that you love it or that you don't like it?

Ask children to choose one of the focus words as their word of the week. Challenge them to use the word as often as they can, both at school and at home.

Follow-up independent sessions

You will need

- Multiple copies of Collins Big Cat *It's Great to Be Small!*
- Paper, coloured pencils
- Resource sheet: Book talk for *It's Great to be Small!*
- Resource sheet: Role on the wall: Tiny

Ask children to work with their Reading Partners and to read the book aloud, each taking on the role of either Ebba or Tiny. Encourage them to use different voices as they read the dialogue.

Ask children to write or draw what they like or dislike about the story on a copy of Resource sheet: Book talk for *It's Great to be Small!* Encourage them to write down two or three questions that they would ask the characters in the book.

Give pairs of children a copy of Resource sheet: Role on the wall: Tiny. The children label the picture with adjectives to describe Tiny's character on the inside and his appearance on the outside.

The Prince and the Parsnip

Book Band: Blue

Princess Sue wants to marry someone kind and caring so she tests ten princes by putting parsnips under their pillows, in this retelling of a traditional tale.

Skills focus

- Draw on knowledge of vocabulary to understand texts
- Make inferences from texts

- Predict what might happen on the basis of what has been read so far
- Read words accurately and fluently

Guided reading session

You will need

- Multiple copies of Collins Big Cat *The Prince and the Parsnip*

Tune in

Ask children to pick up their books so that they are ready to look at the front cover.

Show the children the front cover of the book. Explain that it is a version of a traditional tale called 'The Princess and the Pea'. If the children are familiar with this story, discuss the main events. If not, explore their knowledge of traditional tales in general and their typical features, for example, good and bad characters, magic, characters are set tasks.

Turn to the back cover and read the blurb aloud to the children.

Ask the following questions:

- What do you think it means to have 'feelings'? *(to feel things like love, happiness, worry)*
- What do you think might happen in the story?

If appropriate, introduce the word 'predict' and explain that it means to think about what might happen in a story. Establish that predicting involves thinking about what they already know as well as using clues in the story.

Model how to make some predictions about *The Prince and the Parsnip*, verbalising your thought processes. For example: I know the story of 'The Princess and the Pea'. In that story, the prince wanted to find a wife and he put a pea under the mattress to see who would feel it. He decided to marry the princess who could feel the pea. So, I think something similar might happen in this story, but it's the princess who's looking for a husband and she puts a parsnip under the mattress.

Ask: Can you add any more predictions?

Explore the children's ideas and suggestions.

Turn to pages 2 and 3. Model reading these pages with expression – using different voices for the narrator, queen and king.

Ask children to spot the speech bubbles.

Ask: Who do you think is talking here? *(the queen and the king)*

Encourage the children to try reading the text on pages 2 and 3 with expression.

Ask children to read page 4. Encourage them to predict how Princess Sue will find a kind and caring prince.

Ask the following questions:

- Why do you think Sue wants a kind and caring prince?
- What sort of things do you think a kind and caring prince would do?

Heads together

Ask children to read pages 5 to 13 to find out how Princess Sue finds a prince with feelings.

As they read, work around the group listening to each child. Support them in reading longer words and, if necessary, remind them of why they are reading.

Wrap up

Take feedback from the reading activity, reminding the children of their earlier predictions. **Ask** the following questions:

- Were your predictions right?
- Did Princess Sue find a prince?
- How did she know he was kind and caring? *(He had felt the parsnip under his pillow.)*
- What happened at the end of the story? *(Princess Sue and Prince Tom got married.)*

Vocabulary boost session

You will need

- Multiple copies of Collins Big Cat *The Prince and the Parsnip*
- Resource sheet: Focus word cards

Vocabulary table

Focus word	Child-friendly explanation	Example sentence	Tell me...
handsome	A handsome person is someone who is good looking.	The hero in a story is always a **handsome** man.	Tell me about someone who you think is very handsome.
feelings	Your feelings show that you care about something.	My **feelings** were hurt when someone said horrible things.	Tell me about something you have feelings about.
caring	If someone is caring they are helpful.	My friend is very **caring** because she looks after stray animals.	Tell me about something someone can do to show they are caring.

Tune in

Ask children to tell you about the story *The Prince and the Parsnip*.

Turn to pages 2 and 3. Draw the children's attention to the king's speech bubble where he says the princess should choose a handsome prince.

Ask: Does the princess follow the king's advice? *(No. She wants a kind and caring prince.)*

Read page 5.

Ask: Do you think she is right to look for someone with feelings who is kind and caring instead of someone handsome?

Write up the words 'handsome', 'feelings' and 'caring' on the board. Explain that these are words that the children are going to look at more closely in this lesson.

Use the information in the table, above, to give the children the example sentences and definitions of each of the focus words.

Heads together

Challenge the children to tell you about situations involving the focus words, using the 'Tell me' prompts in the table, above.

Prompt them for more information as they describe their situations in order to develop their understanding of the focus words.

Wrap up

Use the words and definitions from Resource sheet: Focus word cards.

Give out the cards, keeping one for yourself. Hold up and read your card and challenge the child who has the matching word or definition to hold their card up.

Ask another child to hold up and read their card and ask the rest of the group to check if they have the matching word or definition card. Repeat this until all of the words have been explored.

Challenge the children to develop sentences containing the focus words.

Ask children to choose one of the words as their word of the week. Challenge them to try to use the word as often as they can – both at home and at school.

Follow-up independent sessions

You will need

- Multiple copies of Collins Big Cat *The Prince and the Parsnip*
- Resource sheet: Book talk for *The Prince and the Parsnip*

Ask children to work with their Reading Partners. They can read the book together, taking it in turns to read a page each. Give each pair a copy of Resource sheet: Book talk for *The Prince and the Parsnip*. Ask them to think about how they feel about the story and to complete the Resource sheet. Each pair can then share their ideas with the rest of the group.

Ask children to work with their Reading Partners and to turn to pages 14 and 15. They can read the story map and develop an oral version of the story. Remind them to tell the story with expression, using different voices for the characters. Once they have practised their story, they can tell it to the rest of the group.

Animals in Hiding

Book Band: Blue

This information book looks at how animals in the wild use camouflage to hide when they are hunting or being hunted.

Skills focus

- Draw on knowledge of vocabulary to understand texts
- Identify/explain key aspects of fiction and non-fiction texts, e.g. character, events, title
- Make inferences from texts
- Read words accurately and fluently

Guided reading session

You will need

- Multiple copies of Collins Big Cat *Animals in Hiding*

Tune in

Ask children to pick up their books. Introduce the book by asking the children to look closely at the front cover.

Ask the following questions:

- What can you see on the front cover? *(frog, leaves)*
- Can you notice anything about the colours of the frog and the leaves? *(They are the same.)*

Encourage the children to point to the title of the book; then read it aloud to them. Ask them to read it aloud with you.

Draw attention to and read the author's name (Charlotte Guillain).

Turn to the back cover and draw the children's attention to the blurb and the picture. Read the blurb aloud.

Ask the following questions:

- What can you notice about the colours in the picture?
- What do you think the book is about?

Turn to the title page. Ask children to point to the word 'contents'. Explain that the contents tells us what is in the book and where to find it. Read the contents aloud to the children, asking them to follow. As you read, insert the word 'page' before each number so that the children understand that is what the numbers are for.

Heads together

Read the title on page 2. Read back across the word 'camouflage', breaking it down and saying it slowly. Do it again, asking the children to join in with you.

Read pages 2 and 3 aloud to the children, asking them to follow as you read and join in. Model strategies for reading longer words, for example, recognition of tricky words (like, 'they'), using phonic knowledge (h-i-d-e).

Ask the following questions:

- What is camouflage? *(something that makes animals look like the place they are hiding)*
- How do animals use camouflage? *(to hide so that they can hunt or stop themselves from being eaten by other animals)*

Read pages 4 to 11 aloud, modelling reading strategies and encouraging the children to follow and to join in.

Turn back to the title page. Tell the children that you are about to read page 12.

Ask: Can you use the contents to find out what page 12 is about? *(colour change)*

Wrap up

Read pages 12 and 13 together.

Ask the following questions:

- Why do you think that changing colour is the best camouflage?
- Which do you think is the best camouflage? Why?

Explain to the children that you are going to think about how the information is arranged in the whole book.

Ask the following questions:

- What is the first part of the book about? *(introduction, tells us what camouflage is)*
- The books tells us about different sorts of camouflage. Can you tell me one of the sorts and show me where in the book it is? *(in the sea, snow, grass, leaves, colour change)*
- In the book, some animals use camouflage so that they can hide from enemies. Can you tell me and show me an animal that uses camouflage to hide? *(flatfish, baby seals, baby cheetahs, lizards, cuttlefish)*

Vocabulary boost session

You will need

- Multiple copies of Collins Big Cat *Animals in Hiding*

Vocabulary table

Focus word	Child-friendly explanation	Example sentence	Tell me...
hide	If something or someone hides, they go to a place where it is hard to be seen or found.	We play a game where everyone **hides** and someone has to find them.	Tell me about a time when you have played a hiding game.
hunt	If you hunt for someone or something you look for them very carefully.	In the garden, the bird **hunts** for worms.	Tell me about something you might hunt for.
creep up	If you creep up on someone you move slowly closer without being seen by them.	I like to **creep up** on my mum and shout, 'boo!'	Tell me about an animal that creeps up on other animals to catch them.

Tune in

Explain to the children that in this lesson they are going to look closely at some of the words the author has used and what those words mean.

Read the book aloud to the children, asking them to follow and join in as you read.

Refer back to each of the focus words within the context of the story, writing up the word, giving a child-friendly explanation and asking the children to say the focus word with you. For example: The book is about animals that hide. If something or someone hides, they go to a place where it is hard to be seen or found. Now, say the word with me – 'hide'.

Refer to each of the focus words that you have written up and give the children the example sentences. Then ask them to interact with the word meanings by asking the questions in the 'Tell me' column. You may wish to demonstrate by giving some examples of your own.

Ask children to say the words with you once more.

Heads together

Ask children the following questions to explore and develop their understanding of the focus words:

- If I wanted to hide in the classroom where would be a good place?

- If you were hunting for a pencil I had hidden in the classroom, what would you be doing?
- If you were a lion hunting another animal, what would you be doing?
- Show me how a lion might creep up on another animal.

Wrap up

Ask the following questions to review the word meanings:

- Does creep up mean moving quietly or loudly?
- Does hide mean 'going somewhere so that you can't be seen' or 'going somewhere that you can be seen very well'?
- Does hunt mean look for something carefully or close your eyes?
- Do animals hunt because they want food or because they want to sleep?

Ask children to choose one of the focus words as their word of the week. Challenge them to use the word as often as they can, both at school and at home.

Follow-up independent sessions

You will need

- Multiple copies of Collins Big Cat *Animals in Hiding*
- Resource sheet: Book talk for *Animals in Hiding*
- Resource sheet: Animal sort

Ask children to work with their Reading Partners and to read the book aloud.

Give pairs of children a copy of Resource sheet: Book talk for *Animals in Hiding*. Ask them to talk about and write or draw what they like or dislike about the book.

Hand out copies of the cards cut from Resource sheet: Animal sort. The children sort the pictures according to the way the animals hide, either 'pattern', 'shape', 'colour' or 'colour change'.

Arctic Life

Book Band: Blue

This information book explores how animals and people survive in the frozen landscape of the Arctic.

Skills focus

- Draw on knowledge of vocabulary to understand texts

- Identify/explain key aspects of fiction and non-fiction texts, e.g. character, events, title
- Check reading makes sense

Guided reading session

You will need

- Multiple copies of Collins Big Cat *Arctic Life*

Tune in

Tell the children that they are going to read about a part of the world that is different to theirs. Look together at the cover and read the title. Next, read the blurb and reread it together.

Ask:

- Do you know anything about life in the Arctic?
- What do the cover photos show us about life for people and animals? *(tough, hard, cold)*

Turn to page 2 and focus on the globe.

Ask: Where is the Arctic on this globe?

Focus the children on the label 'the Arctic' and the arrow. Elicit how this is a label and explain that labels help us to find things in pictures.

Turn to the contents page and read it to the children. Explain that because this is an information book we can read any sections in any order.

Demonstrate finding the page for something that interests them, for example, 'Homes'.

Ask: Is this the correct page?

Point out the heading 'Homes' and ensure that they know that headings like this tell us the subject of the text below.

Heads together

Ask children to turn to pages 2 and 3 and to follow the words as you read aloud.

Return to page 2 and model how to draw on information from the picture to check understanding. After rereading page 2, say: Is that right, 'The Arctic is at the far north of the Earth'? North means the top part of the world, so let's look at the picture and check that the Arctic is 'far north'.

Turn to page 4 and demonstrate how the children can check their reading by thinking of the context.

Ask: What is this page about?

Point to the heading. Then read the page, pausing after 'thick coats'.

Ask: Have I read that correctly, 'thick coats'? *(Yes, this page is about keeping warm, so this must be right.)*

Read each double page with the children to model fluent reading. Ask children to follow the words as you read. Stop after each double page and ask children to summarise what the page tells us, drawing out important words, then looking at the context (heading) and pictures to check their understanding.

Ask children to reread each double page with you.

Ask children to work with their Reading Partner. Ask them to choose a subject from the contents, find the correct pages and read them.

Move around, listening to each pair. Support them in finding the correct page and reading any words they find difficult, for example, by splitting a word into sounds or looking for shorter words in longer words.

Remind them to look at the pictures after they have read the text, to check everything matches and makes sense, for example, on page 6, point to and read 'poles' in the text.

Ask the following questions:

- Are there 'poles' in the picture?
- Where does it say that in the text?

Wrap up

Ask pairs of children to tell the group about the pages they chose to read.

Ask the following questions:

- What was the heading?
- What did you find out?

Turn to pages 14 and 15. Point to one of the pictures (choose one that has not been mentioned yet).

Ask: Can anyone tell me about this picture?

Encourage children to recall any important words or phrases, such as 'poles' for the 'houses on stilts'.

Encourage the children to find the picture in the body of the book and check what they have remembered by rereading.

Vocabulary boost session

You will need

- Multiple copies of Collins Big Cat *Arctic Life*

Vocabulary table

Focus word	Child-friendly explanation	Example sentence	Tell me...
poles	Poles are specially made long sticks, like the wooden poles that the houses stand on to keep them up off the ice.	Sometimes I tie plants to **poles** to stop them falling over.	Tell me about where you have seen poles.
climate	Climate means all the weather you get in an area. In the book, the Arctic has very cold weather most of the time so it has a cold climate.	The **climate** in the jungles is called tropical because the weather is hot and wet.	Tell me about any climates you know of?
future	Future means the time, or years, that lie ahead.	In the **future**, we might live on the Moon.	Tell me what you think might happen in the future.

Tune in

Ask children to listen carefully and follow the words as you read the book. Explain that you will be looking back at some of the words' meanings more carefully.

Read the book aloud to the children, reading longer words, or words with unusual spellings more slowly, pointing out the letters that make the sounds, for example, f-r-ee-z-er, f-r-o-z-e-n. For 'some', point out how this is an unusual word in the way that 'o-e' makes an /u/ sound.

Point to each focus word in the story and write it on the board. Give a child-friendly explanation for each word and ask children to say the focus word with you.

Refer to each of the focus words that you have written up and give the children example sentences, for example: 'That pole outside is holding wires up.'

Next, ask them to think about the word meaning in the context of their own lives by asking the questions in the 'Tell me' column.

Ask children to say the words with you once more.

Heads together

Ask the following questions to explore and develop the children's understanding of the focus words:

- Might you use a pole to put up a tent or to dig the garden?
- Is climate mainly about the weather or where people live?
- What do we know most about, the past or the future?

Encourage them to elaborate on their answers by asking: Why?

Wrap up

Review the word meanings by asking the children which words go best with the focus word:

- 'poles': bendy, weak, strong, straight
- 'climate': rain, food, fish, snow
- 'future': memories, ahead, tomorrow, yesterday

Put the focus words on the wall and ask children to test a friend on the meaning of one each day.

Follow-up independent sessions

You will need

- Multiple copies of Collins Big Cat *Arctic Life*
- Resource sheet: Arctic world words
- Resource sheet: Arctic facts
- A selection of information books about the Arctic
- Access to the internet (optional)

Ask children to quiz each other in pairs. One child reads a sentence from the book, without showing the page. The other child guesses which section it is in by choosing from the contents list and looking up the page number to see if they are correct. Is the sentence in that section? They then swap roles.

Give each child a copy of Resource sheet: Arctic world words. Explain to them that you want them to copy them in the correct places as labels for the pictures.

Give pairs of children a copy of Resource sheet: Arctic facts. They find four new facts about the Arctic and write them down. They then join with another pair and share their facts.

Fishy Friend

In this poem about friendship, Sam makes an unexpected friend on the beach.

Skills focus

- Draw on knowledge of vocabulary to understand texts
- Identify/explain key aspects of fiction and non-fiction texts, e.g. character, events, title
- Predict what might happen on the basis of what has been read so far
- Read words accurately and fluently

Guided reading session

You will need

- Multiple copies of Collins Big Cat *Fishy Friends*

Tune in

Ask children to look at the picture and then the words as you read the title. Ask them to reread the title with you.

Ask the following questions:

- Where do you think this book is set? *(on a beach, by the seaside)*
- Can you see a 'fishy friend' in the picture?

Discuss whether the crab could be a 'fishy friend' and why.

Challenge the children to identify the similar sound /f/ in 'fishy' and 'friend' as you read the title again.

Ask them if they can hear any similar sounds in any of the words as you read page 2. Emphasise 'beach' and 'each' as you read.

Write 'beach' and 'each' on the board and ask children to find the letters that make the same sounds in both words. Elicit that they are rhyming words.

Ask: What kind of texts have rhyming words?

After the children have suggested answers, ask them to turn to the back cover to check. Point to the blue panel and read: 'a poem'. Explain that poems often have words that rhyme.

Heads together

Read pages 2 and 3 aloud to the children, asking them to follow as you read. Ask them to listen carefully for the rhyming words again.

Next, ask them to read page 3 with you, again listening for the rhyming words.

Ask: Which words rhyme on this page? *(moat, boat)*

Write them on the board.

- Which letters make the /oa/ sound? *(oa)*
- Which two sounds do both these words share? *(/oa/ and /t/)*

Remind them that two letters often make one sound.

Repeat for pages 4 and 5, this time asking the children to read along with you, following the words and then identifying the rhyming words ('top', 'stop').

Ask: What do you think happens next?

Read pages 6 and 7 aloud to the children.

Ask: Were you right?

Discuss what happened and how Sam felt. Prompt them by pointing to 'smiled'.

Ask: What do you think Sam will do next?

Challenge the children to read the rest of the book with their Reading Partner to find out what Sam and the crab did next. Ask them to listen out for words that rhyme. Tell the children that sometimes words that rhyme don't have the same spellings – it's the sound they share that is important.

As they read, circulate, listening to each child. Ask them to point to any pairs of words that they think rhyme. Ask them to read them again and point to the sounds that they share.

Support the children with difficult words, looking for smaller words in large words and then rereading them, for example, 'laugh-ed', 'splash-ed'.

Wrap up

Ask: Can you tell me what happened after Sam met the crab and said 'Hello'.

Encourage the children to look back through the story, using the pictures as prompts to remind them.

Challenge the children to recall any rhyming words. Reread pages 8 and 9 with them.

Ask: Which words rhymed on these pages?

Write the words on the board and ask children to say the words quickly – do they sound similar? Point out and underline the letter sounds they have in common.

Read pages 10 and 11 with the children and ask for the rhyming words again. Point out how 'mate' means the same as 'friend' and that the crab is Sam's 'fishy friend'.

Read the last two pages with the children again.

Ask: What do you think would happen next if the poem had more pages?

Vocabulary boost session

You will need
- Multiple copies of Collins Big Cat *Fishy Friends*

Vocabulary table

Focus word	Child-friendly explanation	Example sentence	Tell me...
emptied	When something has been emptied, everything has been taken out of it, like when Sam took everything out of his bag.	I **emptied** the fish tank so that I could clean it.	Tell me about a time when you have emptied something.
clinging	Clinging means hanging on or holding on tight, just like the crab is hanging on to Sam's jeans with its claws.	The climber was found **clinging** on to a rock after he slipped on the mountainside.	Tell me what you have seen clinging on to something.
cheeky	If you are cheeky, you are a bit rude or naughty. The crab was a bit naughty, or cheeky, to get into Sam's bag.	The **cheeky** dog pulled his new toy out of my bag before I could even unwrap it!	Tell me about a time you, or someone else, has been cheeky.

Tune in

Read the book aloud to the children, demonstrating how to break longer words into syllables to make reading easier, for example, 'wash-ed', 'for-ever'.

Write the focus words on the board and focus the children on where each appears in the book. First read the word, then give a child-friendly explanation, asking the children to say the word, too. For example, say: Emptied means everything has been taken out, so Sam emptied, or took everything out of, his bag when he got home from the beach. Read the word with me – 'emptied'.

Then point to each focus word again and give the children some example sentences (see the table, above). For example: I can use this word to say: 'I emptied my suitcase when I got back home from my holiday.'

Next, challenge them with a 'Tell me' question from the table. Alternatively, make up your own 'Tell me' challenges.

Heads together

Ask the following questions to develop and check the children's understanding of the focus words:

- What would you rather I emptied: your bag of rubbish or your bag of sweets?
- What might you find clinging to a wall: a painting or a fly?
- Which would be cheeky: a friend using your crayons without asking or a thief stealing your crayons?

Encourage the children to explain their answers by prompting with: 'Why do you think that?'

Wrap up

Ask the following questions to revise and review the focus word meanings:

- Might any of these things get emptied: a truck full of bricks, a car, a chocolate bar?
- Which of these might you see clinging: a hat on a head, a spider in a web, a singer on a stage?
- Which of these might be cheeky: a doll, a young child, a policewoman?

Display the words on a word wall and, each day, ask volunteers to mime one of the words for the other children to guess.

Follow-up independent sessions

You will need
- Resource sheet: Rhyming words for *Fishy Friends*
- Resource sheet: What happened next?
- Coloured pencils

Hot-seating: Ask children to work in pairs to take it in turns to be the crab and tell the story from the crab's point of view, explaining why she got in the bag and if she was pleased. The other child can ask questions.

Give pairs of children a copy of Resource sheet: Rhyming words for *Fishy Friends*. Ask them to read the words and then to match the words that rhyme by drawing a line to link them. Can they think of more rhyming pairs of words? They can use the pictures as clues.

Give each child a copy of Resource sheet: What happened next? They draw two pictures of something that might have happened next. Encourage them to write captions that rhyme.

Mojo and Weeza and the New Hat

Book Band: Blue

Weeza's new hat blows away in this fantasy story and the two monkeys set out to find it.

Skills focus

- Draw on knowledge of vocabulary to understand texts
- Identify/explain key aspects of fiction and non-fiction texts, e.g. character, events, title
- Make inferences from texts
- Read words accurately and fluently

Guided reading session

You will need

- Multiple copies of Collins Big Cat *Mojo and Weeza and the New Hat*

Tune in

Introduce the book by reading the title aloud and asking the children to join in.

Ask the following questions:

- What kind of book do you think this is, story or information?
- What makes you think that?

Encourage the children to look closely at the front cover.

Ask the following questions:

- Who do you think Mojo and Weeza are?
- What type of characters are they?
- What do you think the story is about?

Turn to the back cover and draw the children's attention to the blurb. Read the blurb aloud and encourage the children to follow and join in with you.

Ask: Now that you've read the blurb, what do you think the story is about?

Heads together

Read pages 2 and 3 aloud to the children, asking them to follow as you read and to join in if they are able. Model strategies for reading longer words, for example, using phonic knowledge to blend phonemes ('smart', 'wind'), recognition of tricky words ('very', 'new').

Ask the following questions:

- Why did Mojo and Weeza look smart? *(because Mojo had new shoes and Weeza had a new hat)*
- What do you think happens next?

Read pages 4 and 5 aloud to the children, asking them to follow as you read and to join in. As well as modelling strategies for reading, model reading with expression, reading loudly when the sentence ends with an exclamation mark, or using your voice to indicate a question.

Ask: When we are reading, how do we know to change our voice? *(punctuation)*

Point out the exclamation marks.

Ask the following questions:

- What job do you think this is doing? *(telling the reader that s/he needs to read it loudly)*
- What is it called?

Tell the children that as you read the rest of the book you want them to look out for the exclamation marks and change their voices when they are reading those parts.

Read pages 6 to 11 in this way.

Ask the following questions:

- What do you think happens next?

Wrap up

Read pages 12 and 13 aloud, modelling reading strategies and expression and encouraging the children to follow and join in.

Ask the following questions:

- Do you think that Mojo and Weeza liked sploshing through the mud? Why? *(yes, they look happy, smiling)*
- How do you think they felt at the end of the story? *(happy, pleased)*

Refer the children to pages 8 and 10 and encourage them to look at the pictures.

Ask the following questions:

- How do you think the birds and the turtle felt about Weeza? *(angry, annoyed)*
- How do you know? *(pecking, biting)*
- What kind of book is this: story or information?

Vocabulary boost session

You will need

- Multiple copies of Collins Big Cat *Mojo and Weeza and the New Hat*

Vocabulary table

Focus word	Child-friendly explanation	Example sentence	Tell me...
smart	If a person looks smart, it means that they look neat and clean.	I look **smart** in my school uniform.	Tell me about a time when you looked smart.
through	If you move through something, you go from one side to the other.	He walked **through** the flowers.	Tell me about something that you can go through.
better	If something is better, it is nicer than before.	These shoes are **better** than my old ones.	Tell me about something that you have that is better than before.

Tune in

Explain to the children that in this lesson they are going to look closely at some of the words the author has used and what those words mean.

Read the book aloud to the children, modelling how to use the punctuation and dialogue to read aloud with expression.

Refer back to each of the focus words within the context of the story, writing up the word, giving a child-friendly explanation and asking the children to say the focus word with you. For example: At the beginning of the story, Mojo and Weeza look smart. If someone looks smart it means that they look neat and clean. Now, say the word with me – 'smart'.

You may wish to use the examples in the table, above.

Refer to each of the focus words that you have written up and give the children the example sentences. Then ask them to interact with the word meanings by asking the questions in the 'Tell me' column. You may wish to demonstrate by giving some examples of your own.

Ask children to say the words with you once more.

Heads together

Ask the following questions to explore and develop the children's understanding of the focus words:

- After you have been playing outside, do you look smart?
- Pretend you are Mojo or Weeza. Can you act out how you splosh through the mud?
- Pretend you are Weeza. Can you act out him putting his new hat on and saying, "That's better!"?

Encourage the children to make links to their own lives and experiences to help them.

Wrap up

Ask the following questions to review the word meanings:

- Does better mean something good or something bad?
- Which of these would be better – somebody helping you or somebody being nasty to you?
- If you move through something, do you go from one side to the other, or do you go up?
- Does smart mean something good or something bad?
- Which of these would be smart – somebody who is neat and clean or somebody who is messy and dirty?

Ask children to choose one of the focus words as their word of the week. Challenge them to use the word as often as they can, both at school and at home.

Follow-up independent sessions

You will need

- Multiple copies of Collins Big Cat *Mojo and Weeza and the New Hat*
- Resource sheet: What are they saying?
- Resource sheet: What is it? *Mojo and Weeza and the New Hat*

Ask children to work with their Reading Partners and to read the book aloud.

Give each child a copy of Resource sheet: What are they saying? The children use the book to help them to write what Mojo and Weeza are saying in the speech bubbles. The first one has been done as an example.

Give each child a copy of Resource sheet: What is it? *Mojo and Weeza and the New Hat.* They draw lines to match the pictures to the words.

The Magic Pen

Book Band: Green

In this fantasy story, Mr Big discovers that his big new pen has special wish-fulfilling powers.

Skills focus

- Draw on knowledge of vocabulary to understand texts
- Identify/explain the sequence of events in texts
- Predict what might happen on the basis of what has been read so far
- Read words accurately and fluently

Guided reading session

You will need

- Multiple copies of Collins Big Cat *The Magic Pen*
- A collection of items that children might associate with being 'magic' such as a magic wand, a top hat, a broomstick, a magic key, a golden lamp and so on
- A fountain pen

Tune in

Look at a collection of items that children might associate with being 'magic' (see 'You will need' list).

Ask the following questions as you discuss each item:

- Why is it magic?
- What happens to make it magic?

Show the children a fountain pen. Take it apart to show how it is filled with ink. Explain that they are going to read a story about a magic pen.

Introduce the text by looking at the front cover. Model reading the title, segmenting and blending the words 'magic pen' m-a-g-i-c p-e-n.

Ask children to predict how the pen will be magic.

Explain that this is a 'fantasy' story, a story where imaginary things can happen.

Turn the book over to look at the back cover. Ask children to read the text aloud pointing at the words; check if they recognise the high frequency words and can use segmenting and blending.

Ask the following questions to check the children's understanding of the blurb:

- What is the main character called? *(Mr Big)*
- Why do you think he is called Mr Big? *(because he is big)*
- What did Mr Big buy? *(a big new pen)*
- What do you think the surprise could be?

Heads together

Model reading pages 2 and 3 using fluency and accuracy.

Ask the following questions:

- Why do you think Mr Big had a big house? *(because he is big)*

- Can you find the high frequency words: 'called' and 'once'?

Ask children to read pages 4 to 9 in pairs. Discuss the strategies they can use to help with their reading: high frequency word recognition, segmenting and blending, checking it makes sense and using picture clues.

Ask the following questions:

- Why did Mr Big need a big pen? *(He kept breaking the other pens; they were too fragile.)*
- Where did he get the new pen from? *(a shop)*
- Why did he make his own ink? *(The shopkeeper forgot the ink.)*
- What did he put in the ink mixture? *(vinegar, black tea, sugar, jelly, cress, orange juice and water)*
- What do you think will happen next?

Model reading pages 10 and 11 using expression, fluency and accuracy. Discuss how the pen is magic. Ask children to make further predictions now they know how the pen works.

Ask: What do you think Mr Big will write next?

Ask children to read pages 12 to 21 in pairs. Can they find out what else Mr Big writes?

Ask the following questions:

- What did Mr Big write with the magic pen? *(Mrs Big)*
- What happened when Mr Big wrote with the magic pen? *(A big woman rang the doorbell.)*
- Were the cat and the mouse happy? *(no, they wanted fish and cheese)*
- Do you think it was a sensible thing to write?

Wrap up

Turn to page 4. Can the children point out the inverted commas/speech marks? Ask children to practise reading with expression: "I need a big pen," said Mr Big.

Ask the following questions:

- What type of voice would Mr Big have?
- Who else speaks in the story? *(the cat and the mouse)*

In pairs, ask children to reread the text using voices and expression for the speech.

Vocabulary boost session

You will need

- Multiple copies of Collins Big Cat *The Magic Pen*
- Poster paper
- Timer
- A box labelled 'fragile'

Vocabulary table

Focus word	Child-friendly explanation	Example sentence	Tell me…
gigantic	If something is gigantic, it is very big.	I had a **gigantic** ice cream after my dinner.	Tell me another word that means 'big'.
fragile	If something is fragile, it can break easily.	I carried the box labelled '**fragile**' carefully.	Tell me if you have ever broken something fragile.
fantasy	Something imaginary or made up.	I enjoyed reading the **fantasy** story.	Tell me if you like reading fantasy stories.

Tune in

Explain that in this lesson the children are going to look in more detail at some words linked to the text. Write the three focus words clearly for the children to see. Read the words together. Discuss and explain the child-friendly meaning of each word.

Look at page 2.

Ask: How is the main character described? *(a big man)*

Explain that 'gigantic' is another word for big.

Turn to page 4.

Ask the following questions:

- What did Mr Big break? *(ten pens)*
- Why do you think Mr Big kept breaking the pens? *(they were too small)*

Explain we could say Mr Big broke the pens because they were too fragile.

Tell the children *The Magic Pen* is a fantasy story.

Heads together

Write the word 'big' in the middle of a large sheet of paper. Ask children to work with a Reading Partner and think of as many other words for 'big' as they can in one minute (set a timer). The children then share the words and you record them on the sheet of paper. Challenge the children to use some of the words during the week in their writing or conversation.

Show the children a box labelled 'fragile'. Ask them to discuss what might be in the box.

The Magic Pen was a fantasy story. Can they explain what makes it a fantasy story?

Wrap up

Recap the three focus words by discussing the questions in the 'Tell me' column of the table, above.

Challenge the children to think of a sentence using one of the focus words.

Follow-up independent sessions

You will need

- Paints and paper
- Resource sheet: Sentence stems
- Resource sheet: Story order

Ask children to imagine they had a magic pen. What would they write or draw and why? Ask them to paint a picture of what they would ask the magic pen for. Challenge the children to write a sentence to explain what they would write with a magic pen and why. Give them a copy of Resource sheet: Sentence stems. For example, the children might paint a picture of a new bicycle and write: If I had a magic pen, the first thing I would write is 'new red bike' because I like cycling and my bike is getting too small for me.

Using the pictures cut from Resource sheet: Story order, ask children to sort and retell the story in their own words. Challenge them to use interesting adjectives, including alternative words for 'big'. They could also write labels or sentences to match.

Ask children to rewrite the ending of the story. Suggest that perhaps the magic pen starts to be naughty or it doesn't work quite as Mr Big imagines.

Spines, Stings and Teeth

Book Band: Green

This non-chronological report explores the various ways that sea creatures protect themselves from hungry predators.

Skills focus

- Draw on knowledge of vocabulary to understand texts
- Identify/explain key aspects of fiction and non-fiction texts, e.g. character, events, title
- Identify/explain the sequence of events in texts
- Read words accurately and fluently

Guided reading session

You will need

- Multiple copies of Collins Big Cat *Spines, Stings and Teeth*

Tune in

Begin by introducing the book. Explore the front cover together. Read the title 'Spines, Stings and Teeth' and point out the split digraph 'i-e' in spines and the vowel digraph 'ee' in teeth. Explain that this is a non-fiction report.

Ask: What do you think this book is about/ reporting on?

Discuss the photograph of the jellyfish and fish. Do the children know anything about jellyfish? Have they seen one before? Encourage the children to share any relevant experiences. Have they been rock pooling before? Have they seen jellyfish on the beach? Have they been crabbing or sea fishing?

Turn to the back cover and read the blurb. Recap that a blurb tells us more about the book. Discuss that animals use teeth, claws, stings and spines to protect themselves from others.

Create a list of all the animals that live in the sea, which the children can think of.

Ask children to look through the book at the photographs.

Ask the following questions:

- What animals can you see?
- Can you name any of them?

Once they have had a look, call out the following names and challenge the children to find the animals in the book: shark, fish, sea dragon, stonefish, crab, jellyfish, ray, sea urchin, porcupine fish, sea snake, turtle.

Turn to the contents page and read through the headings, modelling fluency and accuracy. Practise using the contents page by asking:

- What is page 16 about? *(stings)*

- On which page can I find out about claws? *(page 9)*

Heads together

Read pages 2 to 5 together, encouraging the children to point to the words as you read and join in where they can.

Recap strategies to use when reading, including: segmenting and blending, picture clues, checking the text makes sense and recognising high frequency words.

Explain that pages 2 to 5 are an introduction to the topic and the other pages in the book focus on the types of different ways animals in the sea protect themselves from being eaten, that is: hiding, claws, shocks, spines, stings, teeth and beaks.

Ask children to choose a topic to find out more about. Challenge them to use the contents page to find their chosen topic. The children read this section independently. Listen to each child read and support where needed.

Share what the children have found out.

Wrap up

Reread the text, demonstrating reading with fluency and accuracy.

Turn to pages 22 and 23 and explore the table.

Ask the following questions:

- Which animals use poison to protect themselves? *(jellyfish and stonefish)*
- Which animals hide? *(stonefish and sea dragon)*
- How does the shark protect itself? *(teeth)*

Explore the diagram on pages 4 and 5 and discuss the sequence of events.

Ask children to choose their favourite page and explain what they like about it.

Vocabulary boost session

You will need

- Multiple copies of Collins Big Cat *Spines, Stings and Teeth*

Vocabulary table

Focus word	Child-friendly explanation	Example sentence	Tell me...
tentacles	Tentacles are the long arms on a jellyfish or octopus.	Do not touch the jellyfish **tentacles**!	Tell me if you have ever seen a jellyfish.
poisonous	If something is poisonous, it is deadly and can kill you.	The cleaning liquids are **poisonous**.	Tell me what sea animals use poison to protect themselves.
protect	To protect something is to keep it safe.	The lioness **protects** her cubs.	Tell me how you protect yourself from the sun.

Tune in

Explain that in this lesson the children are going to look in more detail at some words linked to the text. Write the three focus words clearly for the children to see. Read the words together. Discuss and explain the child-friendly meaning of each word.

Reread the text.

Ask the following questions:

- Which sea animals have tentacles? *(jellyfish and octopuses)*
- How many times can you find the word 'poisonous'? *(nine)*

Heads together

Discuss and create a list of the ways sea creatures protect themselves: hiding, claws, shocks, spines, teeth and beaks.

Ask: How can we protect ourselves from the sun? *(sun hats, sun cream, sunglasses, staying in the shade)*

Ask children to design a poster called 'How to protect yourself from the sun'. They should use the word 'protect' on the poster.

Wrap up

Recap the three focus words by discussing the questions in the 'Tell me' column of the table, above.

Challenge the children to think of a sentence using one of the focus words.

Follow-up independent sessions

You will need

- Collage materials, glue, poster paper
- Resource sheet: My favourite sea creature
- A selection of non-fiction books about sea creatures
- Resource sheet: Book review

Ask children to create a collage of 'under the sea'. They should include some of the creatures from the text (shark, fish, sea dragon, stonefish, crab, jellyfish, sea urchin, turtle).

Give each child a copy of Resource sheet: My favourite sea creature. Ask children to draw their favourite sea creature from the book and label it. They should write a sentence to describe the sea creature.

Ask children to explore a selection of non-fiction books about sea creatures. They should choose one book and write a book review using Resource sheet: Book review, to guide them.

I Want a Pet!

Book Band: Green

In this poem with predictable structure and patterned language, a boy meets some very unusual animals at the Strange Pet Shop before he finds his perfect pet.

Skills focus

- Draw on knowledge of vocabulary to understand texts
- Identify/explain key aspects of fiction and non-fiction texts, e.g. character, events, title
- Make inferences from texts
- Read words accurately and fluently

Guided reading session

You will need

- Multiple copies of Collins Big Cat *I Want a Pet!*

Tune in

Introduce the book by reading the title aloud; ask children to join in.

Encourage the children to look closely at the front cover.

Ask the following questions:

- What animal can you see? *(giraffe)*
- Is there anything strange about the giraffe? *(colour, pattern, eyes)*

Look at the page 1 together.

Ask: Can you point to the author's name? Can you point to the illustrator's name?

Read the names together.

Turn to the back cover and read the first part of the blurb aloud, encouraging the children to follow and join in with you.

Ask: What do you notice about these lines? *(they rhyme)*

Explain that this is a rhyming story, it is a poem.

Read the rest of the blurb together and encourage the children to look closely at the picture.

Ask: What do you think this poem is about?

Heads together

Read pages 2 to 7 aloud to the children, asking them to follow as you read and to join in if they are able. Model strategies for reading longer words, for example, blending phonemes to read CVC, CCVC and CVCC words (pet, shop, want) and recognition of tricky words (here, like).

Focus on the word 'isn't'. Demonstrate how to pronounce it and draw attention to the apostrophe used to show a missing letter. Check the children's understanding of the word. ('is not' contracted to 'isn't')

Check the children's understanding.

Ask the following questions:

- What is the poem about? *(a boy who wants a pet)*
- What is the name of the pet shop? *(Strange Pet Shop)*
- What kind of pets do you think will be in the shop?

Ask children to read the rest of the book, on their own, to find out whether the boy finds a pet.

As they read, move around the group, listening to each child while the others read in their heads. Support them in reading longer words and check their reading strategies.

Wrap up

Check the children's understanding.

Ask the following questions:

- Does he find a pet? *(yes)*
- What kind of pet is it? *(a dog)*

Tell the children that they are going to think about some of the other pets in the shop.

Ask the following questions, encouraging them to use the book to help them answer:

- Can you find the pet with funny feet? *(page 8)*
- Can you find the pet with too much hair? *(page 16)*
- If you could choose any of the pets in the shop, which would it be and why?

Now focus on the words with apostrophes for contractions. Ask children to turn to page 6 and revisit the word 'isn't'. Challenge the children to find any other words in the book with contractions – suggest that they look at page 12 onwards (there are contracted words on pages 14, 15, 16, 18 and 21).

Briefly check understanding of the following words:

'one's' = 'one is' (page 14)

'one's' = 'one has' (page 15)

'here's' = 'here is' (page 16)

'haven't' = 'have not' (page 18)

'I'll' = 'I will' (page 21)

Finish by asking:

- Did you like the poem? Why?

Vocabulary boost session

You will need
- Multiple copies of Collins Big Cat *I Want a Pet!*

Vocabulary table

Focus word	Child-friendly explanation	Example sentence	Tell me...
strange	Something that is strange has not been seen before. It is different to what you usually see or know.	The story was about a **strange** land that was pink and blue.	Tell me about a strange place that you have seen.
wild	If an animal is wild, it is not looked after by people. It lives in places like jungles.	They saw **wild** cats at the zoo.	Tell me what you know about wild animals.
wonder	Wonder means think about. If you wonder about something, you are interested or want to know more about it.	Aran **wondered** what was for lunch.	Tell me about a time that you have wondered about something.

Tune in

Explain to the children that in this lesson they are going to look closely at some of the words the author has used and what those words mean.

Read the book aloud to the children, modelling how to use the punctuation and dialogue to read aloud with expression.

Refer back to each of the focus words within the context of the story, writing up the word, giving a child-friendly explanation and asking the children to say the focus word with you. For example: In the poem, there is a strange pet shop. Something that is strange has not been seen before. It is different to what you usually see or know. Now, say the word with me – 'strange'.

Refer to each of the focus words that you have written up and give the children the example sentences. Then ask them to interact with the word meanings by asking the questions in the 'Tell me' column.

Heads together

Ask the following questions to explore and develop the children's understanding of the focus words:
- Which of these might be strange: a dog with three ears; a cat with whiskers; a tree with bright blue leaves? Explain why or why not.
- Which of these might describe a wild animal: a small animal that lives in someone's house and eats what the people give it; a very large animal that lives in a big place and likes to eat small animals; a small animal that lives in the jungle and catches its own food? Explain why or why not.
- Which of these are things that you might wonder about: what your birthday present might be; where your classroom is; what you will do in the holidays?

Encourage the children to make links to their own lives and experiences to help them.

Wrap up

Tell the children that you will say a sentence that is missing a word and that they have to say one of the focus words that fits into the sentence. Tell them that 'strange', 'wild', or 'wonder' will fit in the blank.
- An animal that is not looked after by people and lives in big places is a… animal. *(wild)*
- If something has not been seen before, or it is different to what you usually see or know, we say it is… *(strange)*
- Another word for 'think about' is… *(wonder)*

Ask children to choose one of the focus words as their word of the week. Challenge them to use the word as often as they can, both at school and at home.

Follow-up independent sessions

You will need
- Multiple copies of Collins Big Cat *I Want a Pet!*
- Resource sheet: Book talk for *I Want a Pet!*
- Resource sheet: Rhyming words for *I Want a Pet!*

Ask children to work with their Reading Partners and to read the book aloud.

Give pairs of children a copy of Resource sheet: Book talk for *I Want a Pet!* Ask them to talk about and write or draw what they like or dislike about the poem.

Hand out copies of Resource sheet: Rhyming words for *I Want a Pet!* The children draw lines to match the words in the top box with the ones they rhyme with in the bottom box.

Worm Looks for Lunch

Book Band: Green

This playscript follows a hungry worm who tries the food that other creatures eat, but gets a shock when he approaches a bird.

Skills focus

- Draw on knowledge of vocabulary to understand texts
- Identify/explain key aspects of fiction and non-fiction texts, e.g. character, events, title
- Identify/explain the sequence of events in texts
- Read words accurately and fluently

Guided reading session

You will need

- Multiple copies of Collins Big Cat *Worm Looks for Lunch*

Tune in

Explain to the children that they are going to read a book that is a 'playscript'. Ask them if they have ever read or seen a play, or if they have ever been in one.

Ask: What was it about?

Explain that plays include the words that characters – animals or people – speak and actors read the words while pretending to be those characters.

Ask children to look carefully at the cover and suggest who some of the characters are in this play.

Turn to pages 2 and 3 and identify the characters and compare them with the children's predictions. Briefly explain that the storyteller is the speaker who tells you what happens during the story.

Point to the circle on page 2 under the storyteller. Ask if they can find the same picture in a circle on page 4. Repeat for the worm picture. Elicit that the circles tell you who is speaking the words.

Focus the children on page 4 and explain the other text features. Point out the text in italics at the top and explain that this tells the actors who are playing the characters what to do and what the setting is.

Read the top lines of text on page 4.

Ask the following questions:

- Where is this part of the play set? *(under a tree)*
- If you were acting Worm on a stage, what would you have to pretend to do? *(wiggle out of the ground)*

Read page 4 and pause after reading 'crossly'. Tell the children that this tells us how Worm should read his words. Demonstrate reading the part crossly.

Heads together

Read pages 4 to 8 aloud to the children, asking them to follow as you read. Model different voices and explain that you are not reading the character names – only the words that the characters are meant to read out.

Point out the exclamation marks on page 4 and remind the children that these mean the words have to be said with extra energy and expression.

On page 8, point to the top line in italics and ask children for advice on what face to pull.

Ask children what has happened so far.

Ask three volunteers to reread pages 4 to 8, each taking a part, while you read the text in italics. Encourage the children to read expressively, helping them to sound out any unfamiliar words.

Ask children to now work in groups to read the whole book to find out what happens so they can report back to the group. Allocate groups of four children to work together to read blocks of pages (4 to 8, 9 to 11, 12 to 14 and 15 to 19) and groups of three children for pages 20 to 21. Each child in the group takes a part. One child can read everything that is in italics, while the others each play a character.

Move around the groups, checking they are making an attempt to allocate parts and are reading their parts fluently and expressively. Support them in reading any difficult words and if necessary ask them to read the sentence containing the word to aid their understanding.

Wrap up

Using the pictures in the book as prompts, ask children from the different groups what happened in the story. Choose groups in the order of the plot.

Ask children to feed back on the ending of the book. Elicit how this section is different to the previous sections. Suggest that they reread pages 15 to 21 as a group to check how the ending differs. Allocate children to read the parts, while you read the text in italics.

Check that the children understand that blackbirds eat worms as well as beetles.

Ask children if they liked the ending and why.

Vocabulary boost session

You will need

- Multiple copies of Collins Big Cat *Worm Looks for Lunch*

Vocabulary table

Focus word	Child-friendly explanation	Example sentence	Tell me...
wiggled	If something wiggled, it moved from side to side, probably quite slowly.	My baby brother **wiggled** when I tickled him in his cot.	Tell me about anything or anyone you that know wiggled.
chewy	If food is chewy, it's hard to break into smaller pieces with your teeth, ready to swallow.	The toffee was so **chewy** I could not swallow it.	Tell me about something that you think is chewy.
towards	If you go towards something or someone, you are moving closer to it or are moving in its direction.	I turned **towards** my friend to speak to him.	Tell me about a time today when you moved towards something, or someone.

Tune in

Read the book to the children, asking them to follow the words closely as you read.

Afterwards ask if there were any words that were unfamiliar to them. Read the words in their context and give a brief child-friendly explanation using everyday language. Encourage the child who queried the word originally to reread the sentence to check their understanding.

Refer to the three focus words within the context of the story. For each, write the word on the board, giving a child-friendly explanation. You could use the definitions in the table, above, or make up your own. Ask children to say the focus words.

Next, challenge the children with the questions in the 'Tell me' column in order to encourage further interaction with the words. The questions will prompt them to look at the words in the context of their own experiences. Support them by giving some examples of your own.

Ask children to say the words with you again.

Heads together

Ask the following questions to develop the children's understanding of the focus words:

- When might you have wiggled?
- What might be chewy?
- What might you move towards?

Discuss the children's answers and decide as a group what other words might go with the focus words.

Wrap up

Ask the following questions to review the word meanings and develop the children's understanding of the focus words:

- Which word goes with 'moving along'?
- Which word goes with 'squirmed'?
- Which word goes with 'tough'?

Ask children to choose one of the focus words each day and suggest another word that goes with it. Add suitable synonyms or linking words to a word wall, around the focus word.

Follow-up independent sessions

You will need

- Multiple copies of Collins Big Cat *Worm Looks for Lunch*
- Resource sheet: Worm food
- Resource sheet: Worm met...

Put the children into groups and ask them to prepare their own expressive reading of the book, doubling up in parts if they wish. Also, you could encourage them to act out the play, experimenting with how they might move as the different animals.

Give pairs of children Resource sheet: Worm food. Ask them to imagine another type of animal Worm might have met and the type of food Worm tried. Why will Worm not like it?

Give pairs of children Resource sheet: Worm met... The children draw lines to link the order that Worm met the animal and the food it ate.

A Day at the Eden Project

Book Band: Green

In this non-fiction recount of a visit, two girls explore the biomes at the Eden Project and look at plants from around the world.

Skills focus

- Draw on knowledge of vocabulary to understand texts
- Identify/explain key aspects of fiction and non-fiction texts, e.g. character, events, title
- Identify/explain the sequence of events in texts
- Check reading makes sense

Guided reading session

You will need

- Multiple copies of Collins Big Cat *A Day at the Eden Project*

Tune in

Explain to the children that they are going to read a recount of a visit or a trip. **Ask** the following questions:

- What day trips have you been on before?
- Where have you visited? (Suggest local attractions, possibly the beach, a castle, a farm park, the zoo/safari park, a museum, a forest or park and so on.)

Introduce the book by looking at the front cover. Read the title: 'A Day at the Eden Project'.

Ask the following questions:

- Has anyone been to the Eden Project?
- What do you think might be there?
- Who do you think went? *(the two girls)*

Turn the book over and explore the back cover. Recap that a blurb tells us more about the book. Look at the blurb together. Can the children recognise any high frequency words? ('on', 'our', 'day', 'at', 'the', 'we', 'saw', 'and', 'a')

Ask the following questions:

- What did the children see? *(oranges, lemons, a chocolate tree and a giant)*
- What do they think might be inside the bubbles in the picture?
- What shapes can they see? *(hexagons)*

Look at the title page. Reread the title.

Ask the following questions:

- Who wrote the book? *(Kate Petty)*
- What do we call someone who wrote the book? *(author)*

Turn to the contents page. Discuss the contents. Explain that a contents page tells us the heading and page numbers in the book.

Ask the following questions to practise using the contents:

- On what page can I find out about 'oranges and lemons'? *(page 14)*
- What is page 6 about? *(the jungle)*

Read through each heading in the contents page.

Heads together

Turn to pages 2 and 3 together. Point out the features of a non-fiction book, such as the heading, the photographs and labels. Model reading the text and ask children to follow with their finger, pointing at each word. Discuss the text and pictures.

Explain where Cornwall is (a county in the South of England). Explain that the big greenhouses allow plants that like different temperatures and weather to be grown.

Ask: Can you describe the 'biomes'? *(like big bubbles)*

Look at pages 4 and 5 together. Point out the apostrophe in the word 'we're' and explain that 'we're' = 'we are'.

Read the text together. Discuss endings such as '–ing' and '–er'. Segment and blend any unknown words, for example, 'down' d-ow-n, 'flower' f-l-ow-er.

Ask: What can you see in the picture?

Continue to explore the recount together. Discuss what the children in the book can see, hear, smell and touch on each page. Read the labels.

Wrap up

Look at the Eden Project map on pages 22 and 23.

Ask the following questions:

- Where did the girls explore first, next, after that...?
- What is the difference between the two biomes? *(different temperatures)*

Return to pages 20 and 21.

Ask the following questions:

- Do you think the girls enjoyed their visit to the Eden Project?
- Would you like to visit the Eden Project?

Vocabulary boost session

You will need

- Multiple copies of Collins Big Cat *A Day at the Eden Project*
- A map or globe that shows the Mediterranean Sea and surrounding countries

Vocabulary table

Focus word	Child-friendly explanation	Example sentence	Tell me...
enormous	If something is enormous, it is big.	My chocolate ice-cream was **enormous**!	Tell me another word meaning enormous.
sculpture	A piece of 3D art work.	There was a metal **sculpture** at the Eden project.	Tell me about a time you have made or seen a sculpture.
Mediterranean	The Mediterranean is a sea. It is also the name given to the countries (region) surrounding that sea.	I went to a **Mediterranean** restaurant.	Tell me something you know about the Mediterranean. (such as the types of food traditionally eaten in the region)

Tune in

Explain that in this lesson the children are going to look in more detail at some words linked to the text. Write the three focus words clearly for the children to see. Read the words together. Discuss and explain the child-friendly meaning of each word.

Reread the text.

Look at page 19 and find the word 'enormous'. Read the text.

Ask: What was enormous? *(bee)*

Explain that there were two sculptures in the book (bee on page 19 and giant on page 19). Challenge the children to find them.

Turn to page 23 and find the word 'Mediterranean'.

Heads together

Find the Mediterranean Sea and surrounding countries and islands on a map or globe. Look at pages 14 to 17.

Ask: What things did the children see in the Mediterranean Biome? *(oranges, lemons, cork oak trees, grapevines)*

Discuss what the Mediterranean is like: food, weather and so on.

Wrap up

Recap the three focus words by discussing the questions in the 'Tell me' column of the table, above.

Challenge the children to think of a sentence using one of the focus words.

Follow-up independent sessions

You will need

- A selection of non-fiction books about chocolate
- Resource sheet: Design a sculpture
- Resource sheet: Missing words
- Paints, paper and crayons

Let the children explore a selection of non-fiction books to find out where chocolate comes from.

Give each child a copy of Resource sheet: Design a sculpture. Ask children to design and draw a picture of a new sculpture for the Eden Project. Can children add labels to their drawing? What would the sculpture be made from?

Give pairs of children a copy of Resource sheet: Missing words. The children use the words from the box to complete the sentences. If they finish early, ask them to create their own missing words sentences to give to another pair to complete.

Ask children to create a painting of the jungle. What plants would be there? When the painting is dry, they should add labels.

Big Cat Babies

Book Band: Green

This non-chronological report looks at the lives of Africa's big cats and their babies.

Skills focus

- Draw on knowledge of vocabulary to understand texts
- Identify/explain key aspects of fiction and non-fiction texts, e.g. character, events, title
- Identify/explain the sequence of events in texts
- Check reading makes sense

Guided reading session

You will need

- Multiple copies of Collins Big *Cat Big Cat Babies*
- A world map or globe
- Resource sheet: Big Cats

Tune in

Ask the following questions to begin the lesson:

- Does anyone have a cat?
- Can you describe your cat?
- What do they look like?
- What do they do?
- What do they eat?
- Where do they live?
- What are baby cats called? *(kittens)*
- Who would like a cat?
- How do you look after a cat?

Display Resource sheet: Big cats. Ask children to identify the different animals (lion, cheetah, leopard, lioness). Explain that these are all 'big cats'.

Ask: What do you know about big cats?

Explain that you are going to read a non-fiction book called 'Big Cat Babies'.

Ask: Does anyone know what a baby lion is called? *(cub)*

Introduce the book by exploring the front cover. Read the title together. Find out who wrote the text and took the photographs. *(Jonathan and Angela Scott)*

Write the words 'leopard', 'lioness' and 'cheetah' on the board for children to practise reading and become familiar with.

Turn the book over and explore the blurb. Recap that a blurb tells us more about the book. Model reading the blurb using fluency and accuracy. Can children point out the question mark?

Look at the word 'climb' and discuss the silent 'b' at the end of the word.

Ask the following questions:

- Where can we find out more? *(in the book)*
- Who can remember what a contents page is? *(a list of the headings and where they are in the book)*
- Where will we find it? *(at the front of the book)*

Challenge the children to find the contents page.

Ask the following questions:

- Who do you think the man and lady in the photograph are? *(the authors)*
- What are they doing? *(on safari/taking photographs of big cats)*

Practise using the contents page; read the headings together.

Ask the following questions:

- On what page can I find out about lions? *(page 4)*
- What is on page 22? *(Big Cat Facts)*

Heads together

Turn to page 2 together. Model reading page 2 using a range of strategies: segmenting and blending ('big' b-i-g; 'cats' c-a-t-s), identifying high frequency words ('in', 'there', 'are', 'where', 'the') and checking it makes sense.

Find Africa on a world map or globe together.

Look at page 3. Ask children to discuss the difference between the three types of big cats. Can they describe the big cats? Model reading the text and ask children to point to the words and join in where they can.

Turn back to the contents page and ask children to work in pairs, each reading and looking at a different big cat: lions, leopards, cheetahs (allocate these as appropriate). Encourage the children to begin by using the contents to turn to the correct page. Listen to the children read and support where needed.

Wrap up

Ask each pairing to share their findings. What have they learned about big cats to tell the rest of the group?

Explore the text together and find facts.

Draw a table on the board. Ask children to say out loud the facts they have found out about each animal as you complete the table.

Lion	Cheetah	Leopard

Ask children to look at pages 22 and 23 together and compare them to their table of facts on the board.

Vocabulary boost session

You will need
- Multiple copies of Collins Big Cat *Big Cat Babies*
- Resource sheet: Baby animals

Vocabulary table

Focus word	Child-friendly explanation	Example sentence	Tell me...
pride	A group of lions that live together.	Lions live in a **pride**.	Tell me who you live with.
cubs	Cubs are baby lions and lionesses.	Lion **cubs** like to play.	Tell me any other names for baby animals that you know.
lioness	A lioness is a female lion.	The **lioness** looks after her cubs.	Tell me how a lioness looks different to a lion.

Tune in

Explain that in this lesson the children are going to look in more detail at some of the words the authors have used. Write the three focus words clearly for the children to see. Read the words together. Discuss and explain the child-friendly meaning of each word.

Reread the text.

Turn to pages 4 and 5. Challenge the children to find all three focus words.

Heads together

Discuss the names for different baby animals that the children might know. For example: a baby cat is a kitten, a baby dog is a puppy, a baby sheep is a lamb, a baby owl is an owlet.

Explain that lots of animals live in groups. A group of cows is a herd. A group of sheep is a flock. A group of lions is a pride. Do the children know of any other names for groups of animals? Challenge them to investigate.

Wrap up

Recap the three focus words by discussing the questions in the 'Tell me' column of the table, above.

Challenge the children to think of a sentence using one of the focus words.

Follow-up independent sessions

You will need
- Paper plates, elastic or string, selection of collage materials
- Resource sheet: Baby animals
- A selection of non-fiction books about big cats
- Pastels and sugar paper
- Magnetic letters and boards

Ask children to use a paper plate and selection of collage materials to create a lion mask.

Using Resource sheet: Baby animals, the children match the animal babies to their mothers.

Ask children to explore a selection of non-fiction texts about lions, leopards and cheetahs.

Let the children use pastels to create a picture of the sunset in Africa, similar to page 2 in the book.

The children can use magnetic letters and boards to make high frequency words from the text: 'in', 'there', 'are', 'where', 'the', 'and', 'all', 'very', 'their', 'too', 'a', 'called', 'her', 'she', 'they', 'can', 'like', 'to', 'of', 'go', 'out', 'on', 'for', 'when', 'will'.

Nick Butterworth: Making Books

Book Band: Green

In this non-fiction recount, Nick Butterworth talks about his life, his work as an author and illustrator, and how he creates his characters like Percy the Park Keeper.

Skills focus

- Draw on knowledge of vocabulary to understand texts
- Identify/explain key aspects of fiction and non-fiction texts, e.g. character, events, title
- Make inferences from texts
- Read words accurately and fluently

Guided reading session

You will need

- Multiple copies of Collins Big Cat *Nick Butterworth: Making Books*

Tune in

Introduce the book by reading the title to the children.

Ask: Does anybody know, or would like to guess, what job Nick Butterworth does? *(author and illustrator)*

Turn to page 3.

Ask the following questions:

- Has anyone read any of Nick Butterworth's books?
- What kind of book do you think this is – information or story? *(information)*
- What makes you think that? *(photographs)*

Turn to the back cover and ask children to read the blurb on their own.

Ask the following questions:

- What is the book about? *(being an author and illustrator)*
- Have you changed your mind about what kind of book you think this is? Is it information or story? *(information)*
- What makes you think that? *(photographs, about real things)*

Heads together

Read pages 2 to 7 aloud to the children, asking them to follow as you read and join in. Model strategies for reading longer words, for example, recognition of tricky words ('some', 'my'), noticing familiar word endings ('–s' for plural, '–ing', '–ed').

Ask: What does the book tell us, so far, about Nick Butterworth?

You may need to model how to look back at the pages and give a short answer. For example, point to the bottom of page 2 and say: It tells us that he writes stories and does the illustrations.

Before you continue reading, tell the children that you want them to think about what the book is telling us as they read.

Read pages 8 to 13 aloud, modelling reading strategies and encouraging the children to follow and join in.

Wrap up

Check the children's understanding.

Ask the following questions:

- What were those pages about? *(where Nick Butterworth gets his ideas from)*
- Where did he get the idea for Percy the Park Keeper from? *(a walk in the park/his grandpa)*

Ask children to read the rest of the book, on their own. As they read, move around the group, listening to each child while the others read in their heads. Support the children in reading longer words and check their reading strategies.

Ask the following questions:

- Do you think Nick Butterworth enjoys his job?
- What makes you think that?
- Is there anything that he doesn't like about his job?
- How do you know?

Vocabulary boost session

You will need
- Multiple copies of Collins Big Cat *Nick Butterworth: Making Books*

Vocabulary table

Focus word	Child-friendly explanation	Example sentence	Tell me...
some	If you talk about 'some' things, it means a small number of things.	I ate **some** sweets.	Tell me what you can see some of in this room.
sometimes	You use 'sometimes' to say something happens only two or three times, not lots of times.	**Sometimes** her dad lets her ride on the back of his bike.	Tell me about something that you do only sometimes.
idea	An idea is something that you think in your head. It could be a picture or a way of doing something.	Miss Brown gave us some **ideas** before we started our painting.	Tell me about a time that you have had a good idea.

Tune in

Explain to the children that in this lesson they are going to look closely at some of the words the author has used and what those words mean.

Read the book aloud to the children, asking them to follow and join in as you read.

Refer back to each of the focus words within the context of the story, writing up the word, giving a child-friendly explanation and asking the children to say the focus word with you. For example: In the book, there are some photographs of Nick Butterworth. 'Some' things means a small number of things. Now, say the word with me – 'some'.

You may wish to use the examples in the table, above.

Refer to each of the focus words that you have written up and give the children the example sentences. Then ask them to interact with the word meanings by asking the questions in the 'Tell me' column. You may wish to demonstrate by giving some examples of your own.

Ask children to say the words with you once more.

Heads together

Explore and develop children's understanding of the focus words by referring to the book. Turn to pages 3 and 4 and read the text.

Ask: Can you tell me what the word 'some' means?

Turn to page 8 and read the text.

Ask: Can you tell me what the word 'sometimes' means?

Turn to page 9 and read the text.

Ask: Can you tell me what the word 'idea' means?

Wrap up

Ask the following questions to review the word meanings:
- What's the word that means something you think in your head?
- What's the word that means a small number of times?
- What's the word that means something that happens only two or three times?

Ask children to choose one of the focus words as their word of the week. Challenge them to use the word as often as they can, both at school and at home.

Follow-up independent sessions

You will need
- Multiple copies of Collins Big Cat *Nick Butterworth: Making Books*
- Resource sheet: Comprehension questions
- Resource sheet: Character notes

Ask children to work with their Reading Partners and to read the book aloud.

Give pairs of children Resource sheet: Comprehension questions. Ask them to use the book to help find the answers to the questions.

Ask children to imagine they are an author like Nick Butterworth. On Resource sheet: Character notes, they should create a fictional character similar to Percy the Park Keeper. Encourage them to think of a person they know on which to base their character. Let children share their notes with the group.

Jodie the Juggler

Book Band: Green

This story with a familiar setting tells us how Jodie gets into trouble as he juggles in lots of places and with lots of things. His mum hopes all will be well if she takes him to play football in the park.

Skills focus

- Draw on knowledge of vocabulary to understand texts
- Identify/explain key aspects of fiction and non-fiction texts, e.g. character, events, title
- Predict what might happen on the basis of what has been read so far
- Read words accurately and fluently

Guided reading session

You will need
- Multiple copies of Collins Big Cat *Jodie the Juggler*

Tune in

Focus the children on the front cover picture and ask them to point to the title and then read it together.

Encourage the children to talk about their experience of juggling and what it involves.

Challenge the children to find the blurb. Read the blurb without stopping, encouraging the children to join in.

Reread the blurb again, this time stopping after the third and fourth sentences to ask children to make predictions about the story.

Ask the following questions:
- Why do you think Mum thought football would be safer?
- What do you think was the 'BIG surprise!'?

Return to the front cover picture and challenge the children to find the cat.

Ask: What do you think the cat is thinking? Why?

Heads together

Read pages 2 and 3 of the story aloud to the children. Ask them to follow the words as you read.

Ask: Did you notice how some phrases were repeated?

Elicit how 'He juggled with…' is repeated three times. Can the children think of any stories they have read where phrases are repeated again and again?

Return to page 3 and reread it, pausing at the ellipsis.

Ask: What do you think happened next?

Point to Mum's and the cat's expressions.

Ask: Why aren't they smiling?

Read pages 3 to 5 aloud with expression. Pause at the ellipsis on page 5.

Ask: What do you think happens next?

Read pages 5 and 6 and ask children to look at the picture on page 6. Discuss Mum and Jodie.

Ask the following questions:
- How do you think Mum is feeling? *(angry)*
- How do you think Jodie is feeling? Why?

Point out how the drama is built up by the bigger font and use of an exclamation mark after 'CRASH!'

Remind them to look for familiar letter patterns and smaller words when reading. Write 'CRASH!' on the board and point out the smaller words 'rash/ash'. Remind them of how 'sh' makes one sound.

Write 'juggling' and 'juggled' on the board and underline the common endings: '–ed' and '–ing'. Explain that remembering these will help them read the rest of the story.

Read page 7 with the children and encourage them to discuss what might happen next. Encourage them to refer to what they know so far (Jodie loves to juggle!)

Ask children to read the rest of the story, to find out if they were right.

Move around the group, listening to each child. Support them in noticing '–ing' and '–ed' endings.

Wrap up

Ask children if they were right about what happened next. Encourage them to explain what happened when Jodie visited his friend's house and what happened at the park.

Focus the children on page 21.

Ask: Do you think Mum is happier now? Why? Why not?

Return to the back cover blurb and reread it with the children.

Ask: Was Mum right – that football would be safer?

Explain that the ending of a story is really important. Say that poor endings can be confusing or boring.

Ask the following questions:
- How did you feel when you read the ending?
- Is it a good ending? Why?

Vocabulary boost session

You will need

- Multiple copies of Collins Big Cat *Jodie the Juggler*

Vocabulary table

Focus word	Child-friendly explanation	Example sentence	Tell me...
safer	When something is safer, there is less danger: people and things are less likely to get hurt or be damaged.	I feel much **safer** in the shallow end of the swimming pool than in the deep end.	Tell me about a time when you have felt safer and why.
splat	'Splat!' is the sound made by something wet or sticky when it hits something hard, like the ground.	When I dropped my ice cream, it went '**Splat!**' on the footpath.	Tell me about something that you have seen go 'splat!'
firmly	If you do something firmly, you do it with certainty or strength.	I told the puppy **firmly**, not to play with my toys.	Tell me about something that you have said or done firmly.

Tune in

Write the focus words on the board in varying sizes and fonts to express their meaning. For example, write 'safer' in rounded thick lettering; 'Splat!' in big, dramatic letters; 'firmly' in strong angular lettering.

Read the words to the children and explain that they are going to learn more about words like these that are in the book.

Read the book aloud to the children, with expression, emphasising words or phrases with exclamation marks and focus words.

Point to each word on the board. Give a child-friendly explanation and ask them to say the word with you. You can use the definitions in the table, above, or make up your own.

For each focus word, give the children an example sentence. Encourage them to interact with the word meanings by asking the questions in the 'Tell me' column, above.

Ask children to say the words with you once again.

Heads together

Ask the following questions to explore and develop the children's understanding of the focus words:

- Do you think it would be safer to climb a mountain on your own or with a team of expert climbers?
- Which would go 'Splat!' if you dropped it – a rock or a rotten tomato?
- Would you firmly open a door or firmly close a door?

Encourage them to elaborate on their answers by following up their responses with the question 'Why?'

Wrap up

Ask the following questions to review the word meanings:

- How would you make a children's playground safer?
- What sort of shape would you draw for a 'splat' – round, wavy or square?
- What sort of voice would you use to say something firmly?

Challenge the children to think of words that can be linked to the focus words and list them in a display.

Follow-up independent sessions

You will need

- Multiple copies of Collins Big Cat *Jodie the Juggler*
- Resource sheet: What happened?
- Resource sheet: Crash! and Splat!
- Coloured pencils or pens

Copy and cut out sets of cards from Resource sheet: What happened? Give pairs (or groups) of children a set of cards. Ask them to put the cards into the correct order to show what happened in the story. Ask them to check the order afterwards by looking at the book. Finally, they can take turns to retell the story using just the cards as prompts.

Give pairs of children Resource sheet: Crash! and Splat! Ask children to draw some things that Jodie is juggling and choose the sound they would make if he dropped them.

Crunch and Munch

Book Band: Green

This instruction text provides four healthy recipes that can be created without cooking.

Skills focus

- Draw on knowledge of vocabulary to understand texts
- Identify/explain key aspects of fiction and non-fiction texts, e.g. character, events, title
- Identify/explain the sequence of events in texts
- Read words accurately and fluently

Guided reading session

You will need

- Multiple copies of Collins Big Cat *Crunch and Munch*
- A selection of cooking utensils: a measuring jug, a mixing bowl, a tablespoon, a lemon squeezer, a cup for measuring, weighing scales, a teaspoon, a wooden spoon and labels from Resource sheet: Labels (create new labels depending on the cooking equipment available)

Tune in

Explain to the children that in this lesson they are going to look at some recipes.

Ask: What is a recipe? *(instructions for making meals or snacks)*

Relate to the children's own experiences.

Ask the following questions:

- What cooking have you done before?
- What have you made?
- What would you like to make?

Introduce the book by looking at the front cover. Read the title by segmenting and blending the words 'crunch' c-r-u-n-ch, 'munch' m-u-n-ch.

Ask the following questions:

- What type of recipes do you think are in this book? *(salad, healthy)*
- What food items crunch? *(vegetables, fruit)*
- What vegetables are your favourite and how do you like them cooked?
- What vegetables can you see on the front cover? *(carrots, celery, cucumber, tomatoes, lettuce)*

Turn the book over and read the blurb. Recap that a blurb tells us more about the book. Can the children predict what recipes will be in the book?

Look at the contents page together. Explain that a contents page lists the headings in the book and what page they are on.

Ask the following questions to practise using the contents page:

- On which page is the Carrot Crunch recipe? *(page 8)*
- What recipe is on page 12? *('Super Salad Dressing')*

Discuss the use of alliteration in the recipe titles.

Find the glossary on page 20. Recap that a glossary tells us the meaning of some tricky words in the text. Read the words and their meanings. Can the children find the words (written in bold) in the text?

Put a selection of cooking utensils on the table and labels from Resource sheet: Labels. Ask children to identify the items and match the objects to the correct label. Then explore pages 2 and 3.

Heads together

Read pages 4 to 7 together. Point out the alliteration in the heading 'Morning Munch'. Ask children what they like to eat for breakfast. Look at the features of instructions, for example, the 'You will need' list, bullet points, numbered steps, instructional language (weigh, put, mix, pour, add).

Give each pair a recipe to read (Carrot Crunch, Super Salad Dressing, Rainbow Kebabs) and ask children to read the recipe in pairs. Can they find out what ingredients they would need, what equipment they would need and what to do? Can they identify the instructional vocabulary? While the children are reading, listen to individuals and support where needed.

Wrap up

Share what the children have found out about the recipes. Can the children ask each other questions about the text?

Ask: Which recipe did you like best and why?

Recap strategies they can use to tackle unknown words when reading, for example, segmenting and blending, high frequency words, checking it makes sense and picture clues.

Recap the features of instructions and challenge children to find them in one of the recipes ('You will need' list, bullet points, numbered steps, instructional language).

Discuss why it is important that instructions are in the correct order.

Vocabulary boost session

You will need

- Multiple copies of Collins Big Cat *Crunch and Munch*
- Oranges/tangerines
- Resource sheet: Tools for the job

Vocabulary table

Focus word	Child-friendly explanation	Example sentence	Tell me...
segments	Pieces of an orange.	I ate three **segments** of orange for my breakfast.	Tell me the name of another fruit that has segments.
ingredients	Parts mixed together to make something.	I bought the **ingredients** at the shops to make a cake.	Tell me what ingredients you would put in a salad.
equipment	The tools or kit to do a task.	I washed up the **equipment** after cooking.	Tell me what equipment you would need as a hairdresser.

Tune in

Explain that in this lesson the children are going to look in more detail at some words linked to the text. Write the three focus words clearly for the children to see. Read the words together. Discuss and explain the child-friendly meaning of each word.

Reread the text.

Ask the following questions:

- Find the word 'segments' in the text. *(page 18)*
- Which recipe do you think it will be in? *(Rainbow Kebabs because they use fruit)*

Look at pages 2 and 3. Discuss the equipment used in the kitchen.

Ask: What ingredients are needed to make Morning Munch? *(porridge oats, dried fruit, nuts, seeds, milk, honey and fresh fruit)*

Heads together

Give each child an orange or tangerine. Can they peel it and find out how many segments it has?

Use Resource sheet: Tools for the job. The children match the equipment to the person or task.

Wrap up

Recap the three focus words by discussing the questions in the 'Tell me' column of the table, above.

Challenge the children to think of a sentence using one of the focus words.

Follow-up independent sessions

You will need

- Wooden skewers
- A selection of fresh fruit cut into pieces, such as grapes, raspberries, slices of banana, strawberries
- A selection of recipe books
- Paper, coloured pencils
- Role-play area set up as a kitchen (pretend food, aprons and cooking equipment)
- Digital recording equipment (optional)

Ask children to make fruit kebabs. Provide them with a selection of fruit pieces and wooden skewers.

The children choose the fruit and thread it on to the skewers.

Ask children to explore a selection of recipe books. What would they like to cook? They can choose a favourite recipe and draw a picture of it.

Set up a role-play area, such as a kitchen or café. Provide the children with pretend food, mixing bowls, aprons, wooden spoons and so on. Ensure children wash their hands before handling food and are accompanied when using sharp objects. Check for any food allergies. The children play at being chefs. If digital recording equipment is available, they can be filmed as if presenting a TV cookery show.

Ella the Superstar

Book Band: Green

Baby Ella's talent for reading turns her into a star, in this story with a familiar setting.

Skills focus

- Draw on knowledge of vocabulary to understand texts
- Make inferences from texts

- Predict what might happen on the basis of what has been read so far
- Check reading makes sense
- Read words accurately and fluently

Guided reading session

You will need

- Multiple copies of Collins Big Cat *Ella the Superstar*
- Photographs/pictures of some superstars, for example famous footballers, actors, singers, chefs, authors

Tune in

Ask the following questions to begin the lesson:

- What is a superstar? *(someone who is famous for a special talent/skill)*
- Do you know of any superstars? *(for example: footballers, singers, actors, authors)*

Show the children some photographs/pictures of some superstars. Discuss what their special talent is.

Ask about each superstar: What are they good at?

Introduce the book. Look at the front cover together and read the title. Show the children how to split the compound word 'super/star'. Can the children predict what Ella might be good at/why she is a superstar?

Ask the following questions:

- What is she doing on the front cover? *(reading)*
- Can babies normally read?

Turn the book over and look at the blurb together. Recap that a blurb tells us more about the book. Model reading the blurb, demonstrating accuracy and fluency.

Ask the following questions:

- Does anyone have a baby sister or brother?
- Are they super at anything?
- Imagine if they were superstars, what do you think it would be like?

Explain that we need to read the book to find out what Ella is so super at!

Look at the title page to find out who the author is and who the illustrator is (Ian Whybrow and Sam McCullen). Recap what an author does and what an illustrator does.

Discuss different strategies the children can use in their reading, such as segmenting and blending, picture clues, high frequency words, checking the text makes sense.

Recap the vowel digraphs: 'er', 'ar', 'ea', 'ee' and 'ai'. Find examples of the digraphs in the book: super, clever, tiger; park, star, car, marched; read; sweet, cheek, beep; fainted.

Heads together

Turn to pages 2 and 3 and read the text together. Encourage the children to point to the words and join in where they can.

Ask the following questions:

- What sort of books do you like best?
- Who do you like reading with?
- Do you think Ella's dad and brother enjoy reading with her?
- Do you think Ella is actually reading the words in the book?

Continue to read and share the text together.

On pages 4 and 5, point out the vowel digraph in 'showed'. Look at the speech marks/inverted commas – can the children identify which words Mum actually said?

Ask: What does Mum think of Ella's reading? *(she likes it, it's funny)*

Turn to pages 6 and 7. Practise reading with expression 'What a sweet little baby!' and 'I'm a tiger. I will bite your nose!' Discuss the different tone and voice.

Ask: Can you explain why the lady might have fainted on pages 8 and 9? *(she was shocked/surprised/scared)*

Read the rest of the book together. Turn to pages 18 and 19.

Ask: Why does the lady think Ella is a superstar? *(she can read)*

Wrap up

Ask: Looking back through the book, what special talents does Ella have? *(reading, driving a car, writing*

a book, presenting a TV show!)

Ask children to predict what Ella will do next.

Vocabulary boost session

You will need

- Multiple copies of Collins Big Cat *Ella the Superstar*
- Coloured pencils or pens, paper

Vocabulary table

Focus word	Child-friendly explanation	Example sentence	Tell me...
superstar	Someone who is well-known for their special talents and skills.	The cyclist was a **superstar**!	Tell me the names of some superstars.
famous	Someone who is well-known, in the newspapers and on TV.	A **famous** footballer came to open the school fete!	Tell me if you think it would be nice to be famous.
talent	If you have a talent for something, you are very good at it.	The guitarist was very **talented**.	Tell me what you are good at.

Tune in

Explain that in this lesson the children are going to look in more detail at some words linked to the text. Write the three focus words clearly for the children to see. Read the words together. Discuss and explain the child-friendly meaning of each word.

Reread the text.

Find the word 'superstar'.

Ask the following questions:

- What does Ella become famous for? *(reading, writing, being a TV presenter)*
- What special talents does Ella have? *(reading with expression)*

Heads together

Ask children to verbally complete the sentence: 'My talent is...'

Ask children to draw a picture of something they are good at or a talent they have. Ask them to label the picture or write a sentence about it.

Wrap up

Recap the three focus words by discussing the questions in the 'Tell me' column of the table, above.

Challenge the children to think of a sentence using one of the focus words.

Follow-up independent sessions

You will need

- Resource sheet: Ella's talents
- Paper and felt-tipped pens
- Resource sheet: Super-baby!

Ask children to reflect on the special talents Ella had. They complete Resource sheet: Ella's talents, by drawing and labelling a picture of each talent.

Ask children to create their own 'Super-baby' character. What special talent will they have? They draw a picture of their Super-baby and write about their talents on Resource sheet: Super-baby!

Scary Hair

Book Band: Green

Rex the dinosaur opens a hairdresser's in this humorous fantasy story and his dad teaches him how to eat the customers. But Rex prefers to give them haircuts and make them happy.

Skills focus

- Draw on knowledge of vocabulary to understand texts
- Identify/explain the sequence of events in texts
- Make inferences from texts
- Read words accurately and fluently

Guided reading session

You will need

- Multiple copies of Collins Big Cat *Scary Hair*

Tune in

Introduce the book by asking the children to look closely at the front cover.

Ask the following questions:

- What can you see? *(two dinosaurs)*
- What do you think the characters' names are? *(The smaller one might be Rex, as that's the name on his bag.)*
- What might they be doing?

Read the title aloud, ask children to join in.

Ask: What do you think the story is about?

Turn to the title page, read the title again and then ask children to point to the part that tells us who wrote and illustrated the book. Read this together.

Turn to the back cover and read the blurb aloud, encouraging the children to follow and join in with you.

Ask: Do you have any more ideas of what the story might be about?

Heads together

Tell the children that they are going to read the first part of the story on their own.

Ask: What strategies can you use to help you if you get stuck on a word? *(look at the pictures; use the initial sound to start you off and then use phonics and blend the phonemes; look for tricky words that you already know)*

Ask children to read pages 2 to 13, on their own. As they read, move around the group, listening to each child while the others read in their heads. Support them in reading longer words and check their reading strategies.

Ask the following questions:

- What kind of dinosaur was Rex? *(kind)* How do you know? *(He liked helping other animals.)*
- What was his dad like and how do you know? *(He was mean because he wanted Rex to eat the animals who came to the shop, but he was kind because he gave Rex a shop.)*
- How did Rex help the dog called Pants? *(gave him a wild haircut)*
- How did Shocker feel after Rex had given her a haircut? *(cool, happy, she could go to a party)*

Wrap up

Before continuing to read the story, turn to page 13 and draw the children's attention to the spoken words. Model how to read them with expression. Read them again, asking the children to follow and join in, practising reading with expression.

Tell children that as they read the last part of the story you are going to be listening out for them using expression when they read speech.

Read pages 14 to 21, modelling reading strategies and reading speech with expression; encourage the children to follow and join in with you.

Ask the following questions:

- How did the story start? *(Rex's dad gave him a shop called 'Scary Hair')*
- What did Rex do next? *(gave animals haircuts that made them feel happy)*
- How did the story end? *(Rex changed his shop name to 'Happy Hair')*

Vocabulary boost session

You will need
- Multiple copies of Collins Big Cat *Scary Hair*

Vocabulary table

Focus word	Child-friendly explanation	Example sentence	Tell me...
first	If something is first, it comes right at the start.	Cho came **first** in the race.	Tell me about a time when you have been first for something.
now	If you do something now you do it straight away.	"**Now** you can go out to play," said the teacher.	Tell me about something you could do now.
soon	Soon tells us when something happens. It means in a short time.	Mum said we were leaving **soon**.	Tell me about something you could do soon.

Tune in

Explain to the children that in this lesson they are going to look closely at some of the words the author has used and what those words mean.

Read the book aloud to the children, modelling how to use the punctuation and dialogue to read aloud with expression.

Refer back to each of the focus words within the context of the story, writing up the word, giving a child-friendly explanation and asking the children to say the focus word with you. For example: In the story, Rex's dad said, "First, they sit in your chair." If something is first, it comes right at the start. Now, say the word with me – 'first' .

You may wish to use the examples in the table, above.

Refer to each of the focus words that you have written up and give the children the example sentences. Then ask them to interact with the word meanings by asking the questions in the 'Tell me' column. You may wish to demonstrate by giving some examples of your own.

Ask children to say the words with you once more.

Heads together

Tell the children that you will say a sentence that is missing a word and that they have to say one of the focus words that fits into the sentence. Tell them that either: 'first', 'now' or 'soon' will fit in the blank.

- … we will wash our hands, after that we will dry them. *(first)*
- It will go dark …. *(soon)*
- Quickly! We have to go …. *(now)*
- The person whose name begins with 'A' will go … in the line. *(first)*
- Mum will … be here. *(soon)*
- We can put our umbrella down … that it's stopped raining. *(now)*

Wrap up

Review the word meanings by doing the following activity. Tell the children you have some sentences that make sense and some that don't make sense. They decide – if it makes sense, they say 'yes'; if it doesn't make sense, they say 'no'. They should listen carefully!

- We will eat our dinner now when it is later. *(no)*
- Soon we will eat our dinner. *(yes)*
- I was the first to finish my work. *(yes)*
- Sarah was first in line, she stood in the middle of it. *(no)*

Challenge the children to use the words as often as they can, both at school and at home.

Follow-up independent sessions

You will need
- Resource sheet: The characters in the story
- Coloured pencils or pens
- Resource sheet: Role on the wall: Rex

Give each child a copy of Resource sheet: The characters in the story. The children draw and write about the characters in the story.

Ask children to work with their Reading Partners and to read the book aloud, remembering to use their voices to show when a character is talking.

Using Resource sheet: Role on the wall: Rex, the children label the picture of Rex with adjectives to describe his character on the inside and his appearance on the outside.

Super Sculptures

Book Band: Green

This information book looks at sculptures made from various materials and of different shapes and sizes.

Skills focus

- Draw on knowledge of vocabulary to understand texts

- Identify/explain key aspects of fiction and non-fiction texts, e.g. character, events, title
- Check reading makes sense

Guided reading session

You will need
- Multiple copies of Collins Big Cat *Super Sculptures*

Tune in

Introduce the book by looking at the cover together. Ask children what the photo shows and what they think the book is about.

Read the title, segmenting the words into syllables as the children follow in their books.

Ask: Have I read the title correctly: Su-per sculp-tures?

Encourage the children to read the title with you again to check it makes sense.

Ask: How can we find out more about this book, before we look inside? *(the blurb)*.

Read the blurb aloud and ask children to think about sculptures they have seen. List the different items on the board and encourage the children to describe their shape, size and what they are made from.

Ask children to turn to the contents page and read the list aloud.

Ask: What are the numbers for?

Elicit that these are the page numbers we need in order to find the chapters that answer each question.

Ask volunteers to say which is the most interesting question and why. Point out how with a non-fiction book like this you can read the text in any order, while for a story you read from the beginning.

Heads together

Demonstrate using the contents to find out 'What is a sculpture?' Read pages 2 and 3 aloud to the children.

Ask the following questions:
- Does that make sense?
- What does the text say a sculpture is? *(work of art)*

Encourage the children to find and read the sentence that answers the question. Repeat with 'What size is a sculpture' on page 6.

Read the speech bubble text on page 6. Briefly explain 'famous', for example: famous means that it is very well known by people.

Ask: Do you think it is famous? Why?

Talk about evidence in the book: its size and the tourists around the bottom of the sculpture.

Point to and identify the caption on page 7, explaining that captions tell us more about a picture. Help the children to read the caption with you and sound out the artist's name. Explain that some of the letters may have different sounds to those we are used to because it is a French name.

Ask children to read the rest of the book in pairs, each pair choosing a question from the contents and reading the correct pages to find the answers. Try to ensure that all the pages will be covered by the pairs.

Move around, encouraging them to check their understanding by looking for information in the picture or other text on the page.

Wrap up

Ask pairs of children to explain the answer they discovered to each question. Afterwards, ask them to point to the sentence on the page that told them this.

Suggest they read the pages together to check everyone understands.

Focus on the speaking sculpture.

Ask: Why do you think the author chose to have a speaking character in a non-fiction book?

Elicit how it provides information but also makes the book more fun for children.

Ask: Have you discovered any new words about sculptures?

Encourage the children to find and point them out so that you can write them on the board. Give a child-friendly definition for each. Afterwards reread the sentence in which each appears.

Ask: Was I correct – does my explanation make sense?

Ask children to say which is their favourite sculpture in the book and to explain why it is 'super'.

Vocabulary boost session

You will need

- Multiple copies of Collins Big Cat *Super Sculptures*

Vocabulary table

Focus word	Child-friendly explanation	Example sentence	Tell me...
spiral	A spiral is a shape that goes round and round and outwards from a central point.	A snail's shell has a **spiral** shape, with a line circling out from the centre.	Tell me about anything you can think of that has a spiral shape.
material	Material is the stuff something is made from – the material a sculpture is made from can be anything, from fur to cloth.	A bicycle is made of different **materials** like rubber and metal.	Tell me what sort of materials your favourite toy is made of.
real	Real is a proper and not a pretend thing.	My doll's house isn't a **real** house.	Tell me about something that isn't real.

Tune in

Explain to the children that they must listen carefully and follow the words as you read the book aloud. Explain that you will be looking back at some of the word meanings more carefully afterwards.

Read the book to the children, segmenting unfamiliar words or longer words and identifying the letters that make the sounds, for example, the words 'material' m-a-t-er-i-a-l and 'Oppenheim' O-pp-e-n-h-ei-m. Point out unusual spellings of sounds, such as 'au' in 'Claude' on page 17.

Point to each focus word in the text and write it on the board. Give a child-friendly explanation for each word (see the table, above, for examples) and ask children to say the focus word with you afterwards.

Next, for each word, offer an example sentence, such as those in the table or your own.

Afterwards, encourage them to use the word in relation to their own experiences by asking the questions in the 'Tell me' column. You could prompt them if necessary, for example: Have you ever seen a spiral staircase?

Ask children to say the words with you once more.

Heads together

Ask the following questions to explore and develop the children's understanding of the focus words:

- Which is more likely to a have a spiral shape: a wallpaper pattern or a ruler?
- Which material would you choose to make a kite: cloth or concrete?
- What is real: a character in a story or a book on a shelf?

Encourage them to elaborate by asking 'Why?'

Wrap up

Review the word meanings by asking the children which of the following words go best with the focus word:

- 'spiral': shape, potato, shoe, music
- 'material': games, cinema, junk, water
- 'real': pretend, dream, school, dragon

Put the focus words on the wall and ask children to test a friend on the meaning of one each day.

Follow-up independent sessions

You will need

- Multiple copies of Collins Big Cat *Super Sculptures*
- Resource sheet: Material words
- Coloured pencils or pens
- Resource sheet: What does it mean?

Ask children to work independently to draw pictures of sculptures made from the different materials, using Resource sheet: Material words. Ask them to think about whether the materials are hard or soft and if they will melt.

Ask children to work in pairs to choose the correct definitions on Resource sheet: What does it mean? Ask them to look for the words in the book to check the meanings make sense.

Too Hot to Stop!

Book Band: Green

In this poem, the desert sand is so hot that Hoppitt and a parade of his friends keep moving as they search for somewhere to cool down.

Skills focus

- Draw on knowledge of vocabulary to understand texts
- Identify/explain key aspects of fiction and non-fiction texts, e.g. character, events, title
- Predict what might happen on the basis of what has been read so far
- Read words accurately and fluently

Guided reading session

You will need

- Multiple copies of Collins Big Cat *Too Hot to Stop!*
- Resource sheet: Desert animals
- A small cactus plant

Tune in

Display Resource sheet: Desert animals. Can the children name the animals? What do they know about these animals, for example, where do they live?

Practise recognising and reading the animal names.

Explain that these animals all live in the desert.

Ask: What do you think the desert is like? *(hot, dry, sunny, sandy)*

Tell the children they are going to read a poem about these animals that live in the desert. Introduce the book by looking at the front cover. Remind the children that the animal on the front cover is a gazelle. Read the title.

Look at the title page.

Ask the following questions:

- Who is the author and illustrator? *(Steve Webb)*
- What does an author do? *(write the words)*
- What is the picture of? *(cactus)*

Show the children a cactus plant and explain that cactus plants grow in the desert.

Turn over to the back cover to share the blurb.

Ask: Can you identify the rhyming words? *(hop, stop)*

Ask the following questions:

- What is the gazelle's name? *(Hoppitt)*
- Why can't Hoppitt stop hopping? *(the sand is hot on his hooves)*
- What might it be too hot to stop doing? *(hopping)*

Heads together

Ask children to look out for rhyming words as they read. Read pages 2 and 3 together. Model reading accurately and fluently.

Ask: Where do you think Hoppitt is going? *(to meet his friends)*

Discuss why the author might have repeated the word 'hop'. *(because it gives the impression of hopping continuously)*

Continue reading pages 4 and 5. Ask children to read the text aloud independently and encourage them to point to each word as they read.

Ask the following questions:

- What does Hoppitt want the sand cat to do? *(follow him)*
- Where do you think they might be going?
- Can you point to the speech marks/ inverted commas?
- Who is speaking? *(Hoppitt)*

Recap strategies the children can use when reading, including high frequency words, segmenting and blending, using picture clues and checking the text makes sense.

Ask children to read pages 6 to 19 with their Reading Partner.

Ask the following questions:

- Who else does Hoppitt meet? *(camel, lizard, fox, snake, falcon)*
- Where do you think they are going?
- What do they think the falcon can see?

Wrap up

Discuss the children's predictions as to what will happen next.

Turn to pages 20 and 21. Model reading the text with accuracy and fluency.

Ask the following questions:

- What happened to the animals? *(They jumped in the pool.)*
- Do you think they liked it?
- Can you find the rhyming words? *(cool, pool, cat, splat, Hoppitt, stop it)*

- Which words are in capital letters? *(SPLASH, SPLOOSH, SPLISH, SPLOSH, SPLAT)*
- What can you tell me about these words? *(they all begin with 'sp', they describe the sound of the water)*

- Why might these words be written in bold? *(to show they are loud, so they stand out)*
- Which is your favourite word and why?

Vocabulary boost session

You will need

- Multiple copies of Collins Big Cat *Too Hot to Stop!* • Water tray

Vocabulary table

Focus word	Child-friendly explanation	Example sentence	Tell me...
warned	If someone warned you, they have given advice or a suggestion.	The lifeguard **warned** us that the sea was very cold today.	Tell me a sentence using the word warned.
parade	A line of people or vehicles marching/travelling.	We watched the **parade** at the carnival.	Can you parade around the room?
splosh	The sound of something entering water.	**Splosh** went the water as I jumped in the puddle.	Tell me as many words that you can think of to describe the sound of water.

Tune in

Explain that in this lesson the children are going to look in more detail at some of the words the author has used. Write the three focus words clearly for the children to see. Read the words together. Discuss and explain the child-friendly meaning of each word.

Reread the text.

Challenge the children to find the word 'warned' in the text (page 16). Read page 16 to the group.

Ask: What was the falcon warning Hoppitt about? *(the lake)*

Turn to page 9 and find the word 'parade'.

Ask: Who is in this parade? *(Hoppitt, sand cat, camel, lizard)*

On pages 20 and 21 find all the words that describe the sound of the water. *(splash, sploosh, splish, splosh, splat)*

Heads together

Let the children play with the water tray. What words can they use to describe the sounds? *(splash, splosh, splat, swish, swash)*

Ask children to choose their favourite word and explain why it is their favourite.

Wrap up

Recap the three focus words by discussing the questions in the 'Tell me' column of the table, above.

Challenge the children to think of a sentence using one of the focus words.

Follow-up independent sessions

You will need

- A selection of non-fiction books about desert animals
- Resource sheet: Word cards *for Too Hot to Stop!*
- Collage materials, paper, glue, scissors

Ask children to explore a range of non-fiction books about desert animals. What can the children find out? What animals live in the desert? How do they survive?

Lay out the cards cut from Resource sheet: Word cards for *Too Hot to Stop!*, on the table. Ask children to match the rhyming words and then to think of some other words that rhyme with them.

Let the children create a collage of the desert and animals in the poem.

I've Just Had a Bright Idea!

Book Band: Green

This information book explores some of the inventors and inventions that have changed the world.

Skills focus

- Draw on knowledge of vocabulary to understand texts
- Identify/explain key aspects of fiction and non-fiction texts, e.g. character, events, title
- Predict what might happen on the basis of what has been read so far
- Check reading makes sense

Guided reading session

You will need

- Multiple copies of Collins Big Cat *I've Just Had a Bright Idea!*
- Resource sheet: Graphic organiser

Tune in

Show the children the front cover of the book and ask them to read the title.

Ask the following questions:

- What do you think 'a bright idea' is? *(a clever thought/a new idea)*
- How does the picture help you to work it out? *(the thought bubble shows that the person is thinking/ having an idea)*
- What do you think the bright idea is? *(a machine to help you brush your hair and clean your teeth)*
- When do you think you would use that machine? *(first thing in the morning)*

Ask children to read the blurb on the back cover.

On the board, write up the words 'inventors', 'invent' and 'inventions'.

Ask: What do you notice about these words? *(they all have the root word 'invent')*

Establish that inventors are people who invent (think of new ideas) for things (inventions) that will help people.

Ask: What sort of book do you think this is? *(non-fiction/information)*

Turn to the contents on the title page. If children are unfamiliar with a contents page, its purpose and how it is organised, explain the feature.

Focus on the first section 'I've just had a bright idea!', explaining that it will give an introduction to the book.

Ask children to turn to page 2 and read the text on pages 2 and 3 aloud to them.

Ask the following questions:

- Have you ever used anything that has Velcro on it? *(shoes, clothing)*
- Why do you think it is a bright idea? *(it makes things easier to fasten)*

Heads together

Return to the contents page. Focus on the section 'An electric idea'. Model how to turn to page 8.

Display Resource sheet: Graphic organiser. This is a representation of the way the double-page spreads in the book have been designed. Identify the position of the main heading and the sub-headings. Read the text on pages 8 and 9, identifying the main heading, the two sub-headings and the question on page 8. Explain that a main heading tells the reader what the double page is about and the sub-headings tell the reader what that part of the text is about.

Focus on the text in bold on page 9: 'Light bulbs'. Explain that it is in bold to show that the word is in the glossary. Turn to the glossary on page 21.

Ask the following questions:

- How is a glossary organised? *(alphabetically)*
- What is a glossary for? *(to explain what words mean)*

Challenge the children to find the entry for 'light bulbs' and to read the definition.

Return to the contents page and allocate one section, from within pages 10 to 18, to each child. Ask them to predict what an invention in their section might be.

Let them then find and read their section, identifying the 'brighter idea'.

As the children read their sections, work around the group, supporting them in reading more challenging words, identifying the brighter ideas and any words that appear in the glossary.

Wrap up

Take feedback from the activity, asking the children to identify the brighter ideas that they have read about.

Ask the following questions:

- Did you look for any words in the glossary?
- Did it help you to understand what you were reading?

Recap on the organisational features of non-fiction books that the children have explored, for example, contents, headings, sub-headings, glossary.

Vocabulary boost session

You will need

- Multiple copies of Collins Big Cat *I've Just Had a Bright Idea!*
- Mini-whiteboards and pens

Vocabulary table

Focus word	Child-friendly explanation	Example sentence	Tell me...
sandwich	Food between two pieces of bread.	My mum made me cheese and pickle **sandwiches** for the school trip.	Tell me what your favourite sandwich filling is.
wellington boots	Boots that keep your feet dry in the rain.	Toby filled his **wellington boots** with tadpoles!	Tell me when you might wear a pair of wellington boots.
macintosh	A coat that keeps you dry in the rain.	The lady was wearing a blue **macintosh**.	Tell me about a time when you have worn a macintosh (raincoat).

Tune in

Ask children to use the contents page to find the section 'Guess what they invented' (page 6).

Read the first sentence stem on page 6 aloud and encourage the children to guess the sentence ending (*cardigan*).

Ask children to read the rest of the sentence stems on these pages and to guess the endings (sandwich, wellington boot, macintosh). If necessary, support them in identifying that a macintosh is another word for a raincoat.

Refer back to each of the focus words within the context of the book, writing up the word, giving a child-friendly explanation and asking the children to say the focus word with you.

Ask: Do these words appear in the glossary? *(no)*

Heads together

On the board write up the word 'cardigan' and explain that you'd like the children to help you to write a definition of the word for the glossary, for example, a top made of wool that has buttons at the front.

Ask children to choose two of the other items on pages 6 and 7 and to write definitions for the glossary on their whiteboards.

Support them as they write their definitions.

Wrap up

Take feedback from the activity, agreeing on the wording of the definitions for the focus words as a group and writing them up on the board. You may wish to refer to the definitions in the table, above, during this activity.

Work with the children to put the glossary entries into alphabetical order: cardigan, macintosh, sandwich, wellington boot.

Turn to the glossary on page 21 and challenge the children to identify where their new glossary entries would fit into the glossary.

Follow-up independent sessions

You will need

- Multiple copies of Collins Big Cat *I've Just Had a Bright Idea!*
- Resource sheet: Timeline for *I've Just Had a Bright Idea!*
- Coloured pencils or pens

Give pairs of children a copy of Resource sheet: Timeline for *I've Just Had a Bright Idea!* Ask children to write the name of the invention in the correct place and draw a picture of it. Ask children to each choose one of the inventions and to write an extra label that explains how the invention helps people.

Olympic Heroes

Book Band: Green

This information book celebrates some of the heroes of the modern Olympics who have had to overcome racial inequality, illness and disabilities to earn their medals.

Skills focus

- Draw on knowledge of vocabulary to understand texts
- Identify/explain key aspects of fiction and non-fiction texts, e.g. character, events, title
- Make inferences from texts
- Read words accurately and fluently

Guided reading session

You will need

- Multiple copies of Collins Big Cat *Olympic Heroes*

Tune in

Introduce the book by reading the title to the children.

Ask: Do you know what 'Olympic' means? *(in this context, related to the Olympic Games – a big sports competition with athletes from all over the world)*

Encourage the children to point to the title of the book and then read it aloud again, asking them to read it aloud with you.

Turn to the back cover and read the blurb aloud, encouraging the children to follow and join in with you. Check that they understand what the book is about.

Turn to the title page, read the title and name of the author together.

Ask children to point to the word 'contents'. Explain that the 'contents' tells us what is in the book and where to find it. Read the contents aloud to the children, asking them to follow. As you read, insert the word 'page' before each number so that the children understand that is what the numbers are for.

Heads together

Turn to page 20, point to the word 'Glossary' and read it aloud.

Ask: What is a glossary and what job does it do? *(a list of special words, it tells us what some of the special words mean)*

Explain that the special words are written in bold in the text.

Say to the children that they are going to choose which chapters to read today by looking at the contents page. Turn back to the title page and ask children which chapter they would like to read (up to page 14). Turn to that chapter and read it aloud, modelling strategies for reading longer words and encouraging the children to follow and join in. Point out words in bold and look them up in the glossary.

Point out captions and labels, read them and check that the children know that they are part of the text and what they are there for.

Now go back to the title page and choose another chapter to read. Follow the same process as before.

Wrap up

Read pages 18 and 19 aloud, modelling strategies for reading longer words; encourage the children to follow and join in.

Ask the following questions:

- Why do you think the book is called 'Olympic Heroes'?
- Do you think that the athletes in the book are special? Why?
- What kind of book is this, information or story? *(information)*
- How do you know? *(real facts, photographs instead of drawings, captions and labels, contents page, glossary)*

Vocabulary boost session

You will need

- Multiple copies of Collins Big Cat *Olympic Heroes*

Vocabulary table

Focus word	Child-friendly explanation	Example sentence	Tell me...
hero	A hero is someone who does something brave or very special. Everybody thinks this person is important because of it.	The man rescued a dog from the river. He was a **hero**.	Tell me about a hero that you know.
athlete	An athlete is a person who does sport.	The **athlete** had to train for three hours every day.	Tell me what an athlete does.
champion	A champion is a person who wins first prize in a competition.	Usain Bolt is a running **champion**.	Tell me about something you could be a champion at.

Tune in

Explain to the children that in this lesson they are going to look closely at some of the words the author has used and what those words mean.

Read up to page 11 aloud to the children.

Refer back to each of the focus words within the context of the story, writing up the word, giving a child-friendly explanation and asking the children to say the focus word with you. For example: The book is called *Olympic Heroes*. A hero is someone who does something brave or very special and everybody thinks this person is important because of it. Now, say the word with me – 'hero'.

You may wish to use the examples in the table, above.

Refer to each of the focus words that you have written up and give the children the example sentences. Then ask them to interact with the word meanings by asking the questions in the 'Tell me' column. You may wish to demonstrate by giving some examples of your own.

Ask children to say the words with you once more.

Heads together

Explore and develop children's understanding of the focus words by doing the following activity. Tell the children that if you say something that is about a hero, they should say 'hero'. If it isn't about a hero, they say nothing.

- A person cleaning their teeth.
- A person rescuing someone in danger.
- A person working really hard so that they can win a competition.

Then tell them that if you say something that is about being an athlete, they should say 'athlete'. If it isn't, they say nothing.

- A person who does lots of sport.
- A person who doesn't do any sport.
- A person who is very good at running.

Now tell them that if you say something that is about a champion, they should say 'champion'. If it isn't, they say nothing.

- A person who wins a writing competition.
- A person who wins a running race.
- A person who is learning to skip.

For each answer, ask children why they responded as they did.

Wrap up

Ask the following questions to review the word meanings:

- What's the word that means a person who wins first prize in a competition?
- What's the word that means someone who does something brave or very special?
- What's the word that means a person who does sport?

Ask children to choose one of the focus words as their word of the week. Challenge them to use the word as often as they can, both at school and at home.

Follow-up independent sessions

You will need

- Multiple copies of Collins Big Cat *Olympic Heroes*
- Resource sheet: Questions for *Olympic Heroes*

Ask children to work with their Reading Partners and to read the book aloud.

Ask children to answer the questions on Resource sheet: Questions for *Olympic Heroes*.

Seahorses

Book Band: Green

This information book looks at the life cycle and facts about the seahorse, from finding its mate, to the young coming out of the male.

Skills focus

- Draw on knowledge of vocabulary to understand texts

- Identify/explain key aspects of fiction and non-fiction texts, e.g. character, events, title
- Read words accurately and fluently

Guided reading session

You will need

- Multiple copies of Collins Big Cat *Seahorses*

Tune in

Look together at the front cover of the book and introduce it by reading the title and subtitle.

Ask: What sort of book do you think this will be?

If necessary, explain that you think this is a non-fiction text but the children must check by looking for things that you would expect to find in a non-fiction text. Call out features of a non-fiction book and ask children if they can find them, for example: photographs, labels, pointer rules, boxes of text, facts, arrows.

Agree that this is an information book.

Ask: What is it about?

Read the title and subtitle again and discuss the meaning of 'Life Cycle'. If necessary, explain it in a child-friendly way, for example, a life cycle is all the stages living things go through from birth, to growing up, to having babies, to dying. Encourage the children to talk about any life cycles with which they are familiar, for example: frogspawn to frogs; eggs to butterflies.

Challenge the children to find the blurb and read it aloud as a group. Help them sound out words they have difficulty with by breaking them down into smaller parts: 'amazing' a-maz-ing; 'cycle' cy-cle. Ask them to reread the blurb to check for fluency.

Ask: What would you like to know about seahorses?

Heads together

Read pages 2 to 5 aloud to the children, asking them to follow as you read.

Remind them to look out for how a letter can have a different sound. Focus on the words 'special', 'curl' and 'centimetres' on pages 2 and 3, writing them on the board. Underline the 'c' in each and ask them to listen out for the different sound it has in each word as they read the words aloud. Then ask children to reread pages 2 and 3 with you.

Focus on pages 4 and 5 and remind the children of how more than one letter together often makes one sound. Reread pages 4 and 5 and ask them to listen out for pairs or groups of letters that make just one sound. If necessary, write examples on the board, underlining the pairs or groups: seahorses, slowest, upright.

Challenge the children to look out for information on the amazing life cycle of the seahorse as you read up to page 21. Ensure the children follow the text as they read, joining in as much as possible. For words or sentences the children find difficult, reread the text, demonstrating how to break down words into letter sounds, for example, the word 'people p-eo-p-le, or smaller words, for example, 'sideways' side-ways.

As they read, move around, listening to each pair. Check that they take turns to read and sound out difficult words slowly, if they are finding them difficult.

Wrap up

Ask children if they found anything surprising or especially interesting about the life cycle of the seahorse.

Ask the group to turn to pages 22 and 23. Discuss each stage with the children. Point to each picture in order.

Ask: What is happening here?

Encourage the children to read the captions.

Point to a 'Fact' panel in the book and read it aloud.

Ask: Which is your favourite fact in the book?

Encourage volunteers to recall a fact, or look for it and read it from the book.

Ask children if they think there is anything missing from this non-fiction book. Point out how it does not have a contents list or headings. Do they think these would have been useful? Why?

Vocabulary boost session

You will need

- Multiple copies of Collins Big Cat *Seahorses*

Vocabulary table

Focus word	Child-friendly explanation	Example sentence	Tell me...
upright	When something is upright it is standing up, like a person who is standing and not lying down.	A horse stands on four legs to stay **upright**.	Tell me about something that was upright but then fell over.
join	When you join two things, you attach them, like when a mother's hand holds the hand of her child.	I **join** two bits of ribbon to make a longer ribbon.	Tell me about anything that you have joined together.
pouch	A pouch is like a big open pocket on the outside of an animal's body.	A kangaroo keeps its baby in a **pouch**.	Tell me what you would keep in a pouch if you had one!

Tune in

Explain to the children that in this lesson you are going to focus on some of the words the author has used and look at their meaning.

Read the book to the children, showing them how pairs or groups of letters make one sound and how longer words can be broken into sounds and then blended. Point to smaller, familiar words within longer words too.

Look at each focus word on the page in which it appears in the book. Read the sentence and write the word on the board. Give a child-friendly explanation, for example: People stay upright when they walk. I am upright now. Seahorses swim upright – see how their head is up at the top. Read the word with me – upright.

Using the table, above, or your own sentences, provide a simple sentence for each focus word so that the children can hear and understand it in a different context. Encourage them to use the word in the context of their own lives by asking the questions in the 'Tell me' column of the table, above. You could offer your own examples to inspire them.

Ask children to say the words with you again.

Heads together

Ask the following questions to explore and develop the children's understanding of the focus words:

- Do you go to sleep upright or walk to school upright?
- Could you use sticky tape or a wooden spoon to join two things together?
- Are you more likely to find a pouch on a building or an animal?

Encourage them to talk about their answers by asking 'Why?'

Wrap up

Ask the following questions to review the word meanings:

- If any of these words link to 'upright', put your hand up: crawl, sleep, roll, walk.
- If any of these words link to 'join', put your hand up: marbles, water, glue, fire.
- If any of these words link to 'pouch', put your hand up: eggs, holidays, aircraft, coral.

Write the focus words on the board and encourage the children to write other words that link to each one alongside.

Follow-up independent sessions

You will need

- Resource sheet: True or false?
- Resource sheet: Hidden words

Cut out the cards from Resource sheet: True or false? Give a set to pairs of children. Ask them to take turns to read a card and the other says whether it is true or false. They can check the book for the answer. If they are correct, they keep the card.

Give the children a copy of Resource sheet: Hidden words, to work on independently. They circle smaller words hidden within the bigger words. They can count how many words they found and swap their work with a partner to check what they have missed.

Wellies

Book Band: Green

In this poem, Wally the penguin enters the welly fashion show and his winning wellies start a new trend.

Skills focus

- Draw on knowledge of vocabulary to understand texts
- Identify/explain the sequence of events in texts
- Predict what might happen on the basis of what has been read so far
- Check reading makes sense

Guided reading session

You will need

- Multiple copies of Collins Big Cat *Wellies*
- Pictures/photos of six pairs of different wellies – some plain, some patterned, different sizes and colours
- Resource sheet: Rhyming words for *Wellies*

Tune in

Ask the following questions:

- Who has a pair of wellington boots?
- When might you wear wellies? *(when it is raining, to walk in mud, to jump in muddy puddles, visit muddy places)*
- Who might wear wellies for their job? *(farmer)*

Show children pictures of different wellies. Ask them to pick their favourite pair and describe them to the group. Can the group guess which wellies they are describing?

Explain that you are going to read a poem about wellies. Introduce the book by looking at the front cover.

Ask the following questions:

- Who might the main character be? *(the penguin)*
- What do you think his job is? *(designing/making wellies)*

Look at the title page.

Ask the following questions:

- Who is the author? Who is the illustrator? *(Steve Webb)*
- What does an illustrator do? *(creates the pictures)*

Provide the children with a set of rhyming word cards from Resource sheet: Rhyming words for *Wellies*. Can they work as a team to match the rhyming words?

Ask: What do you notice about the final sounds?

Challenge the children to find the rhyming words in the book. *(snow/show, himself/shelf, pairs/stares, cakes/flakes, say/today, stop/shop, pair/bear/wear, begun/won, prize/surprise, igloo/you)*

Turn the book over and read the question on the back of the book. Discuss what a fashion show is.

Heads together

Model reading pages 2 and 3 aloud using rhythm. Discuss the use of alliteration.

Ask: Which initial sound is repeated? *(w)*

Explain that this creates rhythm and makes it fun to read.

Ask the following questions:

- Who do you think the main character is? *(a penguin called Wally)*
- What wellingtons is he wearing? *(odd ones!)*
- Where do you think he works?

Read pages 4 to 7 together. Ask children to point to the words as they read. Discuss strategies used: high frequency words, segmenting and blending, picture clues and checking the text makes sense. Can the children point out the rhyming words? *(snow/show, himself/shelf)* Ask children to describe the wellies in the picture on pages 6 and 7.

Look at pages 8 and 9. Discuss the use of commas in a list.

Share pages 10 and 11 together as a group.

Ask the following questions:

- Can you predict which wellies Bertie Bear will pick?
- Which wellies do they think would suit Bertie best and why?

Turn to pages 12 and 13. Ask children to point to the inverted commas/speech marks. Can they explain what these punctuation marks are for?

Ask children to read pages 14 to 21 independently. Can they find out which wellies win at the fashion show? Listen to the children read and support where needed.

Wrap up

Ask children to choose their favourite pair of wellies in the book and say why. Discuss the children's opinion

© HarperCollins*Publishers* 2017

of the winning pair of wellies. Do they think they should have won?

Look at pages 20 and 21.

Ask the following questions:
- Why do all the penguins want white wellies? *(because the white wellies won at the fashion show)*
- Do you think the penguins will suit white wellies?

Reread the poem aloud together.

Vocabulary boost session

You will need
- Multiple copies of Collins Big Cat *Wellies*

Vocabulary table

Focus word	Child-friendly explanation	Example sentence	Tell me…
fashion	Fashion means style.	There was a red dress at the **fashion** show.	Tell me about your favourite pair of shoes or piece of clothing.
wellington boots	A type of waterproof boot often called 'wellies'.	I wore my **wellington boots** to the farm.	Tell me about your wellington boots. What are they like?
waddles	If you are waddling, you are moving from side to side as you walk, or wobbling.	The ducks **waddled** to the pond.	Tell me the name of an animal that waddles.

Tune in

Explain that in this lesson the children are going to look in more detail at some words linked to the text. Write the three focus words clearly for the children to see. Read the words together. Discuss and explain the child-friendly meaning of each word.

Reread the text.

Ask children to find the word 'fashion' in the story. (pages 5, 10, 16)

Ask: What type of fashion show was it? *(a welly fashion show)*

Challenge children to find the word 'waddles' in the text. (pages 2, 15, 20)

Heads together

Ask: What words can you think of that mean 'walking'?

Create a list, for example: 'shuffled', 'wobbled', 'hopped', 'bounced', 'walked', 'ran', 'slide', 'skated', 'skipped'.

Ask children to complete this sentence stem verbally: 'The penguin… to work on the ice.'

Ask the following questions:
- What does waddling look like?
- Can you waddle like a penguin?

Wrap up

Recap the three focus words by discussing the questions in the 'Tell me' column of the table, above.

Challenge the children to think of a sentence using one of the focus words.

Follow-up independent sessions

You will need
- Paint and paper
- A welly or shoe shop role-play area (selection of wellies and shoes, tape measure, till and money)

Ask children to design and make a poster for a welly fashion show.

Let the children explore a 'welly shop' or 'shoe shop' in the role-play area.

Ask children to design and draw their own wellies. What colours or patterns would they paint on their wellies?

The King of the Forest

Book Band: Green

A cunning fox outwits a tiger to save himself from danger, in this traditional story.

Skills focus

- Draw on knowledge of vocabulary to understand texts
- Identify/explain the sequence of events in texts
- Make inferences from texts
- Read words accurately and fluently

Guided reading session

You will need

- Multiple copies of Collins Big Cat *The King of the Forest*

Tune in

Show the children the front cover and ask them to read the title. Challenge them to identify the names of the author (Saviour Pirotta) and the illustrator (Tomislav Zlatic). Turn to the title page to confirm the children's responses.

Ask the following questions:

- What sort of book do you think this is? *(fiction/ story)*
- Where can you find more information about the book? *(back cover blurb)*

Ask children to read the blurb and explore their responses to the question, encouraging them to draw on their knowledge of other stories they have read or heard.

Ask the following questions:

- Who do you think the king of the forest might be?
- Where do you think this story will take place? *(the forest)*

Turn to pages 2 and 3 and read the text without any expression.

Model rereading the text, particularly the dialogue, with expression and ask children what differences they noticed.

Ask children to identify the punctuation marks and how you used them to help you to read with expression, for example, intonation in a question.

Establish that reading with expression makes the story easier to understand and more interesting to a listener.

Heads together

Ask children to read to the end of the story, concentrating on using punctuation marks, meaning and dialogue to help them to read with expression.

As they read, work around the group, listening to individual children. Praise examples of reading with appropriate expression and support them with some of the more challenging vocabulary.

Wrap up

Remind the children of the question in the blurb 'How could he (the fox) save himself (from the tiger)?' Encourage them to reflect on the story and to answer the question.

Turn to page 8.

Ask: What do you think the monkeys were staring at?

If necessary, turn to page 12.

Ask: What do you think the deer saw?

Check that the children realise that the animals saw the shadows of the tiger and the fox and they were scared of the tiger. Challenge them to spot the shadows on other pages in the book.

Turn to page 19 and ask children to read the fox's dialogue with expression.

Vocabulary boost session

You will need

- Multiple copies of Collins Big Cat *The King of the Forest*

Vocabulary table

Focus word	Child-friendly explanation	Example sentence	Tell me...
tremble	To shake with fear.	The mouse **trembled** when it saw the cat.	Tell me about a time when you have trembled.
stare	When you look hard and long at something or someone.	I **stared** at the green alien as it jumped out of the spaceship.	Tell me about a time when you have stared at something.
chuckle	To laugh at quietly.	The baby **chuckled** when he saw the new toy.	Tell me about a time when you have chuckled.

Tune in

Explain that the children are going to look in more detail at some of the words the author has used in the story. Explain that when authors write stories they choose the words they use very carefully to help readers understand what they are reading and to help them make pictures as they read.

Read the story aloud with expression, pausing to briefly explain the meaning of each of the focus words.

Reread the sentences in the book that contain the focus words.

Ask: What pictures do you see in your heads when you hear these sentences?

If necessary, describe the images that you create from the sentences.

Write up the focus words on the board and give the children the example sentences from the table, above, to demonstrate the meanings of the words in a different context.

Heads together

Use the 'Tell me' prompts from the table, above, to explore and develop the children's understanding of the focus words.

You may wish to extend this to include 'Show me' prompts, for example: Show me what it looks like to tremble/stare/chuckle.

Wrap up

Ask children to choose one of the focus words as their word of the week. Challenge them to use it as often as they can – both at home and at school.

Follow-up independent sessions

You will need

- Multiple copies of Collins Big Cat *The King of the Forest*
- Mini-whiteboards and pens
- Resource sheet: Hot seat question cards

Ask children to work with their Reading Partners. Remind them of work they have done previously on creating story maps from stories, for example, drawing pictures of the main events in a story, adding key words, phrases and dialogue. Ask them to reread *The King of the Forest.* They can then identify the main events in the story and create a story map on their whiteboards.

Once each pair has completed their story maps, they can use them to retell the story to the rest of the group. Ask children who are listening to check that the main events are in the correct order.

Hot-seating: explain that the children can use the hot-seating technique to find out how characters felt and why they behaved in a certain way. Give children the question cards from Resource sheet: Hot seat question cards, to support their questioning. Ask them to decide which character to put in the hot seat. Allow them time to choose a question card and to prepare two or three questions for the character in the hot seat. If necessary, demonstrate how to formulate appropriate questions, for example: How did you feel when…? When did you decide…? If there is time, give children the opportunity to repeat the hot-seating activity with other characters from the story.

Wild Dog in the City

Book Band: Green

This information book focuses on the characteristics of North American coyotes and explains how they survive in the city.

Skills focus

- Draw on knowledge of vocabulary to understand texts
- Identify/explain key aspects of fiction and non-fiction texts, e.g. character, events, title
- Make inferences from texts
- Read words accurately and fluently

Guided reading session

You will need

- Multiple copies of Collins Big Cat *Wild Dog in the City*

Tune in

Introduce the book by asking the children to look closely at the front cover.

Ask the following questions:

- What can you see?
- What kind of animal do you think it is?
- Do you think it is friendly?
- What makes you think that?
- Where is it?
- What time of day do you think it is?

Read the title aloud, asking the children to join in.

Turn to the back cover and read the blurb aloud, encouraging the children to follow and join in with you.

Ask: Do you know what a coyote is? *(a type of dog)*

Heads together

Read pages 2 to 6 aloud to the children, asking them to follow as you read and join in. Model strategies for reading, for example, using phonic knowledge ('all', 'them'), breaking words down ('inside' 'in-side').

Ask the following questions:

- What is the difference between a coyote and a pet dog? *(coyotes live outside, pets live in homes with their owners)*
- Which country do coyotes live in? *(North America)*

Tell the children that they are going to read on their own.

Ask: What strategies can you use to help you if you get stuck on a word? *(use the initial sound to start you off and then use phonics and blend the phonemes, look for words that I already know, break long words down)*

Ask children to read up to page 16 on their own. As they read, move around the group, listening to each child while the others read in their heads. Support them in reading longer words and check their reading strategies.

Come back together and then turn to pages 8 and 9.

Ask the following questions:

- Why do you think there is a picture of a coyote next to a pet dog? *(to compare them)*
- What are these pages about? *(the physical differences between coyotes and pet dogs)*

Wrap up

Check the children's understanding.

Ask: What else did you find out about coyotes when you read up to page 16?

Turn to page 12 and point to the word 'dens'.

Ask: Why is this word in bold? *(It's a glossary word.)*

Read pages 17 to 20, modelling reading strategies and pointing out the glossary words. Read the glossary on page 21 together.

Ask: This is an information book. Can you show and tell me what the clues are that this is an information book? *(about real things, labels, glossary)*

Vocabulary boost session

You will need

- Multiple copies of Collins Big Cat *Wild Dog in the City*

Vocabulary table

Focus word	Child-friendly explanation	Example sentence	Tell me...
city	A city is a very big place where people live and work. There are usually offices, shops and houses in cities and very big roads.	My dad works in the **city**; he gets the bus there every day.	Tell me about our nearest city.
country	The country is a place that has farms and fields. It is usually far away from the city and much quieter.	We went to the **country** to see the horses.	Tell me about a time you've been to the country.
neighbourhood	Your neighbourhood is the place where you and the people near to you live.	The children rode their bikes around the **neighbourhood**.	Tell me about your neighbourhood.

Tune in

Explain to the children that in this lesson they are going to look closely at some of the words the author has used and what those words mean.

Read the book aloud to the children.

Refer back to each of the focus words within the context of the book, writing up the word, giving a child-friendly explanation and asking the children to say the focus word with you. For example: The title of the book is *Wild Dog in the City*. A city is a very big place where people live and work. There are usually offices, shops and houses in cities and very big roads. Now, say the word with me – 'city'.

You may wish to use the examples in the table, above.

Refer to each of the focus words that you have written up and give the children the example sentences. Then ask them to interact with the word meanings by asking the questions in the 'Tell me' column. You may wish to demonstrate by giving some examples of your own.

Ask children to say the words with you once more.

Heads together

Explain to the children that you're going to do a thinking activity (word associations). You're going to come up with words that make us think of and remember what the focus words mean.

Take each of the following words in turn and ask children to call out words that pop into their heads when you say them:

- city *(noisy, offices, shops, roads, tower blocks)*
- country *(fields, farms, animals, tractors, quiet)*
- neighbourhood *(relevant answers to the children's own neighbourhoods)*

Encourage the children to make links to their own lives and experiences to help them.

Wrap up

Review the word meanings by doing the following activity.

Refer to the picture on pages 6 and 7 of the book.

Ask: Coyotes live in cities. Can you tell me what a city is?

Refer to the picture on page 12 of the book.

Ask: Can you tell me what the country is?

Refer to the picture on page 18 of the book.

Ask: Can you tell me what a neighbourhood is?

Challenge the children to use the focus words as often as they can, both at school and at home.

Follow-up independent sessions

You will need

- Multiple copies of Collins Big Cat *Wild Dog in the City*
- Resource sheet: Book talk for *Wild Dog in the City*

Ask children to work with their Reading Partners and to read the book aloud.

Give pairs of children a copy of Resource sheet: Book talk for *Wild Dog in the City*. Ask them to talk about and write or draw what they like or dislike about the book.

How the Elephant Got His Trunk

Book Band: Green

This traditional tale tells how the curiosity of Eddie the elephant led to all elephants having trunks.

Skills focus

- Draw on knowledge of vocabulary to understand texts
- Make inferences from texts
- Check reading makes sense

Guided reading session

You will need

- Multiple copies of Collins Big Cat *How the Elephant Got His Trunk*

Tune in

Ask children to look at the front cover and introduce the story by reading the title. Look together at the back cover picture. Do the children notice what is different about the elephant here? *(It has no trunk.)*

Ask: How do you think the elephant got his trunk?

Encourage the children to follow the text as you read pages 2 to 5 expressively. Then ask them to read pages 2 to 5 with you. Pause after page 3 and tell them you are going to check together that this makes sense so far by reading page 3 again.

Reread the speech bubble, emphasising 'I' and 'me'.

Ask the following questions:

- Who is 'I' and who is 'me'? *(Eddie)*
- Is there anything else we can see that shows that this is the elephant speaking? *(the speech bubble and how it points to the elephant)*

Turn to page 5 and read the speech bubble expressively with the children. Tell the children you are going to check that we read this correctly.

Ask: What drove everyone potty? *(Eddie's questions)*

Focus on the picture on page 4 and discuss how each of the animals might be feeling.

Heads together

Read pages 2 and 3 and ask children to follow the text, looking out for some of the questions that Eddie likes to ask. Draw a large question mark on the board and explain how they can check to see if a sentence is a question by looking at the punctuation at the end.

Focus on the words 'can't' and 'doesn't'. Write them on the board and say them aloud. Point to the apostrophe and explain that it shows a missing letter. Write 'cannot' and 'does not' on the board.

Ask the following questions:

- What can Eddie *not* do? *(reach the fruit in the tree)*
- Why do you think Ostrich does *not* look like him? *(Ostrich is a bird, with feathers, beak, long thin legs)*

Work through Eddie's questions so far and encourage the children to infer the answers to the questions.

Tell the children to work with their Reading Partner to read to page 21, with one reading the narrative and the other reading Eddie's words. They can swap halfway through, on page 10. Encourage the children to try to answer Eddie's questions.

As they read, challenge the children to think about what sort of elephant Eddie is.

Support children in reading longer words, breaking down words into syllables and checking they make sense by rereading the sentence in which they appear.

Wrap up

Ask the following questions:

- How did the questions make you feel?
- Did you like Eddie's questions?

Focus on some of the questions and discuss the possible answers.

Write the following words on the board: 'old', 'young', 'wise', 'a bother', 'potty,' 'silly', 'brave'. Focus on each in turn and discuss with the group whether the word matches Eddie and why. Explain the meaning of the word, if necessary.

Focus on page 11 and read the text.

Ask: Do you agree that Eddie was 'curious'?

Explain that if you are curious you want to know about things and ask questions.

Reread pages 20 and 21.

Ask: Do you believe that this is how every elephant got its trunk? Why? Why not?

Vocabulary boost session

You will need

- Multiple copies of Collins Big Cat *How the Elephant Got His Trunk*

Vocabulary table

Focus word	Child-friendly explanation	Example sentence	Tell me...
greasy	If something is greasy it looks slimy and shiny like oil.	The frying pan was very **greasy** after we cooked pancakes.	Tell me about something greasy that you have seen.
curious	If someone is curious they like to find out about things and ask questions.	I am **curious** to know how a radio works so I am reading books about it.	Tell me what you are curious about.
ignore	If you ignore someone you pretend not to hear them or see them.	The naughty puppy **ignored** its mother's bark because it wanted to carry on playing.	Tell me someone you would never ignore and why.

Tune in

Write the three focus words on the board: 'greasy', 'curious' and 'ignore'. Explain that the author has used these words in the book and the children are going to look at them more closely.

Read the book aloud to the children, breaking down and blending longer words so that they can identify the letter sounds.

Return to the pages where the focus words appear ('greasy' on pages 8 and 10, 'curious' on page 11 and 'ignore' on page 19). After finding each, point to it on the board and read it before giving a child-friendly explanation. You can use the explanations in the table, above.

Ask children to read the focus word with you.

Next, give the children an example sentence so that they hear it in another context.

Finally, to encourage them to use the word in the context of their own life, ask them questions like those in the 'Tell me' column. If they struggle, give them your own example answer first.

Ask children to read the words with you once more.

Heads together

Ask the following questions to develop the children's understanding of the focus words further:

- Which of these might be greasy – a butter dish or a football? Why?
- Which job advert is likely to ask for curious people to apply – a shop assistant or a detective? Why?
- What are you more likely to ignore – the sound of a car or someone crying? Why?

Wrap up

Ask the following questions to review the word meanings:

- Is 'greasy' more like dirty or clean? Why?
- Is 'curious' more like clever or questioning?
- Is 'ignore' more like shaking hands or turning away?

Ask children to pick a focus word. How many times can they use it at school or at home?

Follow-up independent sessions

You will need

- Resource sheet: Questions, questions
- Resource sheet: How the...?

Cut out the cards from Resource sheet: Questions, questions and give a set to small groups. Tell the children that they must take it in turns to pick a card and ask the group a question beginning with that word. The questions could be focused on the book, or on the children's own lives and school.

Give the children Resource sheet: How the...? and ask them to choose an animal and think of a story with a partner about how the animal got its horns/stripes/tail.

One Potato

Book Band: Green

In this rhyming story, a potato escapes from the farmer's wife to avoid being turned into soup.

Skills focus

- Draw on knowledge of vocabulary to understand texts
- Make inferences from texts
- Predict what might happen on the basis of what has been read so far
- Read words accurately and fluently

Guided reading session

You will need

- Multiple copies of Collins Big Cat *One Potato*

Tune in

Introduce the book by reading the title to the children. If necessary, explain what a potato is. Encourage them to look carefully at the picture.

Ask the following questions:

- Where do you think the potato is? *(a field, a garden)*
- What do you think the story could be about?

Encourage the children to point to the title of the book; then read it aloud again, asking them to read it aloud with you.

Turn to the back cover and read the blurb aloud, encouraging the children to follow and join in with you.

Ask the following questions:

- Do you have any more ideas what the story could be about? *(a potato that runs away)*
- Do you think the farmer's wife will catch the potato?

Turn to the title page and read the title and the author and illustrator together.

Heads together

Read pages 2 to 5 aloud, modelling strategies for reading, for example: recognition of tricky words ('they', 'what'); reading words with apostrophes ('don't', 'what's'). Encourage the children to follow and join in.

Ask the following questions:

- How do you think the potatoes feel about the farmer coming to dig them out? *(scared, cross, confused)*

- What do you think is going to happen to the potatoes?

Tell the children that they are going to read the story on their own.

Ask: What strategies can you use to help you if you get stuck on a word? *(look at the pictures, use the initial sound to start you off and then use phonics and blend the phonemes, look for tricky words that you already know)*

Ask children to read pages 6 to 21, on their own. As they read, move around the group, listening to each child while the others read in their heads. Support them in reading longer words and check their reading strategies.

Wrap up

Come back together and turn to page 15.

Ask the following questions:

- Can you remember what happened after the potato escaped? *(It ran through the garden, suggesting other vegetables to go in the soup.)*
- How do you think the potato felt?
- What do you think the farmer's wife thought?

Now turn to page 20.

Ask the following questions:

- Where do you think the farmer's wife and dog are? *(outside the farm, by the gate to the farm, on the road)*
- How do you think the dog is feeling? *(tired)*
- How do you know? *(it's sitting down with its tongue hanging out)*
- What do you think the farmer's wife did next?
- Do you think that she made soup?

Vocabulary boost session

You will need

- Multiple copies of Collins Big Cat *One Potato*

Vocabulary table

Focus word	Child-friendly explanation	Example sentence	Tell me...
roll	When something rolls, it moves along, turning over.	The ball **rolled** across the floor.	Tell me about something that rolls.
toss	If you toss something, you throw it a little way without being careful.	He **tossed** the paper into the bin.	Tell me about something that you might toss.
tumble	When something tumbles, it falls and usually it bounces or rolls too.	The grapes **tumbled** on to the floor.	Tell me about a time you have, or something has, tumbled.

Tune in

Explain to the children that in this lesson they are going to look closely at some of the words the author has used and what those words mean.

Read the book aloud to the children, asking them to follow and join in as you read.

Refer back to each of the focus words within the context of the story, writing up the word, giving a child-friendly explanation and asking the children to say the focus word with you. For example: In the story, the potatoes roll around on the ground. When something rolls, it moves along, turning over. Now, say the word with me – 'roll'.

You may wish to use the examples in the table, above.

Refer to each of the focus words that you have written up and give the children the example sentences. Then ask them to interact with the word meanings by asking the questions in the 'Tell me' column. You may wish to demonstrate by giving some examples of your own.

Ask children to say the words with you once more.

Heads together

Ask the following questions to explore and develop children's understanding of the focus words:

- Looking around the room, is there anything you can see that you could roll? Can you roll it or pretend to roll it?
- Is there anything you can see in the room that you could toss? Can you toss it or pretend to toss it?
- Is there a toy or small world figure in the room that could tumble? Can you show me how it would tumble?

Wrap up

Ask the following questions to review the word meanings:

- When would it be better to roll a ball than toss it? Why?
- If I had a piece of rubbish, could I toss it into the bin or roll it? Why?
- If I tossed the rubbish into the bin, might it tumble in or roll in? Why?

Challenge the group to use the words as often as they can, both at school and at home.

Follow-up independent sessions

You will need

- Multiple copies of Collins Big Cat *One Potato*
- Resource sheet: Vegetable story
- Coloured pencils or pens

Ask children to work with their Reading Partners and to read the book aloud, remembering to read with expression.

Hand out copies of Resource sheet: Vegetable story and ask children to make up a new story about a different vegetable.

Happy New Year

Book Band: Green

This information book explores the different ways that New Year is celebrated all over the world.

Skills focus

- Draw on knowledge of vocabulary to understand texts
- Identify/explain key aspects of fiction and non-fiction texts, e.g. character, events, title
- Make inferences from texts
- Check reading makes sense

Guided reading session

You will need
- Multiple copies of Collins Big Cat *Happy New Year*

Tune in

Introduce the book by looking at the front cover. Model reading the title fluently.

Discuss and share children's own experiences of New Year.

Turn the book over and read the back cover. Recap that the blurb tells us more about the book. Explain that this is an information book.

Ask: What will the book tell us about? *(how New Year is celebrated all over the world)*

Discuss the features of an information book including: contents page, glossary, headings, photographs, captions and labels.

Ask children to find the contents page. Explain that a contents page lists the headings and page numbers of the book. Practise using the contents page.

Ask the following questions:
- On what page can we find out about 'Chinese New Year'? *(page 12)*
- On what page would we learn about 'Making noise'? *(page 16)*

Tell children to find page 16. Point out the key features of information text such as the heading, the photographs, the caption and the labels on the diagram.

Challenge children to use the contents page and find the glossary. Explain that a glossary tells us what words mean. Turn to page 21 and discuss the words (ancient, carving, custom, emperor, flasks, symbol, traditions, weave) and what they mean. Explain that these are words in the text and they are in bold writing. Look through the book and find the bold words: ancient (page 6), carving (page 5), custom (page 8), emperor (page 7), flasks (page 7), symbol (page 10), traditions (page 2), weave (page 10).

Heads together

Look at pages 2 and 3 together. Model how to split up compound words, such as 'good/bye' and 'fire/works' to read them easily. Point out the apostrophe in the heading and explain it shows a missing letter: let's = let us. Can the children identify the features: heading, photograph, caption, diagram and labels? Discuss what 'celebrate' means.

Give each pair a heading from the contents page and ask them to turn to the page and read the text carefully. Can they find out what part of the world the celebration is happening in? What is the tradition?

Ask each pair to feed back to the rest of the group what they have found out.

Wrap up

Look at pages 22 and 23 together. Discuss the map of the world. Point out which country the school is in. Relate to children's own experiences by asking if they have visited any other countries and finding them on the map.

Read pages 4 and 5 together. Discuss what a New Year's resolution is.

Ask: Do you think the people are enjoying the celebrations?

Vocabulary boost session

You will need

- Multiple copies of Collins Big Cat *Happy New Year*

Vocabulary table

Focus word	Child-friendly explanation	Example sentence	Tell me...
glossary	A glossary tells you what words in a text mean.	I found out what 'carving' meant by looking at the **glossary**.	Tell me where in a book you can usually find the glossary.
celebrate	To party or show you are pleased about something.	I **celebrated** my fifth birthday last week.	Tell me how you celebrate your birthday.
resolution	A promise or way to make something right.	My New Year's **resolution** was to hand my homework in on time.	Tell me what New Year's resolution you would make.

Tune in

Explain that in this lesson the children are going to look in more detail at some words linked to the text. Write the three focus words clearly for the children to see. Read the words together. Discuss and explain the child-friendly meaning of each word.

Reread the text.

Ask the following questions:

- Can you find the glossary in the book. (page 21)
- Can you find the word 'celebrate' in the text. (page 20)

Turn to page 4 – can children point to the word 'resolutions'?

Ask: What resolution does the carving show? *(to give a borrowed tool back to its owner)*

Heads together

Look at the glossary on page 21. Explore the words and the meanings of each word.

Can the children plan an imaginary party or celebration? What would they eat? What would they wear? What activities would they do? What decorations would there be?

Wrap up

Recap the three focus words by discussing the questions in the 'Tell me' column of the table, above.

Challenge the children to think of a sentence using one of the focus words.

Follow-up independent sessions

You will need

- Black sugar paper, chalks
- Resource sheet: Resolutions
- Paper and felt-tipped pens

Ask children to create a firework picture on black sugar paper using chalks.

Hand out copies of Resource sheet: Resolutions. Ask children to write or draw a New Year's resolution.

Let the children design and create a New Year's Eve party poster or a 'Happy New Year' card as appropriate for your class.

Kind Emma

Book Band: Orange

A traditional story about a lady who helps when some 'thing' is cold and hungry. Her kind act is rewarded with companionship.

Skills focus

- Draw on knowledge of vocabulary to understand texts
- Identify/explain the sequence of events in texts
- Predict what might happen on the basis of what has been read so far
- Read words accurately and fluently

Guided reading session

You will need

- Multiple copies of Collins Big Cat *Kind Emma*

Tune in

Ask the following questions to start the lesson:

- What does 'being kind' mean?
- Can you give me any examples? *(helping someone who has fallen over, playing with someone who has no one to play with, sharing a toy, letting someone else go first, looking after someone who is upset)*

Go around the group and ask children to take turns to verbally complete the sentence: 'I was kind when…'

Introduce the book by looking at the front cover. Read the title together. Discuss the front page.

Ask the following questions:

- What can you see? *(a lady looking out of a window, snow, a little yellow creature)*
- Where is Emma? *(inside her house)*
- What is the little yellow creature in the bottom right of the page?
- What do you think will happen in the story?
- Why do you think she is called 'Kind Emma'?

Turn the book over to read the blurb. Ask children to point out the high frequency words. ('had', 'no', 'one', 'to', 'she', 'for', 'it', 'was' 'and', 'what', 'did', 'she', 'do')

Look at the word 'something' and show children how to split this compound word: 'some/thing'.

Model reading the blurb with accuracy and fluency. Can the children make further predictions? What would they do? What do they think Emma will do?

Practise segmenting and blending the word 'night' n-igh-t. Can the children think of other words with the 'igh' trigraph? Create a list: flight, fight, fright, might, height, bright, sight, light.

Heads together

Read pages 2 and 3 together. Encourage the children to point to the words and join in where they can. Do they notice the split digraph in the word 'alone'?

Ask: How do you think Emma is feeling?

Look at pages 4 and 5 together. Can the children point out the speech marks/inverted commas?

Encourage the children to practise reading using expression; can they use a little voice?

Ask the following questions:

- Where do you think the voice is coming from?
- How does it know Emma's name?

Can the children predict what Emma will do next?

Turn to pages 6 and 7 together. Model reading the text fluently and accurately.

Ask: Why do you think the word 'thing' is in italics? *(to emphasise it is a creature no one has ever seen before)*

Discuss other names that they could give the 'thing'.

Ask: How do you think the 'thing' and Emma are both feeling?

Ask children to read pages 8 to 21 independently. Encourage them to read aloud. Listen as they read and remind them of strategies such as segmenting and blending, picture clues, checking the text makes sense and recognising high frequency words.

Wrap up

Reread the story using accuracy and fluency.

Look at pages 20 and 21 and discuss how the characters feel.

Turn to pages 22 and 23. Explore Emma's diary in detail. Point out it is written from Emma's point of view using 'I'.

Ask the following questions:

- What is a diary? *(a personal recount of what someone has been doing)*
- Does anyone keep a diary?
- What have you done today/this week/this weekend?

Ask children to share what they have been doing with a Reading Partner before feeding back to the whole group.

Vocabulary boost session

You will need

- Multiple copies of Collins Big Cat *Kind Emma*

Vocabulary table

Focus word	Child-friendly explanation	Example sentence	Tell me...
scuttled	If you scuttle across a room, you move quickly and quietly.	The ants **scuttled** across the floor.	Tell me a sentence using the word 'scuttled'.
afraid	If you are afraid of something, you are scared of it.	I was **afraid** of the dark.	Tell me what things you are afraid of.
shiver	If you shiver, your body shakes because it is cold.	I **shivered** as the snow fell to the ground around me.	Tell me about a time you have shivered.

Tune in

Explain that in this lesson the children are going to look in more detail at some words the author has used. Write the three focus words clearly for the children to see. Read the words together. Discuss and explain the child-friendly meaning of each word. Reread the text.

Challenge the children to find the focus words in the text. ('scuttled', page 7; 'afraid', page 13; 'shiver', page 8)

Heads together

How many different words can the children think of that mean 'afraid'?

Working with their Reading Partners, ask children to discuss what they are afraid of or something that they have been afraid of in the past. Ask them to share their thoughts with the whole group, completing the sentence verbally: 'I was afraid when...'

Ask: Look at page 7. What other words could we use instead of 'scuttled'?

Experiment with different words to replace 'scuttled' and discuss the effect: 'She opened the door and a tiny thing... in.'

Discuss different cold settings.

Ask: What colours make you think of cold places? *(blues, whites, silver)*

Wrap up

Recap the three focus words by discussing the questions in the 'Tell me' column of the table, above.

Challenge the children to think of a sentence using one of the focus words.

Follow-up independent sessions

You will need

- Resource sheet: Role on the wall: Emma
- Resource sheet: My diary
- Coloured pencils or pens, paper
- Collage materials, paints, different types of paper including blues, whites and silvers

Use Resource sheet: Role on the wall: Emma. The children label the picture of Emma with adjectives to describe Emma's character on the inside and her appearance on the outside.

Hand out copies of Resource sheet: My diary. Ask children to draw pictures and write sentences about their weekend or day at school in the style of Emma's diary on pages 22 and 23.

Ask children to create a collage of a setting that makes them shiver! They should think about colours that make them think of a cold place.

The Brave Baby

Book Band: Orange

A story from another culture (North America). Find out how brave the baby is when the chief meets her.

Skills focus

- Draw on knowledge of vocabulary to understand texts
- Make inferences from texts
- Predict what might happen on the basis of what has been read so far
- Check reading makes sense

Guided reading session

You will need

- Multiple copies of Collins Big Cat *The Brave Baby*
- Resource sheet: Word cards for *The Brave Baby*

Tune in

Explain to the children that they are going to read a story from another culture – a story from North America about an Indian chief. Check that the children understand the word 'chief'. If necessary, explain it is the person in charge/the leader.

Introduce the book by looking at the front cover.

Ask the following questions:

- Who do you think the characters in the story are? *(an Indian chief and a baby)*
- Where is the setting?

Turn over to the back cover. Read the blurb together, checking reading makes sense.

Ask the following questions:

- Why do you think the baby isn't afraid of the chief?
- Would you be afraid of him?
- Which word makes him sound scary? *(fierce)*
- What do you think will happen in the story?
- What do you think the Indian chief will think of the brave baby?

Point out the digraph 'ie' in 'chief'. Look at the same sound in 'baby'. Use Resource sheet: Word cards for *The Brave Baby*, to sort the words into word families. ('ie', 'ee', 'ea', 'y')

Heads together

Begin by looking at pages 2 and 3 together. Model reading the text using a range of strategies, such as decoding.

Ask the following questions:

- Can you describe the chief? *(big, brave, fierce, angry)*
- What is he wearing? *(a colourful coat, feathers, jewellery)*

Point out the speech marks.

Ask the following questions:

- What did the wise woman say? (*I know someone who is not afraid of you.*)
- Who might be braver than the chief?

Read pages 4 and 5 together. Model reading using expression.

Ask the following questions:

- What did the Indian chief think about someone not being afraid of him? *(He was surprised.)*
- Who do you think is in the tent?

Recap strategies the children can use to help tackle unknown words, such as decoding, picture clues, context clues and checking the text makes sense.

Ask children to work in pairs to read pages 6 to 21. Encourage them to point to words as they read and use expression for the speech marks.

Ask the following questions:

- Can you find out who is in the tent? *(the baby)*
- How does the chief try to get the baby to do as he says? *(He shouts orders; then he dances.)*
- What does the baby do? *(smiles, cries, laughs, falls asleep)*
- Do you think the baby is brave?

Listen to individual children as they read and encourage them to predict what will happen next.

Wrap up

Look at pages 22 and 23 and ask children to work in pairs to retell the story in their own words.

Ask the following questions:

- Did you think the baby was brave?
- Why do you think the baby didn't go to the chief when he asked?
- How did the chief try to get the baby to do as he said? *(shouted, danced)*
- Was the lady wise?

Discuss the different feelings of the chief throughout the book: angry, cross, surprised, tired.

Vocabulary boost session

You will need

- Multiple copies of Collins Big Cat *The Brave Baby*

Vocabulary table

Focus word	Child-friendly explanation	Example sentence	Tell me...
fierce	Very angry and stern.	The dog growled **fiercely**.	Tell me about a time you have been fierce.
brave	If you are brave you do scary things, even if you are worried about them.	The gymnast **bravely** walked along the beam.	Tell me about a time when you have been brave.
surprised	If you are surprised, you are shocked by something.	I was **surprised** to get full marks in my spelling test.	Tell me about something that has surprised you.

Tune in

Explain that in this lesson the children are going to look in more detail at some of the words the author has used. Write the three focus words clearly for the children to see. Read the words together. Discuss and explain the child-friendly meaning of each word.

Reread the text. Challenge the children to find the focus words in the text. ('fierce', page 2; 'brave', page 2; 'surprised', page 4)

Heads together

Play a game of 'You say/I say'. Say a definition and ask children to identify the focus word.

Ask children to think of other words that mean 'surprised' and record their ideas in a word bank. For example: shocked, stunned, astonished, amazed, startled.

Ask children to choose an emotion and make a face to express it. Can the other children correctly guess the emotion?

Wrap up

Recap the three focus words by discussing the questions in the 'Tell me' column of the table, above.

Challenge the children to think of a sentence using one of the focus words.

Follow-up independent sessions

You will need

- Paints and paper
- Resource sheet: Word cards for *The Brave Baby*
- Role on the wall: The chief

Ask children to paint a picture of the setting and write descriptive words around the edges.

Let the children use Resource sheet: Word cards for *The Brave Baby*, to independently sort the words into word families and write a sentence using the word.

Use Resource sheet: Role on the wall: The chief. The children label the picture of the chief with adjectives to describe his character on the inside and his appearance on the outside.

Arthur's Fantastic Party

Book Band: Orange

In this humorous story, Arthur wants only the most fantastic animals to come to his party. But when no one comes, he realises he's made a big mistake.

Skills focus

- Draw on knowledge of vocabulary to understand texts
- Identify/explain the sequence of events in texts
- Make inferences from texts
- Read words accurately and fluently

Guided reading session

You will need

- Multiple copies of Collins Big Cat *Arthur's Fantastic Party*

Tune in

Introduce the book by asking the children to look closely at the front cover.

Ask the following questions:

- What can you see? *(donkey, picnic rug, balloons)*
- What kind of character is in the picture? *(happy)*
- What clues are there? *(smiling, looks cheerful)*
- What else is in the picture? *(trees, flowers, grass, house)*

Read the title aloud, ask children to join in.

Ask: What do you think the story is about?

Tell the children that you are going to turn to the back cover to see if you can find out more about the story.

Ask: What do we call the writing on the back cover of a book? *(blurb)*

Turn to the back cover and encourage the children to look at the picture.

Ask: Does this give you any more clues about the story?

Read the blurb aloud, encouraging the children to follow and join in with you.

Heads together

Tell the children that they are going to read the story on their own.

Ask: What strategies can you use to help you if you get stuck on a word? *(look at the pictures, read the first sound and then think about what the word might be, look for tricky words that you already know)*

Read pages 2 and 3 aloud, with the children following as you read. Model changing your voice for dialogue and reading with expression.

Tell the children that when they read, you want them to think about their reading strategies, changing their voice when someone is speaking and thinking about what is happening in the story. Can they find out why Arthur's party is fantastic?

Ask children to read pages 4 to 23, on their own. As they read, move around the group, listening to each child while the others read in their heads. Check their reading strategies and listen for use of expression as they read.

Wrap up

Identify and praise children's use of reading strategies that you observed them using to help with reading longer or difficult words and their use of expression.

Ask the following questions to check the children's comprehension:

- Why is the story called *Arthur's* Fantastic *Party*? *(because Arthur only wanted fantastic animals at his party/the animals were fantastic/the party was fantastic)*
- What kind of character do you think Arthur is? Why?

Explain that you are going to ask children about the things that happened in the story and that they can use the book to help them answer.

Ask the following questions:

- How did the story start? *(Arthur told Flora about the party.)*
- Then what happened? *(Flora invited the animals and they asked Arthur if they could go to the party – he said no.)*
- What happened after that? *(Arthur set up his party but no one came.)*
- How did the story end? *(Arthur told them all to come to his party and they had a great time.)*

Vocabulary boost session

You will need

- Multiple copies of Collins Big Cat *Arthur's Fantastic Party*

Vocabulary table

Focus word	Child-friendly explanation	Example sentence	Tell me...
fantastic	If you think something is fantastic, you think it is really, really good or you like it a lot.	Jan thought the TV programme was **fantastic**.	Tell me about something you have seen or done that you thought was fantastic.
ready	If someone is ready to do something, they have sorted things out and can start doing it.	"Get **ready** for swimming," said Mum.	Tell me about how you get ready for school.
alone	When you are alone, there is no one else there.	When Clare stayed in during break, she was **alone** in the classroom.	Tell me about a time when you have been alone.

Tune in

Explain to the children that in this lesson they are going to look closely at some of the words the author has used and what those words mean.

Read the book aloud to the children, modelling how to use the punctuation and dialogue to read aloud with expression.

Refer back to each of the focus words within the context of the story, writing up the word, giving a child-friendly explanation and asking the children to say the focus word with you. For example: The title of the story is *Arthur's Fantastic Party*. If you think something is fantastic, you think it is really, really good or you like it a lot. Now, say the word with me – 'fantastic'.

You may wish to use the examples in the table, above.

Refer to each of the focus words that you have written up and give the children the example sentences. Then ask them to interact with the word meanings by asking the questions in the 'Tell me' column. You may wish to demonstrate by giving some examples of your own.

Ask children to say the words with you once more.

Heads together

Ask the following questions to explore and develop the children's understanding of the focus words:

- If you went on a trip to a really great place, you could say, "It was fantastic". When else might you talk about something being fantastic?
- If someone has finished cooking lunch, they could say, "Lunch is ready". When else might you talk about something being ready?
- If someone was playing by themselves, you could say, "They are alone". When else might someone be alone?

Wrap up

Ask the following questions to review the word meanings: What would a fantastic playground look like? What might someone who is ready to ride their bike look like? What feelings might someone who is alone have?

Challenge the group to use the words as often as they can, both at school and at home.

Follow-up independent sessions

You will need

- Multiple copies of Collins Big Cat *Arthur's Fantastic Party*
- Paper, coloured pencils, felt-tipped pens
- Resource sheet: Arthur's reply

Ask children to work with their Reading Partners and to read the book aloud, remembering to use their voices to show when a character is talking.

Challenge the children to draw a story map of *Arthur's Fantastic Party*.

Hand out copies of Resource sheet: Arthur's reply. Ask children to turn to page 23 and read the letter to Arthur. They should write back to one of the animals as if they were Arthur.

Morris Plays Hide and Seek

Book Band: Orange

Morris wants to wait for his biscuits rather than play hide and seek with Tom and Rose, but his mother insists it will be good for him. Morris eventually finds a perfect hiding place – perfect for him at least.

Skills focus

- Draw on knowledge of vocabulary to understand texts
- Make inferences from texts
- Predict what might happen on the basis of what has been read so far
- Check reading makes sense

Guided reading session

You will need

- Multiple copies of Collins Big Cat *Morris Plays Hide and Seek*

Tune in

Look together at the cover of the book and read the title.

Ask: Do you think this is a story book or a non-fiction/information book? Why?

Elicit that the title of the book and the funny illustration suggests it is a story book. Read the title again and the label on the bag in the picture.

Ask: What do you think 'Bics' is short for? *(biscuits)*

Encourage the children to think about any animals that they know and their relationship with food. Do they like food a lot or just some foods?

Ask: How do you think Morris feels about the 'Kitty Bics'?

Turn to the back page and read the blurb.

Ask the following questions:

- What is meant by 'both' in the last question. *(eat his treats and play hide and seek)*
- How might he be able to do both?

Ensure the children know the rules of hide and seek. Ask them to explain them to those who do not know.

Ask: What do you think will happen when Morris plays hide and seek? Why?

Heads together

Turn to pages 2 and 3 and focus on the pictures. Encourage the children to suggest what Morris is thinking. Read the text together.

Ask the following questions:

- What is Morris doing? *(sitting by his bowl waiting for his kitty biscuits)*
- Why do you think he did it all day?
- What does it tell us about him?

Discuss whether they think Morris is greedy or hungry, explaining the meaning of 'greedy', if necessary.

Read pages 4 and 5 aloud to the children and then reread them with the children joining in.

Ask: What has happened in the story so far? *(Mother Cat has told Morris to go and play hide and seek with Tom and Rose. Morris doesn't want to play.)*

Encourage the children to check what they say against the pictures.

Ask the following questions:

- Does that match the pictures?
- Why do you think Mother Cat says "Playing is good for you."?
- Do you think Morris will play or not? Why?

Repeat for pages 6 and 7.

Discuss what might happen in the rest of the story and how it might end. Do their predictions make sense given what they already know about Morris?

Ask children to read the rest of the book individually to find out what happens. As they read, move around the group, checking each child's reading. Support them in checking their understanding by looking at the pictures and rereading, if necessary.

Wrap up

Ask the following questions:

- Did Morris play hide and seek?
- Did he get his biscuits?

Encourage the children to vote on 'yes/no' answers to each question. Say: Let's check we are right.

Encourage the children to take turns to explain the story, stage by stage, using the pictures as prompts. Ask questions with reference to words in the text to check their understanding, for example, on page 17, point to the word 'stuck' and ask why he was stuck.

Encourage the children to describe the ending. Did they think it was sad, funny or happy? Why?

Vocabulary boost session

You will need

- Multiple copies of Collins Big Cat *Morris Plays Hide and Seek*

Vocabulary table

Focus word	Child-friendly explanation	Example sentence	Tell me...
behind	When something is behind an object, it is often hidden by it. So when Tom hides behind the curtain, he is hidden behind it.	I found my purse **hidden** behind a cushion.	Tell me about something in the room that is behind something else.
perfect	A perfect thing is the best. A perfect hiding place is where you cannot be found.	I have made the **perfect** chocolate cake – everyone will love it.	Tell me what would make your day perfect.
squeezed	When Morris squeezed himself into the cupboard, he squashed his body to get it in.	I had to **squeeze** myself through the window because I had lost my front door key.	Tell me about a time you have squeezed into a small space.

Tune in

Read the book aloud to the children, modelling how to read longer words by sounding out the smaller words, for example, in 'sitting' ('sit') and 'squeezed' ('squeeze'). Check that they are familiar with letters that commonly make one sound, such as 'qu' and 'ee' in 'squeezed', 'ng' in 'playing' and 'ai' in 'curtain'.

Explain that you are now going to look at some words the author has used in the book in detail and check what they mean.

Look at each focus word in turn, returning to where they appear in the story, such as 'behind' on page 8. Point out the word, then write it on the board, asking the children to say it out loud. Explain its meaning in a child-friendly way and with reference to the story. For example: 'behind' is when something is hidden or partly hidden by something else. In this story, Tom chose to hide behind the curtain. Now, say the word with me – 'behind'.

Refer to each of the focus words again, using them in example sentences like those in the table, above. Then prompt the children to use each word themselves by answering the questions in the 'Tell me' column.

Help the children to find each word in the book again. When everyone has found the word on a page, reread that sentence as a group.

Heads together

Ask the following questions to explore and develop the children's understanding of the focus words:

- Would you hide your sweets in a cupboard or on a table?
- Would a perfect bike be clean and new or rusty and broken?
- If I squeezed into a cave, would the cave entrance be a bit smaller or bigger than me?

Encourage them to elaborate on their answers by following up their responses with the question: Why?

Wrap up

Review the word meanings by asking the children to choose the missing word from the focus word list to fill the gap:

- I stood in the queue… my friend.
- The budgie… through a gap to get out of the cage.
- The cake tasted…

Put the focus words on a wall chart and challenge the children to place a tick by the word every time they use it in conversation.

Follow-up independent sessions

You will need

- Resource sheet: Story mapping
- Resource sheet: Word link

Hand out cards cut from Resource sheet: Story mapping. Ask children to work with their Reading

Partners to match the pictures with the relevant caption and then to put them in the story order.

Give pairs of children a copy of the Resource sheet: Word link. Ask them to draw lines to connect the word with the correct picture.

How to Make Pop-up Cards

Book Band: Orange

An instruction text with detailed instructions and step-by-step photographs of how to make a pop-up card.

Skills focus

- Draw on knowledge of vocabulary to understand texts
- Identify/explain key aspects of fiction and non-fiction texts, e.g. character, events, title
- Identify/explain the sequence of events in texts
- Check reading makes sense

Guided reading session

You will need

- Multiple copies of Collins Big Cat *How to Make Pop-up Cards*
- A selection of pop-up cards
- Resource sheet: Sentences for *How to Make Pop-up Cards*

Tune in

Look at and explore a selection of pop-up cards.

Ask the following questions:

- How do they work?
- Why do they pop up?
- Has anyone ever been given a pop-up card? Has anyone ever made a pop-up card?

Share experiences.

Explain to the children that they are going to read a book called *How to Make Pop-up Cards*. Look at the front cover together. Read the title. Point out the vowel digraphs 'ow' and 'ar' in the words 'How' and 'Cards'.

Ask: What type of text do you think this is? *(non-fiction/instruction)*

Turn the book over to read the blurb. Model reading the text.

Discuss the key features of instructions: titles, you will need list, introduction, numbered steps, photographs or diagrams, instructional language (fold, press, draw, bend, cut, use) and top tips/handy hints. Write a list of the features on the board. Challenge the children to find examples of each feature in the book.

Using Resource sheet: Sentences for *How to Make Pop-up Cards*, work as a group to read the sentences and sort into 'instructions' and 'not instructions'. Discuss what is different about them.

Look at the contents page together.

Ask the following questions to practise using the contents page:

- On what page will you learn how to make a spring? *(page 10)*
- What will you find out about on page 4? *(making the frame)*

Heads together

Turn to page 2 together to read the introduction.

Ask: What is an introduction? *(a summary/ explanation/starter/it tells you a little bit about the topic)*

Model reading with expression. Ask children to point to the words as you read and join in where they can. Do the children recognise the high frequency words: 'are', 'and', 'to', 'out', 'a', 'them', 'all', 'then', 'your', 'the'?

On page 3 discuss the items needed.

Ask: Why is a 'things you will need' section important? *(so you can make sure you have everything to make the item)*

Look at the labels and practise reading them. Ask what each item is for or does.

Ask children to read pages 4 to 21 in pairs. Listen to them read and support where needed. Remind children to reread sentences and check that they make sense.

Wrap up

Recap strategies used to help with their reading: high frequency words, segmenting and blending, checking the text makes sense and picture clues.

Ask: Were there any words you found tricky?

Explore pages 22 and 23. Talk through the flow chart together. Can the children create an instruction to go with each picture?

Discuss how important it is for instructions to be in the correct order.

Vocabulary boost session

You will need

- Multiple copies of Collins Big Cat *How to Make Pop-up Cards*
- Timer

Vocabulary table

Focus word	Child-friendly explanation	Example sentence	Tell me...
introduction	An introduction tells you a little bit about a topic or person.	Let me **introduce** you to my cousin: Ava.	Tell me what the introduction on page 2 told us.
surprise	A surprise is something that you were not expecting.	We organised a **surprise** party for my uncle's birthday.	Tell me about a time you were surprised by something.
remember	If you remember something, you don't forget it.	I **remember** when I went on holiday with my grandma.	Tell me what you remember doing last weekend.

Tune in

Explain that in this lesson the children are going to look in more detail at some of the words the author has used in the text. Write the three focus words clearly for the children to see. Read the words together. Discuss and explain the child-friendly meaning of each word.

Reread the text.

Challenge the children to find the focus words in the text. ('introduction', page 2; 'surprise', page 2; 'remember', page 14)

Heads together

Explore the focus word 'introduction' by asking children to spend five minutes finding out about their Reading Partner; then ask each child to feed back a brief introduction verbally about their Reading Partner. For example: 'This is Ava. She is six years old and has two brothers. Ava likes painting and bouncing as high as she can on her trampoline.'

Explore the focus word 'remember' by playing a memory game. The children complete the sentence 'I went to the zoo and I saw…' Each time a player has a turn they must remember what the previous person said and add something else. The more detail included, the harder the game becomes. For example: 'I went to the zoo and I saw a monkey eating a banana, an elephant squirting water...'

Wrap up

Recap the three focus words by discussing the questions in the 'Tell me' column of the table, above.

Challenge the children to think of a sentence using one of the focus words.

Follow-up independent sessions

You will need

- Multiple copies of Collins Big Cat *How to Make Pop-up Cards*
- Construction kits and instructions
- Thin coloured card, coloured paper, glue stick, stapler, ruler, scissors, pencil, felt-tipped pens, a pebble, photographs or pictures
- Resource sheet: Instruction order
- Scissors

Ask children to make something from a construction kit by following the instructions.

Ask children to follow the instructions in the book to make a pop-up card.

Give the children a copy of Resource sheet: Instruction order. Ask them to cut out the cards and put the instructions in order. They should also write a sentence to go with each picture.

Bounce Catch Kick Throw

Book Band: Orange

A non-fiction text about different types of balls. Included are instructions for how to juggle and how to make a bouncy ball.

Skills focus

- Draw on knowledge of vocabulary to understand texts
- Identify/explain key aspects of fiction and non-fiction texts, e.g. character, events, title
- Identify/explain the sequence of events in texts
- Read words accurately and fluently

Guided reading session

You will need

- Multiple copies of Collins Big Cat *Bounce Catch Kick Throw*
- Sticky notes

Tune in

Begin the lesson by linking to the children's own experiences.

Ask the following questions:

- Who likes football/netball/tennis?
- What type of ball games do you like playing best?

Create a list of all the different types of balls the children can think of, for example: rugby ball, tennis ball, beach ball, ten-pin bowling ball, bouncy ball, hockey ball, cricket ball. Write their suggestions on the board.

Introduce the book by looking at the front cover. Model reading the title. Point out the vowel digraphs 'ou' and 'ow'. Explain that this is a non-fiction book.

Ask: What do you think it is about?

Turn the book over to read the blurb. Look at the questions. Ask children to work in pairs to record their own question about balls on a sticky note and save these for the 'Wrap up' session.

Explore the contents page together.

Ask the following questions:

- What page will tell me how to make a bouncy ball? *(page 12)*
- What is page 8 about? *(how to juggle)*

Heads together

Turn to pages 2 and 3 and read together. Model reading fluently. Can the children answer the questions? Turn to page 4 to find out.

Ask children to read pages 5 to 7 with their Reading Partner. Listen to the children read and support them where needed. The children can discuss what type of ball games they like playing.

Turn to pages 8 and 9 and read about how to juggle.

Ask the following questions:

- What type of text is this? *(instruction)*
- Can you point to and tell me about the features? *(heading, you will need list, numbered points, instructional language)*

Read through the instructions together.

Ask: Do you start with one ball or two balls first? *(one ball)*

Ask children to read pages 10 to 21 with their Reading Partners. Encourage them to use a range of reading strategies and to support each other.

Wrap up

Turn to page 22. Read and answer the questions together, finding the answers in the text by using the contents page and rereading the text if necessary.

Look at the questions the children wrote at the beginning of the lesson. Can they answer them now? Help children to find the answers in the book or discuss where else they could look.

Vocabulary boost session

You will need

- Multiple copies of Collins Big Cat *Bounce Catch Kick Throw*

Vocabulary table

Focus word	Child-friendly explanation	Example sentence	Tell me...
stadium	An arena where people can go to watch sport.	The **stadium** was full for the football match.	Tell me about a stadium you have visited or seen on TV.
springs	If something springs, it bounces up. Springs are also coiled pieces of wire, like the ones used on a trampoline.	The spider **springs** back up to its web. The **springs** on the trampoline had gone rusty.	Tell me the names of some items that have springs in them.
popular	If something is popular, lots of people like it.	Salt and vinegar crisps are the most **popular** flavour in our class.	Tell me which fruit you think will be the most popular in your class.

Tune in

Explain that in this lesson the children are going to look in more detail at some of the words the author has used. Write the three focus words clearly for the children to see. Read the words together. Discuss and explain the child-friendly meaning of each word.

Reread the text. Challenge the children to find the focus words in the text. ('stadium', page 2; 'springs', page 14; 'popular', page 18)

Heads together

Ask children to look at the picture of the stadium on page 2.

Ask: Has anyone been to a stadium before?

Write stadium in the middle of the board and ask children to describe it. Record their ideas. Ask them to think about what they might hear, smell, see, taste or feel in a stadium.

Ask the following questions:

- What would it sound like?
- What would you be able to smell?
- What might you see in a stadium?
- What might you have to eat or drink?
- How would you feel?

Ask children which is their favourite ball game: football or tennis? Record the results for children to see; then ask which is most popular – tennis or football? (If the result was equal, you could include your own preference.)

Wrap up

Recap the three focus words by discussing the questions in the 'Tell me' column of the table, above.

Challenge the children to think of a sentence using one of the focus words.

Follow-up independent sessions

You will need

- Multiple copies of Collins Big Cat *Bounce Catch Kick Throw*
- Juggling balls or bean bags
- Three different types of balls
- Resource sheet: Bouncing balls
- Resource sheet: Senses

Ask children to follow the instructions on pages 8 and 9 of the book and to learn how to juggle with two balls or bean bags.

Ask children to carry out the investigation on pages 16 and 17 of the book to see which ball bounces the highest. They use Resource sheet: Bouncing balls, to record results.

The children should imagine that they are in a football stadium. Ask them to record words on Resource sheet: Senses, to describe what it would be like using all five of their senses.

Fire! Fire!

Book Band: Orange

This information book explores the past, present and future of firefighting.

Skills focus

- Draw on knowledge of vocabulary to understand texts
- Identify/explain key aspects of fiction and non-fiction texts, e.g. character, events, title
- Make inferences from texts
- Read words accurately and fluently

Guided reading session

You will need

- Multiple copies of Collins Big Cat *Fire! Fire!*

Tune in

Introduce the book by encouraging the children to look closely at the front cover.

Ask the following questions:

- What do you think the book is about?
- What kind of book do you think this is, information or story? *(information)*
- What makes you think that? *(photograph)*

Ask children to point to the title of the book; then read it aloud together. Point to the exclamation marks.

Ask the following questions:

- What are these called? *(exclamation marks)*
- Why are they there? *(for emphasis)*
- Why might someone shout 'fire!'? *(to get help, warn others)*

Turn to the back cover and read the blurb aloud, encouraging the children to follow and join in with you.

Explain that you are going to turn to the title page. In some information books, the title page has a list of what is in the book.

Ask: Do you know what the list is called? *(contents)*

Turn to the contents page and read the contents aloud to the children, asking them to follow. As you read, insert the word 'page' before each number so that the children understand that is what the numbers are for.

Ask: Who wrote this book? *(Maureen Haselhurst)*

Heads together

Before you start reading, tell the children that for this session you will be focusing on:

- Reading strategies; recognising tricky words, blending phonemes to read longer words, looking out for words that end in '–s', '–ing', '–er' and '–ed'.
- The features of information texts: photographs, captions, labels, glossary words in bold.

Read pages 2 to 5 aloud, asking them to follow as you read and to join in. Model the reading strategies and discuss the features of information texts as you come across them.

Ask children to read up to page 23 alone. As they read, move around the group, listening to each child. If necessary, support them in reading longer words and observe their use of the range of strategies.

Wrap up

Ask the following questions to check the children's understanding:

- What are the features of information texts that you have seen? *(contents list, photographs, captions, labels, glossary words in bold, glossary, index)*
- Why do you think that they are there? *(to help the reader to understand the text, to make it easier to read)*

Ask children to turn to the title page.

Ask: Which is your favourite part of the book? Why?

Play 'Who can find it first?' Give the children each of these to find and see who can find it first: photograph, glossary, caption, contents, label, index.

Vocabulary boost session

You will need

- Multiple copies of Collins Big Cat *Fire! Fire!*

Vocabulary table

Focus word	Child-friendly explanation	Example sentence	Tell me...
firefighter	Firefighters are people whose job it is to put out fires.	The **firefighters** put out the flames.	Tell me what special equipment firefighters might need to do their job.
dangerous	If something is dangerous, it might hurt you.	Cars can be **dangerous**.	Tell me about something that is dangerous.
powerful	Something that is powerful is very strong.	The **powerful** wind blew down a tree.	Tell me about something that is powerful.

Tune in

Explain to the children that in this lesson they are going to look closely at some of the words the author has used and what those words mean.

Read the book aloud to the children, asking them to follow and join in as you read.

Refer back to each of the focus words within the context of the story, writing up the word, giving a child-friendly explanation and asking the children to say the focus word with you. For example: The book talks about 'firefighters'. Firefighters are people whose job it is to put out fires. Now, say the word with me – 'firefighter'.

You may wish to use the examples in the table, above.

Refer to each of the focus words that you have written up and give the children the example sentences. Then ask them to interact with the word meanings by asking the questions in the 'Tell me' column. You may wish to demonstrate by giving some examples of your own.

Ask children to say the words with you once more.

Heads together

Explore and develop the children's understanding of the focus words.

Ask the following questions, referring to the book:

- Can you find me a picture of a firefighter? What is s/he doing?
- Can you find me a picture of something dangerous? Why is it dangerous?

Turn to page 17 and read the text.

Ask: Can you explain what a 'powerful' hose is?

Wrap up

Ask the following questions to review the word meanings:

- What's the word that means 'very strong'?
- What's the word that means 'someone whose job it is to put out fires'?
- What's the word that means 'something that might hurt you'?

Ask children to choose one of the focus words as their word of the week. Challenge them to use the word as often as they can, both at school and at home.

Follow-up independent sessions

You will need

- Multiple copies of Collins Big Cat *Fire! Fire!*
- Resource sheet: Contents race

Ask children to work with their Reading Partners and to read the book aloud.

Hand out copies of Resource sheet: Contents race, to each pair. Ask children to race to see who can answer the questions first. The winners are the first pair to have all of the correct answers.

A Letter to New Zealand

Book Band: Orange

Jack in the UK writes a letter to his penpal, Tama, in New Zealand and we follow the letter's journey through its many stages, from collection to delivery.

Skills focus

- Draw on knowledge of vocabulary to understand texts
- Identify/explain key aspects of fiction and non-fiction texts, e.g. character, events, title
- Identify/explain the sequence of events in texts
- Check reading makes sense

Guided reading session

You will need

- Multiple copies of Collins Big Cat *A Letter to New Zealand*

Tune in

Ask children to look at the back and front cover.

Ask: Is this a fiction or non-fiction book?

Discuss the children's views and elicit how this is a non-fiction book. The clues are: a photo and not an illustration; maps on the front; the blurb.

Read the blurb with the children.

Ask: What does this book tell us about? (how Jack's letter gets to New Zealand)

Return to the front cover and look more carefully at the maps together. Discuss what they show. Turn to the map on page 3 and point to labels. Ask children if they know anything about New Zealand and how far away it might be.

Ask the following questions:
- Have you ever written a letter? Where to? Who was it to?
- Have you ever received a letter? Where from? Who was it from?

Heads together

Look together at the contents. Focus on the '–ing' words, asking the children to find the small words within each. Check their understanding of each word.

Ask the following questions:
- What do you think happens when someone posts a letter?
- Who do you think collects a letter?

Explain to the children that it is often helpful to look at the pictures on a page before reading the text.

Ask the following questions, for example:
- What is the boy doing on page 2? (writing a letter)
- Where does it show he lives?

Point out the address in the photo. Ask children to look at page 3.

Ask the following questions:
- What is UK short for? (United Kingdom)
- Why is this map here? (It shows where the letter was written and where it is going to.)

Reread the text on pages 2 and 3 with the children. Return to words the children were unsure of. Point out unfamiliar spellings of sounds, such as the 'ur' sound in 'journey'.

Ask the following questions:
- Can they find any '–ing' words? (sending, writing, going)
- What are the smaller words in them? (send, go)
- Does the text make sense against the pictures?
- What more have we found out about the pictures? (the boy is Jack; he is writing to a penpal; it is a long journey from the UK to New Zealand)

Ask children to read the rest of the book, using the pictures to check that the text makes sense. Challenge them to find out what different stages were involved in the letter's journey to New Zealand. As you circulate, ask questions about the pictures.

Wrap up

Write the following on the board but in a mixed-up order: 'write', 'post', 'collect', 'sort', 'airmail', 'New Zealand'. Ask the group to explain what happened at the first stage of the letter (write).

Ask children to turn to pages 2 and 3 to check that they are correct.

Continue in this way until the items on the board have been numbered in the correct order and each stage has been checked and explained.

Ask: What are the main words that explain what happened once the letter got to New Zealand? (delivery, open, send)

Ask children if they found any of the stages confusing. Together, return to the pages, reread and check their understanding.

Vocabulary boost session

You will need

- Multiple copies of Collins Big Cat *A Letter to New Zealand*

Vocabulary table

Focus word	Child-friendly explanation	Example sentence	Tell me...
pops	If someone 'pops' something in, they quickly drop it in. Jack quickly drops the letter in the postbox.	My friend **pops** in on Mondays to help me with my Maths.	Tell me about something you have popped into something else.
collects	When a postman collects letters, it means that they gather them together to take them away.	The farmer **collects** the eggs from the hens.	Tell me about anything you collect or have seen collected.
sorts	If someone sorts things, they put them into order or into groups.	The factory **sorts** the apples into good and bad.	Tell me what you might sort.

Tune in

Ask children if they can think of any words that they might use explaining how the post works or how a letter gets from one address to another. Start the children off with, for example, 'stamp'. Write the children's ideas on the board, encouraging them to try to help you with spellings.

Read the book aloud to the children, modelling how to break words down into syllables (for example, 'jour/ney') and look for familiar spellings (for example, '–ing' endings) as they read. Ask if they have heard any other words to do with the post and add their ideas to the board.

Explain that you are going to look at some of the words the author has used in the book more closely. Refer to each of the focus words, rereading them in their context, writing them on the board and giving a child-friendly explanation. You may wish to use the definition in the table, above.

Ask children to say the focus words with you.

Give the children the example sentences for each word. Then encourage them to interact with the word meanings further by asking the questions in the 'Tell me' column of the table, above. You may wish to support them by giving some examples of your own.

Heads together

Ask the following questions to explore and develop the children's understanding of the focus words:

- If someone pops in, do they arrive slowly or quickly?
- When someone collects things, do they end with more of them or less?
- Do you sort letters before they are posted or afterwards?

Encourage children to elaborate on their answers by following up their responses with the question 'Why?'

Wrap up

Review the word meanings by asking the children to raise a hand when they hear a similar word to the focus word:

- 'pops': picks, puts, sticks, runs
- 'collects': displays, gathers, sorts
- 'sorts': picks, sticks, turns, organises

Ask the group to try to use these words and to put a tick against them on a display board, every time that they have used them.

Follow-up independent sessions

You will need

- Multiple copies of Collins Big Cat *A Letter to New Zealand*
- Resource sheet: Picture clues
- Resource sheet: Interesting letter words

Ask children to work with their Reading Partners and take turns to take a picture card from Resource sheet: Picture clues. They should explain everything that they know about the picture and its part in a letter's journey.

Give pairs of children the Resource sheet: Interesting letter words. Challenge them to work with their Reading Partner to decide on the meaning of each word. They can discuss their answers, or write words or notes about the meaning. Some children could draw pictures. The children's work can be used to create a 'Post A Letter' dictionary or glossary.

First Day

Book Band: Orange

A boy's parents reassure him there is no need to worry about your first day at school; they tell him all about things that went wrong for some different people's first day at work.

Skills focus

- Draw on knowledge of vocabulary to understand texts
- Identify/explain the sequence of events in texts
- Predict what might happen on the basis of what has been read so far
- Check reading makes sense

Guided reading session

You will need

- Multiple copies of Collins Big Cat *First Day*

Tune in

Begin by showing the children the front cover. Model reading the title by segmenting and blending the words 'first' f-ir-s-t and 'day' d-ay.

Point out the vowel diagraphs 'ir' and 'ay'. Practise reading words using the 'ir' and 'ay' digraphs. Write these on the board for children to read: say, day, pay, play, away, May; bird, girl, twirl, dirt, shirt, stir.

Discuss the picture on the front cover. Can the children make any predictions? **Ask** the following questions:

- Who do you think the characters are?
- Where do you think the boy is going?
- How do you think he is feeling?

Model reading the blurb using fluency and accuracy.

Ask the following questions to check the children's understanding:

- Who is Flynn? *(the boy on the front cover)*
- Where is he going? *(to school)*
- Has he been to school before? *(no)*
- How is he feeling? *(nervous)*

Relate to the children's own experiences. Discuss and share their memories of their first day at school.

Ask the following questions:

- How were they feeling?
- Can they remember what they did?

Having read the blurb, can the children make predictions of what will happen on Flynn's first day at school?

Heads together

Look at pages 2 and 3 together. Model reading using a range of strategies, including decoding, checking for sense, picture clues and recognising high frequency words. Encourage the children to point to the words as you read and join in if they can.

Ask the following questions:

- Why do you think Flynn is nervous?
- What might he be worried about?

Ask children to work in pairs and to discuss what they can see in the picture. **Ask** them the following questions:

- What is Flynn having for breakfast? *(cereal)*
- What day is it? *(Monday 8th September)*
- What time is it? *(8:20 a.m.)*
- Why do they think most of the picture is blue?

Turn to pages 4 and 5 together. Ask children to point to the speech marks/inverted commas and discuss that these show the reader a character is speaking. Model reading to the children.

Ask: Can you suggest what type of things people might get wrong on their first day? *(wrong time, not knowing where to put things or where to go)*

Still working in pairs, ask children to flick through the book (pages 6 to 17) and skim/scan to find out what people Flynn's mum and dad are talking about. Share what they have found. (Police officer, builder, farm worker, gardener, hairdresser, cook, zookeeper, stuntman) Turn to pages 22 and 23 and discuss each character and what they might have done wrong on their first day. Can the children make predictions?

Ask children to read pages 6 to 17 in detail. Recap different strategies that they could use to help them. Support them where needed.

Wrap up

Check the children's understanding.

Ask: Do you think Flynn will feel less worried now?

Read pages 18 and 19 together. Ask children to predict what will happen next. Will Flynn do something silly on his first day?

Finally, read pages 20 and 21. Discuss what the children think of the ending. Is it funny?

Vocabulary boost session

You will need

- Multiple copies of Collins Big Cat *First Day*

Vocabulary table

Focus word	Child-friendly explanation	Example sentence	Tell me...
nervous	If you are feeling nervous, you are worried or unsure.	I was **nervous** on my first day of school.	Tell me about a time you have felt nervous.
confident	If you are feeling confident, you are sure of yourself.	I felt **confident** I would get my spellings correct.	Tell me about a time you have felt confident.
shocked	If you are shocked, you are surprised or were not expecting something.	I was **shocked** when I saw Jim's new haircut.	Tell me about a time you have been shocked.

Tune in

Explain that in this lesson the children are going to look in more detail at some words linked to the text. Write the three focus words clearly for the children to see. Read the words together. Discuss and explain the child-friendly meaning of each word.

Reread the text.

Discuss how Flynn is feeling throughout the text: nervous on pages 2 to 5; confident on pages 18 and 19; shocked on pages 20 and 21.

Heads together

The children work together to make a list of words that describe emotions and how characters are feeling. Write their suggestions on the board.

Ask children to make some 'emotion' faces together: make a nervous face, a confident face, an upset face, a shocked face.

Play a game where one child makes an emotion face and the rest of the group guess how they are feeling.

Wrap up

Recap the three focus words by discussing the questions in the 'Tell me' column of the table, above.

Challenge the children to think of a sentence using one of the focus words.

Follow-up independent sessions

You will need

- Paper, coloured pencils or pens
- Resource sheet: First days
- Resource sheet: Word sort

Ask children to draw a picture of their favourite part in the story. Challenge them to write a sentence explaining what they liked about it.

Ask children to draw a picture and write about their first day at school.

Hand out copies of Resource sheet: First days. The children write or draw what a nurse, racing car driver, a football player, a plumber, a shopkeeper or a vet might do wrong on their first day.

Give children a set of cards cut from Resource sheet: Word sort. The children sort the 'er', 'ur' and 'ir' words.

What is CGI?

A non-fiction book about computer-generated images, written in the first person. The artist explains how he created the images.

Skills focus

- Draw on knowledge of vocabulary to understand texts
- Identify/explain key aspects of fiction and non-fiction texts, e.g. character, events, title
- Identify/explain the sequence of events in texts
- Read words accurately and fluently

Guided reading session

You will need

- Multiple copies of Collins Big Cat *What is CGI?*

Tune in

Read the title together. Point out that 'CGI' is written in capital letters and explain that this is because it represents a phrase: computer-generated images.

Ask: What do you think computer-generated images are?

Turn to the back cover. Model reading the blurb accurately and fluently.

Ask: Where might you have seen computer-generated images? *(films, TV programmes, books, advertising posters, computer games)*

Explore the glossary on page 20 together and play a game of 'I say/You say' by saying a word from the glossary and asking the children to tell you the definition.

Discuss the difference between the index page (page 21) and the contents page (page 1). Look in detail at the contents page.

Ask the following questions:

- On which page can you find out about lighting? *(page 16)*
- On which page will you learn about texture? *(page 8)*

Discuss the features of non-fiction texts, such as headings, photographs, captions, diagrams, labels, glossary, index. Challenge the children to scan through the book in pairs to find examples of each feature.

Heads together

Begin on pages 2 and 3. Ask children to point at the words in bold ('computer-generated images' (CGI), 'characters'). Look up these words in the glossary.

Turn back to pages 2 and 3 and model reading the text accurately. Discuss the characters.

Ask the following questions:

- What do you like about the characters?
- Which is your favourite?
- How do you think that they are made?

Turn to pages 4 and 5 together. Read through the text together. Ask children what they think the words 'studio' and 'models' mean. Check the glossary for the meaning. Discuss how the text is written from Jon Stuart's 'point of view', as if he is talking to us.

Recap the different strategies the children can use to help them read: high frequency word recognition, decoding, picture clues, checking the text makes sense.

Ask children to read pages 6 to 19 with their Reading Partners. Can they find out how the models are made? Listen to the children as they read and support them where needed.

Wrap up

Ask children to choose their favourite page and to tell you what they like about it.

Turn to the flow chart on pages 22 and 23 and read through the chart together. Discuss the importance of the order and the numbered points. Recap how the computer-generated image is made.

Vocabulary boost session

You will need

- Multiple copies of Collins Big Cat *What is CGI?*
- A selection of materials with different textures, for example: silk, bubble wrap, velvet, cotton, foil, something fluffy
- Resource sheet: Settings cube
- Scissors, glue or sticky tape

Vocabulary table

Focus word	Child-friendly explanation	Example sentence	Tell me...
'computer-generated images'	Pictures created on the computer.	The characters on this computer game are **computer-generated images**.	Tell me the name of a film/TV programme character that might be a CGI.
character	Characters are the fictional people or animals in plays, TV programmes, films and books.	The main **character** of my story was a rabbit.	Tell me what characters might be in a story set in a castle.
texture	Texture is how something feels; it may have a bumpy, smooth or shiny texture.	The inside of my coat has a fluffy **texture**.	Tell me how you would describe the texture of your school uniform or the clothes you are wearing.

Tune in

Explain that in this lesson the children are going to look in more detail at some words the author has used in the text. Write the three focus words clearly for the children to see. Read the words together. Discuss and explain the child-friendly meaning of each word.

Reread the text. Challenge the children to find the focus words in the text. ('computer-generated images', page 2; 'characters', page 2; 'texture', page 8)

Heads together

Look at the selection of different textured materials. Give the children time to feel each one. Can they describe the texture? Use a range of vocabulary to describe the textures, for example: smooth, bumpy, rough, shiny, fluffy, soft, slippery.

Use Resource sheet: Settings cube. Cut out and make the cube using glue or sticky tape. Roll it like a dice. Can the children think of characters that might be found in this setting? (For example: forest – owl, rabbit, fox; castle – prince, princess, knight, cook, king, queen, butler.) Roll the cube and repeat.

Wrap up

Recap the three focus words by discussing the questions in the 'Tell me' column of the table, above.

Challenge the children to think of a sentence using one of the focus words.

Follow-up independent sessions

You will need

- Resource sheet: Flow chart
- Resource sheet: Settings cube
- Coloured pencils or pens or paints, paper

Using the cards cut from Resource sheet: Flow chart, the children order the pictures to create a flow chart and add their own sentences/captions.

Using the Resource sheet: Settings cube, the children roll the cube and then design/create their own character for this setting. They draw or paint a picture and label the picture with descriptive words.

When Arthur Wouldn't Sleep

Book Band: Orange

This humorous story follows Arthur's bedtime adventures when he visits a place where no one ever sleeps.

Skills focus

- Draw on knowledge of vocabulary to understand texts
- Make inferences from texts
- Predict what might happen on the basis of what has been read so far
- Read words accurately and fluently

Guided reading session

You will need

- Multiple copies of Collins Big Cat *When Arthur Wouldn't Sleep*

Tune in

Introduce the book by asking the children to look closely at the front cover.

Ask the following questions:

- What can you see?
- What is happening in the picture?
- Is it a happy picture? Why?

Read the title aloud, asking children to join in.

Ask: What do you think the story is about?

Turn to the back cover, encouraging the children to follow and join in with you as you read the blurb aloud.

Ask the following questions:

- Do you know of a place where no one goes to sleep?
- What kind of place do you think Arthur finds?
- Do you think it is a real place? Why?

Turn to the title page.

Ask: Who wrote and illustrated the book? *(Joseph Theobald)*

Encourage the children to point to where it tells us this.

Heads together

Tell the children that they are going to read the story on their own.

Ask: What strategies can you use to help you if you get stuck on a word? *(look at the pictures; break down longer words, for example, feel-ing, lady-bird; look for tricky words that you already know)*

Tell the children that when they read, you want them to think about: their reading strategies; changing their voice when someone is speaking; and the answer to the question: 'Where is the place where no one sleeps?'

Ask children to read pages 2 to 17, on their own. As they read, move around the group, listening to each child while the others read in their heads. Check their reading strategies and listen for use of expression as they read.

Wrap up

Identify and praise the children's use of reading strategies that you observed them using to help with reading longer or difficult words and their use of expression.

Ask the following questions:

- Where is the place where no one sleeps? *(See if the children have noticed that Arthur is dreaming – in your dreams, no one sleeps. If not, allow them to describe and discuss the world that Arthur is visiting.)*
- Do you think it is a nice place to visit? Why?

Turn to page 17.

Ask the following questions:

- What do you think happens next in the story?
- How do you think the story ends?

Read pages 18 to 21 together and discuss the ending in the light of the children's predictions.

Vocabulary boost session

You will need

- Multiple copies of Collins Big Cat *When Arthur Wouldn't Sleep*

Vocabulary table

Focus word	Child-friendly explanation	Example sentence	Tell me...
mumble	If you mumble, you speak very quietly and it is hard to understand what you are saying.	"I don't want to go to bed," **mumbled** Jo.	Tell me about a time you have heard someone mumble.
grumble	If you grumble, you say you are not happy about something. You usually say it in an angry way.	Asad **grumbled** about his lunch.	Tell me when you've grumbled about something.
gaze	If you gaze at something, you look at it for a long time or in a way that means you really like it.	When we were at the beach, Mum **gazed** at the sea.	Tell me about something that you would gaze at.

Tune in

Explain to the children that in this lesson they are going to look closely at some of the words the author has used and what those words mean.

Read the book aloud to the children, modelling how to use the punctuation and dialogue to read aloud with expression.

Refer back to each of the focus words within the context of the story, writing up the word, giving a child-friendly explanation and asking the children to say the focus word with you. For example: In the story, Flora mumbles "Ssssh! It's bedtime. Time to go to sleep". If you mumble, you speak very quietly and it is hard to understand what you are saying. Now, say the word with me – 'mumble'.

You may wish to use the examples in the table, above.

Refer to each of the focus words that you have written up and give the children the example sentences. Then ask them to interact with the word meanings by asking the questions in the 'Tell me' column. You may wish to demonstrate by giving some examples of your own.

Ask children to say the words with you once more.

Heads together

Ask the following questions to explore and develop children's understanding of the focus words:

- Which word goes with 'seeing' or 'looking'?
- Which word goes with talking quietly?
- Which word goes with talking unhappily?

For each question, ask children why they answered in that way. Encourage them to make connections with their own lives and experiences.

Wrap up

Ask the following questions to review the word meanings:

- Describe a time when you have mumbled.
- Describe a time when you have grumbled about something.
- Describe a time when you have gazed at something.

Challenge the children to use the focus words as often as they can, both at school and at home.

Follow-up independent sessions

You will need

- Multiple copies of Collins Big Cat *When Arthur Wouldn't Sleep*
- Resource sheet: Where no one sleeps
- Coloured pencils or pens

Ask children to work with their Reading Partners and to read the book aloud, remembering to use their voices to show when a character is talking.

Challenge the children to think of a new place where no one sleeps. Can they draw it and talk with their partner about what happens there?

Ask children to turn to page 22 and read the advert for the place where no one sleeps. Ask them to write an advert about the new place where no one sleeps on Resource sheet: Where no one sleeps.

Marathon

Book Band: Orange

An information book on the history of the marathon, the start and finish of a marathon and its runners and winners.

Skills focus

- Draw on knowledge of vocabulary to understand texts
- Identify/explain key aspects of fiction and non-fiction texts, e.g. character, events, title
- Read words accurately and fluently

Guided reading session

You will need

- Multiple copies of Collins Big Cat *Marathon*

Tune in

Introduce the book by asking a volunteer to read the title.

Ask the following questions:

- What do you know about marathons already?
- Have you seen one or do you know anyone who ran in one?

Encourage them to spend five minutes flicking through the pages to find out what they will learn. Ask children what they discovered.

Ask: Did you look at the headings?

Read a few of the headings with the children. Elicit how these and the pictures are good clues as to what they will learn from the book.

Turn to the contents and point out how this is a list of the main headings.

Ask: What order should we read the pages in? Why?

Point out how you can often read non-fiction books in any order, although turning to page 2 first might be a good idea – to check what a marathon is!

Before turning to page 2, turn to the back cover and focus the children on the blurb.

Ask: Can you suggest how to tackle reading some of the long words here?

Remind the children of ways of breaking words down into syllables (for example, 'running' runn/ing) and into letter sounds (for example, 'thousands' th-ou-s-an-d-s) and then blending.

Heads together

Read pages 2 and 5 aloud to the children, asking them to follow as you read.

Return to the words in bold type and explain that the meanings of these words are in the 'glossary'. Demonstrate finding and reading the glossary definition for 'Ancient Greeks'; then encourage a volunteer to do the same for 'Olympic Games'.

Check the children understand the meaning of 'BC'.

Focus on the word 'incidents' in the photograph on page 5. Read it out letter by letter and give a simple child-friendly explanation if necessary, such as: Incidents are special events that might be reported in newspapers and people are more likely to remember. Car crashes are sometimes called incidents.

Point out how information books are full of facts.

Ask: What facts have we discovered already?

Ask children to read the rest of the book to find out more facts. Ask them to look out for the bit of information or fact that they like the most.

As the children read, listen to each child, supporting them with reading longer or unfamiliar words, such as people's names. Encourage them to reread any sentences where they have stumbled on a word.

Ask occasionally: Have you found an interesting fact on this page?

Wrap up

Ask children which information they found was the most interesting. Ask them to explain it and why they thought it was interesting.

Ask: Were there any words you found difficult to read?

Encourage the children to share ideas on how they tackled any of these words. Read them, together with the sentences that they are in, as a group.

Ask the following questions:

- Did you find the book easy to understand?
- Was the glossary useful?

Discuss whether the children think there should have been more words in the glossary and what the definitions would be.

Focus on and demonstrate using the index. Encourage the children to work in pairs to take it in turns to look something up and read about it to their partner.

Vocabulary boost session

You will need

- Multiple copies of Collins Big Cat *Marathon*

Vocabulary table

Focus word	Child-friendly explanation	Example sentence	Tell me...
imagine (from the blurb)	Imagine means to picture something in your mind, like picturing yourself running a marathon.	I **imagine** how exciting it would be to ride on a camel across a desert.	Tell me about something that you imagine.
incident	An incident is an event that is rare or unusual.	The police arrived when there was an **incident** on the motorway between two cars.	Tell me about an incident you have seen on television or in real life.
nowadays	Nowadays is the present time – today and the days just before and ahead of today.	**Nowadays** nearly everyone has a mobile phone.	Tell me about something people do nowadays.

Tune in

Explain to the children that they are going to look carefully at some of the words in the book and what the words mean.

Read the book aloud to the children, modelling how to break down larger words into smaller words, syllables or sounds.

Point to each of the focus words in the book, read the sentence and write the focus word on the board. Give a child-friendly explanation of the word. For example: Imagine means to picture something in your mind, like picturing yourself running a marathon. Now, say the word with me – 'imagine'.

Child-friendly explanations for the focus words are provided in the table, above.

Give the children example sentences for each focus word, again using those in the table, above, if necessary. Then ask them to think of the word meanings in the context of their own lives by asking them questions from the 'Tell me' column. You could demonstrate by giving some examples of your own.

Ask children to say the words with you again.

Heads together

Ask the following questions to explore and develop the children's understanding of the focus words:

- Do you think a robot can imagine?
- Can incidents be dangerous?
- Do you think people drive horses and carts a lot nowadays?

Encourage them to elaborate on their answers by asking: Why?

Wrap up

Review the word meanings by asking the children which word goes best with the focus word:

- 'imagine': fantasy, happy, running
- 'incident': decision, event, lunch
- 'nowadays': past, future, present

Ask children to choose one of the focus words as their word of the week. Challenge them to use the word as often as they can, both at school and at home.

Follow-up independent sessions

You will need

- Multiple copies of Collins Big Cat *Marathon*
- Resource sheet: Marathon fact file

Encourage the children to look at pages 16–17 and then design and draw their own charity outfit for a marathon. Ask them to include the name of their charity (which they could make up) and to remember that they would have to be able to run in the outfit and wear it for many hours.

Ask children to use Resource sheet: Marathon fact file, to gather their favourite information from the book. Encourage them to find the facts in the body of the book rather than copy facts from page 22. They could research additional facts if there is an opportunity to do so, too.

Bugs!

Book Band: Orange

A poem (with rhyming words) all about the good and bad things bugs do.

Skills focus

- Draw on knowledge of vocabulary to understand texts
- Identify/explain key aspects of fiction and non-fiction texts, e.g. character, events, title
- Identify/explain the sequence of events in texts
- Read words accurately and fluently

Guided reading session

You will need

- Multiple copies of Collins Big Cat *Bugs!*
- Resource sheet: Rhyming words for *Bugs!*
- Mini-whiteboards and pens

Tune in

Begin with a rhyming words activity. Use the words from Resource sheet: Rhyming words for *Bugs!*, to practise reading the words. Recap some of the digraphs: 'ee', 'ea', 'ou', 'er', 'ay', 'ow', 'air', 'ear'. Ask children to match the rhyming words. You could extend the activity by asking them to pick one of the words and to write more words to rhyme with it on their mini-whiteboards, for example: 'me' rhymes with 'be', 'tea', 'sea', 'Lee', 'he', 'we'.

Explain to the children that they are going to read a poem using these rhyming words. Challenge the children to look out for the rhyming words.

Explore the front cover together.

Ask the following questions:

- Do the bugs look friendly?
- What do bugs do?
- Are bugs bad or good?
- Can you think of any other names for bugs? (germs, bacteria, infections)

Turn the book over to read the blurb. Model reading the blurb using fluency and accuracy.

Ask the following questions:

- From whose point of view is the poem written? (the bugs')
- Which words rhyme? (see, me)

Discuss how small bugs are and that we cannot see them.

Ask: Do you think bugs are useful in any way?

Turn to the title page. Recap the role of an author and illustrator. Find out who wrote and illustrated this poem. (Sam McBratney and Eric Smith)

Recap the strategies the children can use in their reading: decoding; picture clues; identifying high frequency words; checking for sense.

Heads together

Read pages 2 and 3. Model reading using fluency and expression and focus on the rhythm of the poem. Discuss the picture of the bugs.

Ask the following questions:

- What colours/shapes are there?
- Do the bugs look friendly or fierce?
- What do you think bugs look like?

Continue on to pages 4 and 5 together. Ask children to join in with the reading.

Ask: Can you point out the rhyming words? (everywhere/air, underground/found, hair/wear)

Discuss compound words in the text: 'every/where', 'in/doors', 'out/doors', 'under/ground'.

Ask: Why are there magnifying glasses in the picture? (Because the bugs are so very tiny, you can't see them with the naked eye.)

Ask children to work in pairs to read pages 6 to 20 of the poem. Encourage them to support each other and read aloud. Can they find out what bugs do? Can they find the rhyming words?

Wrap up

Reread the poem to the group using fluency and accuracy and focus on the rhythm of the poem. Ask children what the bugs do. Make a list of all the things bugs do. Encourage children to look back through the book to check. Then add a tick or a cross to each item on the list to show if it is a good or a bad thing.

Turn to pages 22 and 23. Discuss each picture – what does it show? Compare it to the chart/list you have made as a group – is it the same?

Ask the following questions:
- What do you think of bugs now? Are they all bad?

- What do you need to do to protect yourself from bugs? *(Wash your hands after using the toilet and before eating.)*
- How do you wash your hands properly? *(soap, water, dry)*

Vocabulary boost session

You will need
- Multiple copies of Collins Big Cat *Bugs!*
- A washing-up bowl, soap and warm water, paper towels
- Example posters on how to wash your hands properly and how to clean your teeth

Vocabulary table

Focus word	Child-friendly explanation	Example sentence	Tell me...
decay	If something is decaying, it is falling apart and breaking down.	Clean your teeth to stop tooth **decay**.	Tell me why it is important to clean your teeth.
infection	Bugs can cause an infection making you unwell or stopping a cut from healing.	I had an ear **infection**.	Tell me if you have ever had an infection.
microscopic	Something very small which can only be seen through a microscope.	Bugs are **microscopic**.	Tell me what you think microscopes are used for.

Tune in

Explain that in this lesson the children are going to look in more detail at some words linked to the text. Write the three focus words clearly for the children to see. Read the words together. Discuss and explain the child-friendly meaning of each word.

Reread the text.

Challenge children to find the focus word 'decay' (on pages 14 and 16).

Explain that the bugs are microscopic.

Heads together

Discuss different words for 'small' and create a word bank, for example: small, tiny, mini, miniature, microscopic, little, baby, miniscule.

Talk about tooth decay and how to clean our teeth twice a day.

Explore how we can avoid tummy infections by washing our hands properly. Using a bowl of water, soap and paper towels let the children practise washing their hands properly. In pairs, the children can talk each other through how to wash their hands thoroughly.

Wrap up

Recap the three focus words by discussing the questions in the 'Tell me' column of the table, above.

Challenge the children to think of a sentence using one of the focus words.

Follow-up independent sessions

You will need
- Poster paper, coloured pencils or pens
- Resource sheet: Good and bad
- A selection of poetry books for children
- Microscope and magnifying glasses and a selection of items to look at closely

Ask children to design and create a 'wash your hands' poster to display in the school cloakrooms.

Hand out cards cut from Resource sheet: Good and bad. The children sort the pictures into 'good things bugs do' and 'bad things bugs do'. They then write sentences to match each picture.

Let the children read and explore a selection of poetry and poetry books.

Let the children explore using a microscope and magnifying glasses, either investigating small things or looking at items in detail.

A Day in India

Book Band: Orange

This non-fiction recount follows Gini through a day in her life in Jaipur and reveals what it's like to live in India today.

Skills focus

- Draw on knowledge of vocabulary to understand texts
- Identify/explain key aspects of fiction and non-fiction texts, e.g. character, events, title
- Identify/explain the sequence of events in texts
- Check reading makes sense

Guided reading session

You will need

- Multiple copies of Collins Big Cat *A Day in India*
- Mini-whiteboards and pens

Tune in

Ask children to look closely at the front cover of the book.

Ask the following questions:

- What sort of book is this? *(non-fiction)*
- What clues are there to tell us? *(title and photograph)*
- Where else can we look to help us? *(back cover blurb)*

Turn to and read the blurb. Model how to read 'Jaipur' and explain that it is a large city in India.

If necessary, explain that non-fiction books give information about things, whereas fiction books are stories that are made up and we need to use our imagination when we read them.

Turn to the contents and explain that each entry is the heading of a section in the book.

Ask: What do you notice about how the contents is organised? *(by page number)*

Explain that the first section ('Where I live' on page 2) should give an introduction to the rest of the book. Ask children to turn to page 2 and to identify the heading. Read the text on page 2 aloud. Explain that, in non-fiction books, we are given information in words and through pictures. Point out the map and the two photographs. Identify the labels on the map and the caption on the photograph on page 3. Establish that the labels tell us which country is India and where Jaipur is in India. The caption tells us where the photo was taken and what it shows.

Ask: Who do you think the girl in the photo is? *(Gini)*

Make the connection between the information in the text and the photo.

Return to the contents.

Ask: How is Gini's day organised? *(chronologically, starting in the morning and ending with bedtime)*

Ask children to find and turn to the index (page 21).

Explain that an index is always near the back of a book.

Ask: What do you notice about the entries in the index? *(single words, alphabetical order)*

Establish that we use an index to help us to quickly find information about something. Challenge the children to find the entry for 'cows' and demonstrate how to flick to page 15. Once the children have found page 15, challenge them to find the word 'cow' and 'cows' in the text. If necessary, remind them to look at the caption as well.

Ask children to look at pages 14 and 15 and to identify how we are being given information (text, photos, caption, label).

Ask: Is there a heading on these pages? *(no)*

Model how to flick back to the previous pages and identify the heading 'Home time'. Establish that the information on pages 14 and 15 is all part of the section on 'Home time'.

Ask children to work with their Reading Partners and on their mini-whiteboards to list the non-fiction features that they have come across so far in the book: headings, text, photographs, map, labels, captions. Write these up on the board and ask children to clean their whiteboards.

Heads together

Ask children to return to the contents and choose a section they would like to read. They can read their section and list the non-fiction features on their mini-whiteboards.

Wrap up

Ask children to hold up their whiteboards so you can check the non-fiction features they have found.

Ask the following questions:

- Did anything in the section you read remind you of things that you do during the day?
- Was there anything that was different?

Encourage the children to refer to the book as they respond to your questions.

Vocabulary boost session

You will need
- Multiple copies of Collins Big Cat *A Day in India*
- Mini-whiteboards and pens

Vocabulary table

Focus word	Child-friendly explanation	Example sentence	Tell me...
wander	If you wander, you move around slowly.	I **wandered** through the market.	Tell me about a time when you might wander around.
whizz	If you whizz, you move around quickly.	I **whizzed** around the supermarket.	Tell me about a time when you might whizz somewhere.
chatting	If you are chatting, you are talking.	Mum was **chatting** to her friend.	Tell me what you might be chatting about.

Tune in

Explain to the children that you noticed some words that you think the authors have chosen very carefully because the words add to the information that we are being given. On the board write up the three focus words.

Challenge the children to quickly find the word 'wander' (page 8) and to read the sentence in which it appears. Ask them to turn to page 15 and to find 'wander' on that page.

Ask: On page 8, who wanders? *(Gini and her aunt)*

This response means that the children have to read back to page 7 to identify who the pronoun 'we' refers to.

Ask the following questions:
- On page 15, what wanders. *(cows)*
- What do you think 'wander' means? *(to walk about slowly, to walk about with no real purpose)*

Demonstrate 'wander' by moving slowly around the classroom, pausing every now and then. Repeat this activity with the word 'whizz'.

Heads together

Move to an open space and encourage the children to join in with wandering and whizzing.

Ask the following questions:
- What is the difference between wandering and whizzing?
- How do you feel when you wander?
- How do you feel when you whizz?

Use the 'Tell me' prompts from the table, above, to develop the children's understanding of the meaning of the words. Encourage them to explain why they might wander or whizz. Establish that if you wander, you move around without a real reason or purpose. When you whizz, you move around quickly.

Focus on the word 'chatting' and use the 'Tell me' prompt to encourage them to think about something that they might chat about.

Wrap up

Ask children to work with their Reading Partners and to create three sentences on their whiteboards that each include one of the focus words.

Check the sentences that they have written to monitor understanding of the meanings of the words.

Ask them to choose one of the focus words as their word of the week. Challenge them to use it as often as they can, both at school and at home, over the coming week.

Follow-up independent sessions

You will need
- Multiple copies of Collins Big Cat *A Day in India*
- Resource sheet: Spidergram

Ask children to look at the spidergram on pages 22 and 23. Ask them to choose something that Gini likes and to use the contents and index to find the section that gives more information about it. Ask them to read the section and to note down why she likes that thing.

You may wish to demonstrate this process using the example 'lassi' on page 11. *(Gini likes it because it is delicious, especially when the weather is hot.)*

Hand out copies of Resource sheet: Spidergram. Ask children to work with their Reading Partners and to create their own spidergram of 'Things I like about where I live', drawing on the content of the book for ideas and examples. Once they have completed their spidergram, each pair can share it with the rest of the group, explaining what they chose to include and why.

The Titanic

Book Band: Orange

The *Titanic* set sail for America in 1912, but never arrived. This information book explores what happened to the ship and her passengers on that tragic voyage.

Skills focus

- Draw on knowledge of vocabulary to understand texts
- Identify/explain key aspects of fiction and non-fiction texts, e.g. character, events, title
- Identify/explain the sequence of events in texts
- Read words accurately and fluently

Guided reading session

You will need
- Multiple copies of Collins Big Cat *The Titanic*

Tune in

Introduce the book by encouraging the children to look closely at the front cover.

Ask the following questions:
- What do you think the book is about?
- What kind of book do you think this is, information or story? *(information)*
- What makes you think that?

Ask children to point to the title of the book; then read it aloud together.

Ask the following questions:
- Have you ever heard of the *Titanic*?
- Does anyone know anything about it?

Turn to the back cover and read the blurb aloud, encouraging the children to follow and join in with you.

Ask the following questions before you turn to the title page:
- Can you name the features of an information book? *(contents list, photographs, captions, labels, glossary, index)*
- Where in the book can we find the contents list? *(title page)*

Turn to the title page for the contents list and check for the glossary and the index.

Heads together

Before you start reading tell the children that you will be focusing on reading strategies for this session, that is, recognising tricky words, blending phonemes to read longer words and breaking words up, for example, 'ship/builders', 'South/ampton'. You will also focus on the order of events in the recount of what happened to the *Titanic*.

Tell the children that the word 'passenger' comes up a lot. Write the word on the board.

Ask: What does 'passenger' mean? *(somebody who travelled on the boat)*

Read the word together.

Ask children to read up to page 20 alone. As they read, move around the group, listening to each child. If necessary, support them in reading longer words and observe their use of the range of strategies.

Wrap up

Ask the following questions to check the children's understanding:
- What happened to the *Titanic*? *(It hit an iceberg and sank.)*
- Can you use the book to help you to put the events in order – what happened first? Next? After that?

Turn to pages 22 and 23 and use these pages to check the order of events.

Ask the following questions:
- Where is the *Titanic* now? *(on the seabed)*
- What do you think about the *Titanic*?
- Do you think that this is a good information book? Why?

Vocabulary boost session

You will need

- Multiple copies of Collins Big Cat *The Titanic*

Vocabulary table

Focus word	Child-friendly explanation	Example sentence	Tell me...
flooded	If something is flooded, it is covered with water.	The playground was **flooded** after it rained all night.	Tell me about a flood that you have seen.
doomed	If something is doomed, it means something bad is going to happen or it won't go well.	Outdoor play was **doomed** because of the thunderstorm.	Tell me about the kind of things that would happen to doom playtime.
disaster	A disaster is a very bad accident or something very bad that happens.	The train crash was a **disaster**.	Tell me about a disaster that you know about.

Tune in

Explain to the children that in this lesson they are going to look closely at some of the words the author has used and what those words mean.

Read the book aloud to the children, asking them to follow and join in as you read.

Refer back to each of the focus words within the context of the story, writing up the word, giving a child-friendly explanation and asking the children to say the focus word with you. For example: The book talks about how the *Titanic* was flooded with icy seawater. If something is flooded, it is covered with water. Now, say the word with me – 'flooded'.

You may wish to use the examples in the table, above.

Refer to each of the focus words that you have written up and give the children the example sentences. Then ask them to interact with the word meanings by asking the questions in the 'Tell me' column. You may wish to demonstrate by giving some examples of your own.

Ask children to say the words with you once more.

Heads together

Explain to the children that they are going to do a thinking activity (word associations). They are going to come up with words that make us think of and remember what the focus words mean.

Take each of the following words in turn and ask children to call out words that pop into their heads when you say them:

- flooded (water, wet, cold, sad, sea, river)
- doomed (bad, trouble, accident, sad)
- disaster (ship sinking, plane crashing, bad, accident)

Encourage the children to make links to their own lives and experiences to help them.

Wrap up

Review the word meanings by doing the following activity.

Turn to page 10 of the book.

Ask the following questions:

- It says that the seawater 'flooded' in. Can you tell me what this means?
- It says the *Titanic* was 'doomed'. Can you tell me what doomed means?

Turn to page 18 of the book.

Ask: It says 'the *Titanic* disaster'. Can you tell me what disaster means?

Ask children to choose one of the focus words as their word of the week. Challenge them to use the word as often as they can, both at school and at home.

Follow-up independent sessions

You will need

- Multiple copies of Collins Big Cat *The Titanic*
- Resource sheet: Glossary words for *The Titanic*

Ask children to work with their Reading Partners and to read the book aloud.

Hand out copies of Resource sheet: Glossary words for *The Titanic*. Ask children to complete the three activities.

Pompeii The Lost City

Book Band: Orange

This information book looks at the history of Pompeii, including its destruction and discovery and the world-famous remains today.

Skills focus

- Draw on knowledge of vocabulary to understand texts
- Identify/explain key aspects of fiction and non-fiction texts, e.g. character, events, title
- Check reading makes sense

Guided reading session

You will need

- Multiple copies of Collins Big Cat *Pompeii The Lost City*

Tune in

Introduce the book by looking together at the cover and reading the title with the children.

Ask: Why do you think it is 'lost'?

Ask children if anyone is familiar with Pompeii and its history and to explain or describe what they already know.

Ask children to turn to the contents page. Read the list aloud with them and then ask them to read it with you. Focus on the word 'volcano' and discuss its meaning: a mountain made from rock that has melted and from which more molten rock might burst.

Point to the word 'timeline' near the bottom of the contents and discuss what it is, pointing out as a clue that it is made from two words: 'time/line'.

Ask children which sections in the contents look the most interesting and why.

Heads together

Demonstrate using the contents to find 'A fine city'. Read pages 2 and 3 aloud to the children.

Ask: Does the text make sense?

Encourage the children to discuss the connection between the volcano and the city and what the maps show.

Remind them of what they discussed about volcanoes and point to the bold type on page 3. Explain that this links to a glossary where they can check the meaning of the word.

Read the glossary definition for 'volcano' and ask if it makes sense against what they already know about volcanoes.

Point to the labels on pages 2 and 3, asking what these are called.

Ask: Are they different to captions?

Elicit how captions are often longer than labels and how labels usually have pointer rules to different parts of a picture.

Ask children to read the rest of the book in pairs, challenging them to find out what happened to Pompeii. Remind them to read the glossary definitions and the captions and labels too.

Move around the pairs, checking that the children take turns to read a sentence or page. Encourage them to check their understanding by looking for information in the picture or other text on the page to see that it makes sense.

Support the children with simple definitions of any unfamiliar words.

Wrap up

Using the timeline and pictures on pages 22 and 23 as a prompt, ask pairs of children to take it in turns to explain what happened in time order. Encourage the listeners to look back at the relevant pages to check that they are correct.

Reread any pages as a group where the children disagree on what happened.

To check children's understanding suggest that they hold a quiz. Give the children time to think of a question and note the page where the answer can be found. To begin the quiz:

Ask: How many people lived in Pompeii? *(about 20,000)*

If the children can't find the answer, give them the page number as a clue (page 4). The first to answer asks the next question.

Continue in this way, discussing answers and checking them by rereading relevant pages if necessary.

Vocabulary boost session

You will need

- Multiple copies of Collins Big Cat *Pompeii The Lost City*

Vocabulary table

Focus word	Child-friendly explanation	Example sentence	Tell me...
ancient	Ancient means a long time ago, like the Egyptians who built pyramids and the Romans who rode chariots.	The **ancient** building had crumbled over hundreds of years.	Tell me about anything ancient you have seen.
massive	Massive means very, very large rather than just big.	There was a **massive** clap of thunder that shook the whole town.	Tell me about anything massive you have seen or read about.
terrified	Terrified means very frightened rather than a bit scared.	The **terrified** people ran away screaming when they saw the monster.	Tell me about a time when you, or a story character, were terrified.

Tune in

Tell the children to follow the words closely as you read the book to them.

Next, ask them to read the book with you, letting them take the lead. Stop when they stumble over a word and segment it into letter sounds or syllables to help them work it out.

Point to each focus word in the text and write it on the board. Give an easy explanation for each word in child-friendly language. You can use the explanations in the table, above, or your own. Ask children to say the focus word with you afterwards.

Next, for each word, give them an example sentence that incorporates the word. Use those in the table above or make up your own.

To encourage the children to use the words in the context of their own experiences, challenge them with the 'Tell me' questions in the table, above.

You could support them by offering your own answer, for example: "I saw an ancient castle on the television."

Finally, ask children to say the words with you again.

Heads together

Ask the following questions to explore and develop the children's understanding of the focus words:

- Which is more likely be ancient – a plastic toy or a stone statue?
- What might you describe as massive – a mountain or a hill?
- What might terrify people – a book or a film?

Encourage them to elaborate on their answers by asking: Why?

Wrap up

Review the word meanings by asking the children which words are closest in meaning:

- ancient: old, elderly, antique, worn
- massive: big, gigantic, impressive, amazing
- terrified: scared, horrified, nervous, shy

Put the focus words on the wall and ask children to test a friend on the meaning of one each day.

Follow-up independent sessions

You will need

- Multiple copies of Collins Big Cat *Pompeii The Lost City*
- Resource sheet: The eruption!
- Resource sheet: Visit Pompeii!

Ask children to think about what the people might be saying in the scene on Resource sheet: The eruption! They could use their ideas to act out a scene in which the people of Pompeii see the volcano begin to erupt.

Challenge the children to design an advert that encourages tourists to come to Pompeii. They can use the Resource sheet: Visit Pompeii! for ideas for the texts and the book itself for images to copy.

Lost Sock

Book Band: Orange

A delightful story about a boy who has lost his lucky sock. But Grandad knows just where it is! It's gone to sock land...

Skills focus

- Draw on knowledge of vocabulary to understand texts
- Make inferences from texts
- Predict what might happen on the basis of what has been read so far
- Check reading makes sense

Guided reading session

You will need

- Multiple copies of Collins Big Cat *Lost Sock*
- A pile of clean socks! (a mixture of big, small, thick, thin, long, short, stripy, spotty, patterned, plain and so on.)
- Mini-whiteboards and pens

Tune in

Tip a pile of socks on to the table! Ask children to discuss the socks. What colours are there? What patterns? Are they thick or thin? Are they soft or itchy? Can they describe the socks? Ask children to write words to describe the socks on their whiteboards.

Ask the following questions:

- What different types of socks do you have? *(for example: football socks, ballet socks, slipper socks, welly socks, school socks)*
- Do you have a favourite pair of socks?

Introduce the book by looking at the front cover. Read the title together by segmenting and blending l-o-s-t s-o-ck. Ask children to predict what might have happened to the sock; where could the sock have gone?

Ask:

- Has anyone ever lost a sock?
- Did you find it?
- Where was it?
- How do you think the boy on the front cover is feeling? *(sad, cross, annoyed, frustrated, upset)*

Turn the book over and read the blurb together, encouraging the children to join in. Point out the 'ck' digraph in 'sock' and 'lucky'. Discuss the apostrophe in 'isn't' and 'can't'. Do the children know 'isn't' = 'is not' and 'can't' = 'cannot'? Explore other contractions such as: don't, haven't, couldn't, wouldn't, shouldn't.

Heads together

Begin by sharing pages 2 and 3 together. Model reading and encourage the children to point to each word and join in where they can. Discuss the apostrophe in 'they're'. Do the children know 'they're' = 'they are'?

Give children one minute to find out their Reading Partner's favourite colour and why; then feed back to the rest of the group. For example: My partner Lucy's favourite colour is yellow because it reminds her of sunshine and the sand.

Can the children predict what will happen next?

Ask the following questions:

- Why do you think his socks are his favourites?
- What do you think will happen to his socks?

Recap strategies the children can use when reading.

Ask children to read aloud pages 4 to 17 independently and to point at each word. Listen to children read and support where needed.

Ask the following questions:

- Can you find out what happened to the sock? *(it gets lost)*
- Where does the boy look? *(in the wash basket, under his bed)*

Encourage them to consider the boy's feelings at each point in the story.

Wrap up

Model reading pages 4 to 17 fluently. Look at pages 16 and 17.

Ask the following questions:

- How do you think the boy is feeling?
- What might cheer him up?
- What do you think is in the present?

Read pages 18 to 20. Discuss the character Grandad. How would the children describe him?

Ask: What do you think about Grandad? *(He is thoughtful because he gets the boy a present.)*

Explore the posters on pages 22 and 23.

Ask: What are the posters for?

Ask children to work in pairs. Give each pair a sock from the pile and ask them to write a brief description of it on their whiteboard. Read the descriptions aloud – can the group find the socks being described?

Vocabulary boost session

You will need

- Multiple copies of Collins Big Cat *Lost Sock*

Vocabulary table

Focus word	Child-friendly explanation	Example sentence	Tell me...
favourite	If something is your favourite, then it is your best or the thing you like most.	My **favourite** colour is pale blue.	Tell me what is your favourite food.
probably	Probably means most likely.	I will **probably** go swimming on the weekend.	Tell me something that will probably happen tomorrow.
vanished	If something has vanished, it has disappeared or gone missing.	The sock had **vanished**! I couldn't find it anywhere.	Tell me what things you have lost.

Tune in

Explain that in this lesson the children are going to look in more detail at some words linked to the text. Write the three focus words clearly for the children to see. Read the words together. Discuss and explain the child-friendly meaning of each word.

Reread the text.

Ask children to find the words 'favourite' and 'probably' in the text.

Challenge the children to find a word that means the same as 'vanished'.

Heads together

Working as a group, ask children to think of all the words that mean 'vanished'. Write their suggestions on the board; prompt if needed. (For example: disappeared, missing, lost, gone, extinct, misplaced, no longer here.)

Say a sentence to the children and ask them to decide if it will 'probably happen tomorrow' or if it will be 'unlikely to happen tomorrow'. For example:

- It will snow.
- The Queen will visit the school.
- There will be an assembly in the school hall.
- You will play in the playground.
- You will clean your teeth.
- You will visit a castle.

Wrap up

The children work in pairs to role-play a newspaper reporter interviewing a child about the vanishing sock; challenge them to use all three focus words.

Recap the three focus words by discussing the questions in the 'Tell me' column of the table, above.

Follow-up independent sessions

You will need

- Old clean socks, googly eyes, pom-poms, sequins, buttons, felt, pipe cleaners, glue, scissors
- Paints, pencils, paper
- Resource sheet: My lucky sock
- Resource sheet: Match the contractions to the words

Ask children to make a sock puppet (see 'You will need' list) and to use the puppet to tell stories.	They should record this on Resource sheet: My lucky sock.
Let the children paint a picture of the Sock Land setting in the story or draw a map of the setting in the story.	Ask children to create a poster to collect smelly socks to feed the hungry dragon.
Ask children to design their own lucky socks. What colour would they be? What pattern would they have on them? What material would they be made from?	More able children could write a story about visiting Sock Land or a description of Sock Land.
	Hand out copies of the cards cut from Resource sheet: Match the contractions to the words and ask children to complete the activity.

Clementine's Smile

Book Band: Orange

In this rhyming text, Clementine the crocodile pays a visit to the dentist and swallows him whole! Luckily, the dentist is rescued and is able to give Clementine some advice about caring for her teeth.

Skills focus

- Draw on knowledge of vocabulary to understand texts
- Make inferences from texts
- Predict what might happen on the basis of what has been read so far
- Read words accurately and fluently

Guided reading session

You will need

- Multiple copies of Collins Big Cat *Clementine's Smile*

Tune in

Ask children to look closely at the front cover of the book and to read the title.

Ask the following questions:

- Can you identify the animal on the cover? *(a crocodile)*
- What do you know about crocodiles?
- Where can we find more information about what is in the book? *(back cover blurb)*

Turn to the back cover and read the blurb to the children, emphasising the rhythm and rhyme. Focus on the final two sentences in the blurb.

Ask: Where would you go if you had a sore tooth? *(dentist)*

Explore children's experience of dentists.

Ask: What do you think is going to happen in the book?

Note down the children's predictions on the board, encouraging them to support their predictions with reasons and evidence. If necessary, model how to make predictions by drawing on knowledge of stories and using personal experience.

Ask children to revisit the front and back cover and to spot the words 'Clementine' and 'Clementine's'. Challenge them to tell you what the difference is between the two words. If appropriate, explain the use of the possessive apostrophe in 'Clementine's'.

Heads together

Ask children to turn to page 2 and to follow as you read. Read to page 8, using the rhythm, rhyme, dialogue and meaning to help you read with fluency and expression. Pause at the end of page 8.

Ask the following questions:

- What has happened so far?
- Is that what you thought would happen?
- How do you think Clementine's friends feel about her?
- Why do you think Clementine is saying that she's fine?

Establish that Clementine doesn't seem to want to go to the dentist.

Ask: What do you think is going to happen next?

Note down the children's predictions on the board, encouraging them to support their predictions with reasons and evidence.

Ask children to read to page 19 to find out whether their predictions were correct. Remind them to try to read with expression, just as you demonstrated.

As they read, move around the group, commenting positively on children who are using expression when they read.

Remind them, if necessary, why they are reading.

Wrap up

Take feedback from the reading, asking the children to say what has happened.

Refer to the predictions on the board.

Ask the following questions:

- Were you right about what you thought would happen?
- Why do you think Clementine ate the dentist?
- How do you think the dentist felt after Mum pulled him free?

Read pages 20 and 21 aloud to the children.

Ask: Why do you think the dentist hopes that Clementine won't be back soon? *(because she ate him)*

Establish that thinking about what might happen in a book, before and during reading, can help to understand what is happening.

Vocabulary boost session

You will need

- Multiple copies of Collins Big Cat *Clementine's Smile*

Vocabulary table

Focus word	Child-friendly explanation	Example sentence	Tell me...
sparkling	If something is sparkling, it is very shiny.	The sequins on her dress were **sparkling** in the sunlight.	Tell me about something that is sparkling.
painful	If something is painful, it hurts a lot.	My thumb is very **painful**.	Tell me about something that might be painful.
resist	If you can't resist something, you have to do it.	I can't **resist** eating chocolate cake!	Tell me about something that you can't resist doing.

Tune in

Explain to the children that when authors write stories and poems, they choose the words that they use very carefully and that sometimes these words are more unusual than words we use when we talk.

Explain that in this lesson they are going to be looking at some of these words and what they mean.

Read the text aloud, using expression to help the children understand the content. When you read the focus words, give a brief explanation of their meanings using the information in the table, above.

Once you have finished reading, write up the three focus words on the board and once more explain the meanings of the words.

Heads together

Refer to the focus words on the board.

Ask: Which of these words do you know?

Encourage the children to help you to write up sentences that contain the focus words, for example: The sunshine is sparkling in the puddles. I bumped my arm and it is very painful. The strawberries looked so juicy that I couldn't resist eating one.

Write up 'Tell me' on the board and explain that you'd like the children to think of an example of each of the focus words that they can talk about with their Reading Partner. Demonstrate by giving a couple of examples of your own, for example: Something that is sparkling is the sea when it is sunny. Something that might be painful is if I fell off my chair. Something I can't resist is singing really loudly when I have the radio on in my car.

Give the children time to think about their 'Tell me' examples and to share them with their Reading Partner.

Wrap up

Ask each pair to feed back on the 'Tell me' examples that they came up with. Encourage the rest of the group to ask questions, for example: Why can't you resist singing really loudly?

Ask children to choose one of the focus words as their word of the week and challenge them to use it as often as they can – both at home and at school.

Follow-up independent sessions

You will need

- Multiple copies of Collins Big Cat *Clementine's Smile*
- Resource sheet: Story map for *Clementine's Smile*
- Coloured pencils or pens

Ask children to reread the book aloud to their Reading Partner, taking it in turns to read a page each. Encourage them to think about using expression as they read.

With their Reading Partner, children can use Resource sheet: Story map for *Clementine's Smile*, to create a story map that shows the main events in the poem.

Ask them to use their story maps to retell the poem together and then to think about how Clementine was feeling at different points. Encourage them to note down Clementine's feelings on their story maps.

Slumbery Stumble in the Jungle

Book Band: Orange

In this adventure story, Monkey saves the jungle from a big yellow monster and shows the other animals that he is brave and clever.

Skills focus

- Draw on knowledge of vocabulary to understand texts
- Make inferences from texts
- Predict what might happen on the basis of what has been read so far
- Read accurately and fluently

Guided reading session

You will need

- Multiple copies of Collins Big Cat *Slumbery Stumble in the Jungle*

Tune in

Introduce the book by reading the title to the children.

Ask the following questions:

- Does anyone know what 'slumber' is?
- Can you guess?

Encourage them to look carefully at the picture.

Ask the following questions:

- Who do you think the character is?
- Where do you think it is?
- Can you guess (predict) what kind of character it is?
- What do you think the story could be about?

Encourage the children to point to the title of the book; then read it aloud again, asking them to read it aloud with you.

Turn to the back cover and read the blurb aloud, encouraging the children to follow and join in with you.

Ask the following questions:

- What do you think it means by 'the forest is getting smaller'?
- Apart from a monster, could the 'big yellow monster' be something else? What?
- Do you think that the story has a happy ending? What makes you think that?

Heads together

Tell the children that they are going to read the story on their own. While they are reading you would like them to be thinking about what might happen next in the story (predict). You want them to think particularly about what or who the big yellow monster is and how the story is going to end.

Ask: What strategies can you use to help you if you get stuck on a word? *(look at the pictures, blend phonemes, look for words in words, segment words into syllables)*

Ask children to read pages 2 to 21, on their own. As they read, move around the group, listening to each child while the others read in their heads. Check their reading strategies, listen for use of expression as they read and, if appropriate, ask a prediction question.

Wrap up

Identify and praise children's use of reading strategies that you observed them using to help with reading longer or difficult words and their use of expression.

Ask the following questions:

- Did anyone think about what or who the big yellow monster was?
- Were you right?
- Did you predict the ending? (All predictions should be valued, even if they are not in line with your thinking.)

Explain that you are going to ask children some 'clue' questions about the story. They will have to think about them – the answers aren't right there in the story.

Ask the following questions:

- Do you think that the other animals in the jungle like Monkey? What makes you think that?
- Do you think that Monkey is a good sleeper? Why?
- Do you think that Monkey is brave? Why?
- At the end of the story, do you think that the animals change their minds about Monkey? What makes you think that?

Vocabulary boost session

You will need

- Multiple copies of Collins Big Cat *Slumbery Stumble in the Jungle*

Vocabulary table

Focus word	Child-friendly explanation	Example sentence	Tell me...
gentle	Someone who is gentle is kind. They don't fight and they touch things softly.	We had to be very **gentle** when we played with the baby.	Tell me about a time when you are gentle.
scared	If you are scared of someone or something, you are frightened of them.	Jen is **scared** of wasps.	Tell me about something that you are scared of.
brave	Someone who is brave doesn't feel as frightened as others or doesn't show it if they are feeling frightened or upset.	John was **brave** when the wasp flew near to him.	Tell me about a time when you have been brave.

Tune in

Explain to the children that in this lesson they are going to look closely at some of the words the author has used and what those words mean.

Read the book aloud to the children, modelling how to use the punctuation and dialogue to read aloud with expression.

Refer back to each of the focus words within the context of the story, writing up the word, giving a child-friendly explanation and asking the children to say the focus word with you. For example: In the story, there is a gentle wind blowing. If something or someone is gentle, they touch things softly. Now, say the word with me – 'gentle'.

You may wish to use the examples in the table, above.

Refer to each of the focus words that you have written up and give the children the example sentences. Then ask them to interact with the word meanings by asking the questions in the 'Tell me' column. You may wish to demonstrate by giving some examples of your own.

Ask children to say the words with you once more.

Heads together

Ask the following questions to explore and develop the children's understanding of the focus words:

- If I am in a garden, am I being gentle when I touch the flowers or climb the trees? Can you mime being gentle when you touch something?
- If I am on the playground and I think a ball is going to hit me, I feel scared. Can you mime feeling scared?
- If I am on the playground and a ball hits me, I might be brave about it. Can you mime being brave after something like that has happened?

Wrap up

Ask the following questions to review the word meanings:

- Can you explain what 'gentle' means?
- Can you explain what 'scared' means?
- Can you explain what 'brave' means?

Challenge the children to use the focus words as often as they can, both at school and at home.

Follow-up independent sessions

You will need

- Multiple copies of Collins Big Cat *Slumbery Stumble in the Jungle*
- Resource sheet: Animal names
- Coloured pencils or pens

Ask children to work with their Reading Partners and to read the book aloud, remembering to use their voices to show when a character is talking.

Hand out copies of Resource sheet: Animal names. Ask children to name the animals in the story.

Turtle's Party in the Clouds

Book Band: Orange

All the birds decide to have a party in the clouds and Turtle finds a way to join them, but will he be safe?

Skills focus

- Draw on knowledge of vocabulary to understand texts
- Make inferences from texts
- Predict what might happen on the basis of what has been read so far
- Check reading makes sense

Guided reading session

You will need
- Multiple copies of Collins Big Cat *Turtle's Party in the Clouds*

Tune in

Introduce the book by beginning with its title. Ask children to point to the title on the front cover as you read it aloud.

Ask: Does 'a party in the clouds' make sense? Let's look at the picture to check.

Ask children to look at the picture on the front cover.

Ask the following questions:
- Which is Turtle?
- Can you see clouds?

Turn to the back cover and read the blurb together. Help the children break down the longer words into parts, then blend to aid their reading (with/out, un/fort/un/ate/ly).

Discuss the blurb and ask the following questions:
- Do you think all goes well for Turtle?
- Which words make you think it might not go well? ('but', 'unfortunately', 'didn't')

Turn back to the front cover and ask children to 'jump' into the picture. If they were there, what might they be afraid of?

Ask children to predict what might happen in the story. Will Turtle get to the party and what will happen next?

Heads together

Read pages 2 to 5 expressively, with the children following the words closely. Return to longer words they might be unfamiliar with, breaking them down, then asking the children to read them with you.

Point out the words in capitals on page 4.

Ask the following questions:
- Why are these words in capital letters? *(for emphasis)*
- What does it tell us about how Turtle said these words?

Elicit how it means we read these words more loudly. Demonstrate reading 'PLEASE take me!' with and then without emphasis. Ask how each version makes the children feel.

Reread the pages again, but this time together and with the spoken words of Turtle and Vulture allocated to separate groups of children or individuals.

Ask the following questions:
- How would you have felt if you were Tortoise?
- Do you think Vulture was right to call Turtle 'silly'? Why?

Read page 6 with the children, emphasising the words in italics.

Ask: What do you think will happen next?

Challenge the children to read the rest of the book as a group with you. Pause occasionally to ask them to check the picture to see if the text makes sense.

At the end of the book:

Ask: How would you feel if you were Turtle now?

Ask children to work with their Reading Partner and read their favourite pages, practising reading it together with emphasis and feeling. Suggest they check that what they are reading makes sense and read it again if in doubt.

Wrap up

Ask pairs of children to read their favourite pages to the group. Ask questions about the readings, such as: How did Turtle feel? Why did that happen?

Return to the ending and reread pages 20 and 21.

Ask the following questions:
- Where are the birds?
- What do you think Vulture would say if he knew what happened to Turtle? Why?

Hold a group discussion on which animal or bird is the children's favourite and why? Ensure that they refer to the text or pictures to back up their opinion.

Conclude by rereading page 5. Ask children if what Vulture said was true. Was Turtle silly? Why?

Vocabulary boost session

You will need
- Multiple copies of Collins Big Cat *Turtle's Party in the Clouds*

Vocabulary table

Focus word	Child-friendly explanation	Example sentence	Tell me...
polishing	Polishing means rubbing something so clean that it is shiny.	I was **polishing** my shoes to make them shine.	Tell me about anything you have that needs polishing.
hurtled	Hurtled means moved very, very fast.	A rocket **hurtled** through space to the Moon.	Tell me about something you have seen that hurtled.
sobbed	Sobbed means cried hard, gasping and shedding tears.	The little boy **sobbed** because he'd lost his favourite teddy bear.	Tell me about a time you have sobbed.

Tune in

On the board, write some '–ing' and '–ed' words, that are not focus words, from the book, for example, twirling, whirling, listened, looked. Provide simple child-friendly explanations of their meaning, if necessary, pointing out the smaller words in the bigger words as the main clue to their meaning .

Ask children to follow the words carefully as you read the book aloud to them. Ask them to look out for words with '–ing' and '–ed' endings.

After reading the book, write 'polishing' on the board and explain that you are going to look very closely at this and other words from the book. Read the word 'polishing' on the board and explain its meaning.

Focus the children on the word where it appears in the story (page 2). Ask them to read the word with you again. Give them another example sentence of the word, for example: I was polishing my shoes to make them shine.

To encourage the children to use the word again, challenge them with a 'Tell me' question.

Ask children to say the word ('polishing') with you once again before moving on to the next focus word.

Heads together

Ask the following questions to develop the children's understanding of the focus words:
- Which would you polish: a drinking glass or a frying pan?
- Which do you think hurtled: a balloon or a racing car?
- Do you think a girl sobbed because she fell over in the playground or because she had finished her lunch?

Encourage the children to explain their answers and discuss them as a group.

Wrap up

Ask the following questions to review the word meanings:
- If I said I had been polishing my table, what would that mean?
- If I said I said a dog hurtled towards me, what would that mean?
- If I said my baby niece sobbed, what would that mean?

Use the focus words to start a display list of '–ing' and '–ed' words. For the focus words and any that follow on the lists, ask children to look for pictures that link with the words, to display alongside the lists.

Follow-up independent sessions

You will need
- Resource sheet: Whirling words
- Resource sheet: Animals

Provide the children with the Resource sheet: Whirling words. Ask them to circle any words that you could add '–ing' to. Ask children to read the words that they have circled but add an '–ing' on when they say them.

Give individual children Resource sheet: Animals. Ask them to draw a line from each word to the correct animal. Encourage them to compare their answers with a friend.

The Gardening Year

Book Band: Orange

This information book looks at how gardens change throughout the year's seasons and explains the jobs to be done, along with giving helpful tips.

Skills focus

- Draw on knowledge of vocabulary to understand texts
- Identify/explain key aspects of fiction and non-fiction texts, e.g. character, events, title
- Identify/explain the sequence of events in texts
- Read words accurately and fluently

Guided reading session

You will need

- Multiple copies of Collins Big Cat *The Gardening Year*

Tune in

Look together at the cover and read the title with the children; then read the back cover blurb.

Ask the following questions:

- What kind of changes have you seen in gardens through the year?
- Have you done any gardening?
- What did you do?

Ensure the children understand the word 'season'. Give a child-friendly definition if necessary, for example: One of the four times of year when the weather is usually different.

Point out the spelling of the word 'Aut-umn' and how the 'n' is silent. And the /oo/ sound in 'new' – n-(y)-oo.

Ensure the children understand this is an information book. Challenge them to flick through the pages to find other features found in information books. If necessary, prompt by pointing at the circular diagram on page 3, the 'top tip' boxes and photos with labels.

Turn to the contents and read it with the children.

Ask: What is a glossary? *(a list of important words found in the book with explanations)*

Turn to page 21 and help the children read the words – demonstrating how to break longer words into syllables, for example, 'decidious' de/cid/u/ous.

Heads together

Read pages 2 to 5 with the children, focusing on unfamiliar words and breaking them down into letter sounds if necessary, for example, the words 'produce' p-r-o-d-u-ce, 'cycle' c-y-c-le, 'again' a-g-ai-n.

Check the children's understanding of word meanings, for example, point to 'surprises' and offer a simple explanation, if necessary (things you don't expect).

Point to the word 'shoots' in bold on page 3 and ensure that they understand that the bold text means it is a word in the glossary. Demonstrate looking the word up and read the definition on page 21.

Return to page 3. Discuss how information is often shown in diagrams. Talk about how it is a 'cycle' that goes round and round (new plant, flower, dying plant [that drops seeds], seeds, new plant).

Write the four seasons as headings on the board. Ask children to read the rest of the book in pairs and look out for at least one important word for each season as they read.

Move around the group, listening to check that both children in the pair take turns at reading and checking that they attempt to read difficult words by breaking down sounds and blending.

Ask the pairs the following questions to check their understanding:

- What does this picture show?
- Have you found an important word from the Spring pages yet?

Wrap up

Ask children to close their eyes and challenge them to say the four seasons in order without looking.

Ask the pairs for the words that they found for each season and list them on the board. Together as a group discuss each season in turn, recalling the changes and jobs to be done. Reread the pages as a group on the changes and jobs to be done in that season.

Ask children if there was anything that they did not understand.

Ask: Did you find any pages very difficult?

Return to those pages and offer definitions for words as necessary and reread the text together.

Hold a group discussion about which season in the garden the children like most and why. Focus them on pages 22 and 23.

Ask: Which jobs would you like to do or not? Why?

Vocabulary boost session

You will need
- Multiple copies of Collins Big Cat *The Gardening Year*

Vocabulary table

Focus word	Child-friendly explanation	Example sentence	Tell me...
cycle	A number of events that keep happening in the same order over and over again.	The Sun rises, then sets, then rises, then sets in a never-ending **cycle**.	Tell me about any kind of cycle that you know about, where events happen over and over again.
contain	To contain means to have something inside, so fruits that contain seeds have seeds inside them.	The money box **contains** all the money I have saved up this year.	Tell me about anything you have that contains something.
worst	Worst means the most bad, so the book says that the absolutely most awful (or worst) pest to have in your garden is a slug.	The **worst** day of the week for me is Monday because I have to go to work.	Tell me the worst joke you know.

Tune in

Read the book with the children, ensuring that they follow the words closely with you. When you read a word in bold, refer to the glossary, read the word's meaning and check that the children understand it.

Ask children for suggestions on which pages they would like you to read again, which they found more difficult. Read them again, this time encouraging the children to join in. Discuss the pages, checking that they understand the vocabulary.

Explain that you are going to look at three words now more carefully and write the focus words on the board.

Refer back to each of the focus words in the book, giving a child-friendly explanation (suggestions can be found in the table, above).

Ask children to read the word with you again and then give them an example sentence containing the word to broaden their understanding.

Next, ask them to interact with the word meanings by asking the questions in the 'Tell me' column. You could demonstrate by giving some examples of your own.

Ask children to say the words with you again.

Heads together

Ask the following questions to explore and develop the children's understanding of the focus words:
- Which is more likely to be a cycle – a shopping list or the life of a forest?
- Which might contain something – a plate or a cupboard?
- What would be the worst – a broken leg or a scratch?

Encourage them to elaborate on their answers by asking: Why?

Wrap up

Review the word meanings by asking the children which words are closest in meaning:
- cycle: circular, timeline, list
- contain: compare, empty, hold
- worst: unhelpful, okay, awful

List the focus words as a display, asking children to suggest similar words to list below each, or pictures that link with their meaning.

Follow-up independent sessions

You will need
- Multiple copies of Collins Big Cat *The Gardening Year*
- Resource sheet: Seasons
- Resource sheet: Gardening book
- Old gardening magazines, scissors, glue
- A selection of plant books

Give the children a copy of Resource sheet: Seasons. Ask them to look at the pictures and add a label to each for: Spring, Summer, Autumn or Winter. Ask them to swap their work with a friend to check by looking through the book.

Challenge the children to use the Resource sheet: Gardening book, to complete two pages for a class book on gardening. Encourage them to write a sentence for each page.

Holidays: Then and Now

Book Band: Orange

A non-fiction information book about how holidays have changed over the years. It looks at how people travel, destinations and activities to do on holiday.

Skills focus

- Draw on knowledge of vocabulary to understand texts
- Identify/explain key aspects of fiction and non-fiction texts, e.g. character, events, title
- Make inferences from texts
- Check reading makes sense

Guided reading session

You will need

- Multiple copies of Collins Big Cat *Holidays: Then and Now*
- Mini-whiteboards and pens

Tune in

Give the children a chance to discuss holidays with their Reading Partners. What holidays have they been on? What holidays would they like to go on? Where do people go on holiday? How do people get there? Why do people go on holiday?

Introduce the book by looking at the front cover. Read the title.

Ask the following questions:

- What do you think this book is about?
- Do you think holidays were the same in the past?

Turn to the back cover and read the blurb.

Ask: What type of book is this? *(information text)*

Ask children to work in pairs to record any questions that they have about holidays in the past on their whiteboards.

Challenge the children to find the contents page. Read through the contents page together.

Ask the following questions:

- On what page can you find out about a Spanish holiday? *(page 16)*
- What will you find out about on page 10? *(the age of the car)*

Write the following digraphs 'ea', 'ar', 'sh', 'ay', 'i-e', 'a-e' on the board and challenge the children to find them on the contents page. Practise sounding out the words.

Recap what the features of an information text are: headings, photographs, diagrams, labels, captions, glossary, contents page. Ask children to work in pairs to scan through the book and find examples of the features.

Heads together

Turn to pages 4 and 5. Model reading the text using a range of strategies, such as decoding, high frequency words, checking the text makes sense, picture clues and context.

Ask the following questions:

- How did people travel to the seaside? *(by train)*
- How do people travel to their holidays now? *(car, ferry, plane, train)*

Look at the map of the UK. Can children find where they are on the map? Read through the seaside locations. Has anyone been to any of these places on holiday?

Move on to pages 6 and 7 together. Model reading the text.

Ask: What things do people spend money on at the seaside?

Point out that some of the words are in bold writing ('tourists', 'holidaymakers') and explain that this means that those words are in the glossary. Turn to the glossary and find the words 'tourists' and 'holidaymakers'. Read the definitions.

Turn back to the contents page. Allocate each pair a heading/topic. The children use the contents to find the correct page. Ask them to read through the page that they have been allocated. What can they find out? Listen to the children as they read independently and support them where needed. Provide time for each pair to feed back what they have found out.

Wrap up

Read page 20 together.

Ask: Where would you like to go on holiday in the future?

Explore the timeline on pages 22 and 23.

Ask: What has changed about people's holidays? *(where they go, how they travel, how long they go for)*

Look back at the questions the children wrote on their whiteboards. Can they answer them now?

Vocabulary boost session

You will need

- Multiple copies of Collins Big Cat *Holidays: Then and Now*

Vocabulary table

Focus word	Child-friendly explanation	Example sentence	Tell me...
flamenco	This is a type of dance from Spain.	The **flamenco** dresses are beautiful.	Tell me what type of dance you would like to learn.
guest house	A house where people can stay on holiday.	I stayed in a **guest house** on holiday in Wales.	Tell me where would like to stay on holiday.
tourists	people on their holidays	The **tourists** mainly visit in the summer.	Tell me what types of things tourists like to do.

Tune in

Explain that in this lesson the children are going to look in more detail at some of the words the author has used. Write the three focus words clearly for the children to see. Read the words together. Discuss and explain the child-friendly meaning of each word.

Reread the text. Challenge the children to find the focus words in the text: ('flamenco', page 17; 'guest house', page 12; 'tourists', page 6).

Heads together

Play a game of 'You say/I say'. Read a child-friendly explanation or definition and ask children to tell you the correct word. Repeat.

Make a list together, with the teacher scribing, of all the places people might stay when on holiday, for example: tent, hostel, hotel, guest house, apartment, villa, self-catering, holiday park and caravan.

Play 'I went to the dance studio and saw...' Each child repeats the sentence, adding on a type of dance. For example, the first person might say: I went to the dance studio and saw flamenco dancers. The second person could say: I went to the dance studio and saw flamenco and ballet dancers and so on.

Wrap up

Recap the three focus words by discussing the questions in the 'Tell me' column of the table, above.

Challenge the children to think of a sentence using one of the focus words.

Follow-up independent sessions

You will need

- Old holiday brochures, scissors, glue
- Resource sheet: Timeline for *Holidays: Then and Now*
- Paper, paints
- Resource sheet: Space holiday
- Poster paper, coloured pens or pencils

Ask children to look through a selection of holiday brochures and pick out their favourite pictures to create a collage of their ideal holiday. Where would they go? How would they get there? What would they do on holiday?

The children should order pictures and descriptions of holidays on to Resource sheet: Timeline for *Holidays: Then and Now*.

Let the children paint a picture of the seaside and add labels.

Ask children to use Resource sheet: Space holiday, to create a poster to advertise a holiday into space. What would they see, hear, smell, taste, feel?

The Bogeyman

Book Band: Turquoise

A story about a boy who was afraid to step on the lines and cracks in the pavement in case the Bogeyman got him, *until* one day he faced his fear.

Skills focus

- Draw on knowledge of vocabulary to understand texts
- Identify/explain key aspects of fiction and non-fiction texts, e.g. character, events, title
- Make inferences from texts
- Check reading makes sense

Guided reading session

You will need

- Multiple copies of Collins Big Cat *The Bogeyman*
- Resource sheet: Rhyming words for *The Bogeyman*

Tune in

Introduce the book by looking at the back cover. Read the title and the blurb together. Point out the speech marks and read with expression and different voices.

Ask the following questions:

- Who do you think Carrie and Harry are? *(friends/children)*
- Do any of the words rhyme? *(Harry/Carrie, game/lane)*
- Who do you think the Bogeyman might be?
- Have you ever tried not to step on the lines in the pavement?

Turn to the front cover. Reread the title. Discuss the picture.

Ask the following questions:

- What do you think the shadow is?
- How do you think the characters are feeling? *(The girl looks like she is playing; the boy looks scared.)*
- What types of things are people frightened of? *(the dark, monsters, ghosts, spiders, snakes)*

Look at the title page. Find out who wrote the story and who illustrated the story. Consider the picture together.

Ask the following questions:

- What is Harry doing? *(running away)*
- How do you think Harry is feeling? *(worried)*
- What can you do if you are worried or frightened about something? *(talk to a grown-up, such as a parent or teacher)*

Explain that there are lots of rhyming words in the story. Give the children a copy of Resource sheet: Rhyming words for *The Bogeyman* and ask them to match the rhyming words.

Recap strategies to use when reading, such as: decoding, high frequency words, checking it makes sense, picture clues and context clues.

Heads together

Begin on pages 2 and 3. Read these together and encourage the children to join in where they can. Point out the speech marks/inverted commas. Can the children use voices and expression to read the speech? Check their understanding.

Ask: How did the world change? *(Harry now knew about the Bogeyman.)*

Explore pages 4 and 5 together. Remind the children Carrie is playing a game/trick on Harry. Read through the text, modelling expression.

Ask: Why are the words 'SNIP SNAP' in capital letters? *(to emphasise them/say them loudly and suddenly)*

Look at pages 6 to 9 together.

Ask the following questions:

- Can you identify any rhyming words used? *(street/feet; bed/head)*
- How has Harry's world changed? *(he can't step on the cracks, he is scared, he has nightmares)*

Share pages 10 and 11. Read the text together, modelling how to use a range of strategies.

Ask: What does it mean 'rising up through the cracks when he was trying to play'? *(Harry couldn't concentrate on playing because he kept thinking of his fear of the Bogeyman.)*

Read pages 12 and 13 together.

Ask the following questions:

- Why did Harry pretend to be brave?
- How was he really feeling?
- What do you think he should have done? *(talked to someone he trusts)*

Ask children to read pages 14 to 21 in pairs. Can they find out what happens?

Ask the following questions:

- Where is the safest place in the world? *(home)*
- How does Harry's world change back to how it was before? *(he feels safe, he isn't scared)*
- What does Harry discover? *(Bogeyman is not real)*

Listen to the children read and support where needed. Discuss the questions once the children have finished reading.

Wrap up

Look closely at the description of the Bogeyman (on page 4) and the similes used. Record these on the board: as thin as a knife; eyes like fried eggs; hair like string.

Can the children come up with their own similes? For example: as green as the grass, as hot as the Sun.

Vocabulary boost session

You will need

- Multiple copies of Collins Big Cat *The Bogeyman*

Vocabulary table

Focus word	Child-friendly explanation	Example sentence	Tell me...
afraid	If you are afraid, you are scared.	I am **afraid** of the dark.	Tell me two other words that mean 'afraid'.
fear	If you have a fear, you are frightened of something.	I have a **fear** of snakes.	Tell me how you can tackle a fear.
embarrassed	If you are embarrassed, you feel silly or ashamed about something.	I was **embarrassed** when I fell over on sports day.	Tell me about a time when you have been embarrassed.

Tune in

Explain that in this lesson the children are going to look in more detail at some words that the author has used. Write the three focus words clearly for the children to see. Read the words together. Discuss and explain the child-friendly meaning of each word.

Reread the text.

Challenge children to find the focus words in the text ('embarrassed', page 11; 'afraid', page 12; 'fear', page 15).

Heads together

Use the focus words to pose some questions to the children.

Ask the following questions:

- What was Harry afraid of? *(the Bogeyman)*

- What was Harry's fear? *(that the Bogeyman would get him)*
- What was Harry embarrassed about? *(his fear of the Bogeyman)*

Create a list of all the words that mean 'afraid' and 'fear'.

Discuss how to help people who are afraid of something, for example, spiders, going on stage, jumping in the swimming pool.

Ask: How can you be a good friend?

Wrap up

Recap the three focus words by discussing the questions in the 'Tell me' column of the table, above.

Challenge the children to use the focus words as often as they can, both at school and at home.

Follow-up independent sessions

You will need

- Paints, paper
- Coloured pencils or pens
- Poster paper
- Resource sheet: Role on the wall: Harry

Ask children to paint a picture of the Bogeyman using the description in the book on page 4.

Ask children to draw a picture of 'the monster under the bed' that Carrie mentions on page 20. What do

the children think it might look like? Ask them to label the drawing and write a description. Encourage the children to use similes such as 'eyes as big as...'

In pairs, children can create a warning poster about the Bogeyman.

Using Resource sheet: Role on the wall: Harry, children label the picture with adjectives to describe Harry's character on the inside and his appearance on the outside. Encourage the children to use similes, for example: as brave as a lion.

Castles

Book Band: Turquoise

An information and explanation text all about castles and what life in a castle would have been like. Children learn all about the different parts of a castle.

Skills focus

- Draw on knowledge of vocabulary to understand texts
- Identify/explain key aspects of fiction and non-fiction texts, e.g. character, events, title
- Identify/explain the sequence of events in texts
- Check reading makes sense

Guided reading session

You will need

- Multiple copies of Collins Big Cat *Castles*

Tune in

Ask the following questions to relate to the children's personal experiences:

- Who has visited a castle before?
- Which castle did you go to?
- What are castles like?
- What do you know about castles?
- Would you like to go to a castle?
- Who do you think lived in castles?

Write 'castles' in the middle of the board and record what children know around it.

Introduce the book by exploring the front cover together. Read the title.

Ask the following questions:

- Can you describe the castle?
- What do you think it is made from?
- What shapes can you see?
- Do you know what any parts of the castle are called?

Turn the book over to look at the back cover. Model reading the blurb. Recap what a blurb is: it tells you what the book is about.

Ask the following questions:

- What is an enemy? *(someone who is against you)*
- What type of book do you think this is? *(information/explanation)*

Challenge the children to find the contents page. Read through the headings together.

Ask the following questions:

- What can you find out about on page 17? *(castle windows)*
- On which page will you find out where castles were built? *(page 4)*
- Does anyone know what a 'garderobe' is? *(a toilet)*

Look at pages 22 and 23 together. Read through the labels and discuss the different parts of the castle.

Discuss the features of non-fiction texts and write a list on the board: headings, photographs, captions, diagrams, labels. Challenge the children to work in pairs and skim through the book to find examples of each feature.

Heads together

Begin by reading pages 2 and 3 together. Discuss the picture of the castle.

Ask: What do you think made the castle a safe place to live?

Recap different strategies for tackling unknown words, such as: identifying high frequency words, decoding, picture clues, context clues and checking the text makes sense.

Turn back to the contents page and ask children to work in pairs and choose a page to research. What would they like to find out about? Remind them that you don't have to read non-fiction books in order. Encourage the children to explore their chosen pages. Listen to them read and offer support where needed.

Wrap up

Ask children to report back to the rest of the group on their chosen pages. What did they find out?

Turn to pages 19 and 20 and discuss how castles today are different to those in the past.

Vocabulary boost session

You will need

- Multiple copies of Collins Big Cat *Castles*
- Resource sheet: Castle

Vocabulary table

Focus word	Child-friendly explanation	Example sentence	Tell me...
portcullis	Bars that can be lowered and raised to block the doorway and stop people getting in.	The **portcullis** also had sharp points on the bottom.	Tell me what a portcullis is used for.
garderobe	a type of toilet	The toilet in a castle was called a **garderobe**.	Tell me how a garderobe is different to a modern toilet.
drawbridge	A drawbridge is a bridge that can be lowered and raised over the moat.	The **drawbridge** is raised to stop people entering the castle.	Tell me when the drawbridge would be down.

Tune in

Explain that in this lesson the children are going to look in more detail at some words that the author has used. Write the three focus words clearly for the children to see. Read the words together. Discuss and explain the child-friendly meaning of each word.

Reread the text. Challenge children to find the focus words in the text.

Heads together

Using Resource sheet: Castle, children work as a group or in pairs to add labels in the correct places.

Wrap up

Recap the three focus words by discussing the questions in the 'Tell me' column of the table above.

Challenge the children to think of a sentence using one of the focus words.

Follow-up independent sessions

You will need

- A selection of cardboard boxes and tubes, glue
- A selection of 2D shapes, paper, pencils
- Resource sheet: What is it like in a castle?
- Non-fiction books about castles

Let the children use a selection of cardboard boxes and cardboard tubes to design and build their very own castle.

The children can use 2D shapes to draw around and create a castle picture. They should label the different parts of the castle.

Tell the children that they should imagine that they are in a castle. What would it feel like? What would it smell like? What would you see? What would you hear? What would you eat? Let them record their ideas on Resource sheet: What is it like in a castle?

Ask children to explore a range of non-fiction books about castles

Horses' Holiday

Book Band: Turquoise

Follow the horses as they enjoy a lively holiday by the sea in this humorous rhyming story.

Skills focus

- Draw on knowledge of vocabulary to understand texts
- Identify/explain the sequence of events in texts
- Make inferences from texts
- Read words accurately and fluently

Guided reading session

You will need
- Multiple copies of Collins Big Cat *Horses' Holiday*

Tune in

Introduce the book by asking children to read the title together.

Ask the following questions:
- What kind of book do you think this is?
- What makes you think that?

Encourage them to look carefully at the front cover.

Ask the following questions:
- What do you think the story could be about?
- Do you think that this is a happy story or a sad one?
- What makes you think that?
- Who wrote this story? *(Kaye Umansky)*

Turn to the title page and ask children to point to the names of the author and illustrator. Encourage them to look at the picture.

Ask the following questions:
- Are there any more clues about the story? *(suitcase, sun block, sunglasses)*
- Whose suitcase could this be? *(one of the horses)*

Turn to the back cover and read the blurb aloud, encouraging the children to follow and join in with you.

Heads together

Read page 2 aloud, with the children following and joining in as you read. Model reading with expression, paying particular attention to the rhyme.

Tell the children that they are going to read the story on their own.

Ask: What strategies can you use to help you if you get stuck on a word? *(read the first sound then think about what the word might be; look at the pictures and guess what word would make sense; break words into parts)*

Tell the children that when they read, you want them to think about: their reading strategies; using expression, particularly at the end of the lines that rhyme; and the different things that the horses do on their holidays.

Ask children to read pages 4 to 21, on their own. As they read, move around the group, listening to each child while the others read in their heads. Check their reading strategies and listen for use of expression as they read.

Wrap up

Identify and praise the children's use of reading strategies that you observed them using to help with reading longer or difficult words and their use of expression.

Ask the following questions:
- What are the different things that the horses in the story like doing on their holidays? *(encourage the children to refer back to the book to help them)*
- What do the mums do while the babies play in rock pools? *(sit around and neigh)*

Turn to page 14.

Ask the following questions:
- What can you notice about these three pictures? *(elicit that the tide is coming in/sea water is rising)*
- What does that tell us about how long the horse is taking to write his postcards? *(He is taking a long time.)*

Ask the following questions, encouraging the children to use the book to help them to think about the answers:
- What times of day are in the book? *(daytime, evening, night-time)*
- How do you know?
- In the story, what activities are there for horses who like to be quiet? *(lounging by the poolside, writing postcards, strolling on the pier)*
- In the story, what activities are there for horses who like to be busy? *(swimming in the pool, going on the slide, water skis, splashing in rock pools, dancing, fireworks)*
- Would you like to go on a horses' holiday? Why?

Vocabulary boost session

You will need

- Multiple copies of Collins Big Cat *Horses' Holiday*

Vocabulary table

Focus word	Child-friendly explanation	Example sentence	Tell me...
lounge	If you lounge somewhere, you sit or lie there in a relaxed or lazy way.	Sadia **lounged** on the sofa watching television.	Tell me about somewhere that you can lounge.
zoom	If you zoom somewhere, you go there very quickly.	The rocket **zoomed** up into the sky.	Tell me what zooms.
stroll	If you stroll somewhere, you walk there slowly or in a relaxed way.	They **strolled** through the park listening to the birds singing.	Tell me about a time when you have strolled along.

Tune in

Explain to the children that in this lesson they are going to look closely at some of the words the author has used and what those words mean.

Read the book aloud to the children, modelling how to use the punctuation and dialogue to read aloud with expression.

Refer back to each of the focus words within the context of the story, writing up the word, giving a child-friendly explanation and asking children to say the focus word with you. For example: In the story, some horses 'lounge' by the pool. If you lounge somewhere, you sit or lie there in a relaxed or lazy way. Now, say the word with me – 'lounge'.

You may wish to use the examples in the table, above.

Refer to each of the focus words that you have written up and give the children the example sentences. Then ask them to interact with the word meanings by asking the questions in the 'Tell me' column. You may wish to demonstrate by giving some examples of your own.

Ask children to say the words with you once more.

Heads together

Ask the following questions to explore and develop the children's understanding of the focus words:

- In the story, the horses lounge by the pool. Where else might you lounge? Can you show me 'lounging'?
- In the story, the horses zoom around the bay. Where else might you zoom? Can you show me 'zooming'?
- In the story, the horses stroll along the pier. Where else might you stroll? Can you show me 'strolling'?

Wrap up

Ask the following questions to review the focus word meanings:

- Does 'lounge' mean running around or sitting down quietly?
- Does 'zoom' mean moving really slowly or really quickly?
- Does 'stroll' mean moving slowly or quickly?

Challenge the children to use the words as often as they can, both at school and at home.

Follow-up independent sessions

You will need

- Multiple copies of Collins Big Cat *Horses' Holiday*
- Coloured pencils or pens
- Resource sheet: Postcard

Ask children to work with their Reading Partners and to read the book aloud, remembering to use expression at the rhyming words.

Challenge the children to draw a story map of the things that the horses did on their holiday.

Ask children to turn to page 23 and read the postcard from Tolly. Hand out copies of Resource sheet: Postcard. The children write a postcard from one of the other horses.

Good Fun Farm

Book Band: Turquoise

This story is about animals on a farm that get bored and stop doing their work, until they find something that is really fun to do and includes everyone.

Skills focus

- Draw on knowledge of vocabulary to understand texts
- Make inferences from texts
- Check reading makes sense

Guided reading session

You will need

- Multiple copies of Collins Big Cat *Good Fun Farm*

Tune in

Show children the cover and read the title.

Ask: Have you ever been to a farm or seen one on television in detail?

Encourage the children to describe their experiences, drawing out language associated with the animals that are in the book (cows, hens, horses, ducks, pigs and sheep) and ask if they know the noises that they make. Write relevant words on the board, for example, moo, grunt, neigh.

Reread the title with the group.

Ask: What do you think this farm would be like?

Turn to the back cover and draw the children's attention to the blurb. Read it as the children follow the words closely.

Ask the following questions:

- Would you be bored if you were an animal on a farm? Why?
- What do you think the duckling's idea is?

Heads together

Tell the children that you are going to read some of the story and they must follow the words closely, looking out for where animals make noises or speak and where humans speak.

Read pages 2 to 7, using emphasis and expression for the animal sounds and speaking voices.

Ask: How did I know when a person or an animal was talking?

Remind the children of speech bubbles (pages 2 and 3) and speech marks (pages 6 and 7).

Focus on page 6 and tell the children that you are going to reread the text but differently. Read the text without any expression and read the questions like statements and the shout like a whisper.

Ask: Does it make sense?

Discuss how your reading did not make sense. Focus on the punctuation (question mark, exclamation mark) and the words 'shouted', 'cried' and 'asked'.

Ask the following questions:

- Why did the farmer shout? *(he is angry, annoyed)*
- Why did the farmer's wife cry out? *(There are no eggs or milk for market.)*

Ask children to work in small groups, taking it in turns to read a page, while the others listen to check the reading make sense. Ask them to focus on how spoken words or noises are said.

Circulate around the groups, checking if children have noticed speech punctuation and verbs and have attempted to read with these in mind. Also, support them in sounding out any unfamiliar words.

Ask the groups to tell you what has happened so far in the story. Correct any misunderstandings by focusing the children on relevant phrases or pictures.

Wrap up

Ask children if they enjoyed reading the animals' words and if they enjoyed the story and why.

Ask children to read the story again with you as a group; remind them to read the spoken words and sounds with expression, as if they were the people/ animals talking. **Ask** the following questions:

- Could the humans hear the animals talking? *(focus on page 8 for a clue)*
- Why was football better than having more mud, a bigger pond or racing? *(all the animals enjoyed football)*
- Why do you think the farmer changed the name of the farm (on page 21)?
- Do you think it is a 'good fun farm' too? Why?

Turn to pages 22 and 23 and read the words together, focusing on the positions of the different animals. Encourage the children with a knowledge of football to explain what the different team members do.

Vocabulary boost session

You will need

- Multiple copies of Collins Big Cat *Good Fun Farm*

Vocabulary table

Focus word	Child-friendly explanation	Example sentence	Tell me...
moaned	To moan means to complain or be cross about something.	The boy **moaned** because he had peas for tea and didn't like them.	Tell me about a time when you or someone else has moaned.
hard	Hard can mean with extra effort and care.	She worked **hard** to get her dancing certificate.	Tell me about something you've tried hard to do.
fair	Fair means to be good and just.	It isn't **fair** that some people are poor and others are rich.	Tell me about something you think isn't fair.

Tune in

Tell the children that in this lesson they are going to explore some of the words in the story and look at their meaning. Read the book aloud expressively to the children, modelling how to sound out and blend longer words.

Write the focus words on the board and ask children to read them.

First, refer to where they appear in the story. Give child-friendly explanations (see the table, above). Ask children to read the words again.

Next, give the children the example sentences. Then ask them to think of the word meanings by asking the questions in the 'Tell me' column. You could support them by giving some examples of your own.

Ask children to say the words with you once again.

Heads together

Ask the following questions to explore and develop the children's understanding:

- When is someone more likely to have moaned – after a walk in the rain, after a birthday party or while reading a book?
- Would you think that someone is more likely to sleep hard, sing hard or practise hard?
- Would you think it was fair if grown-ups got free sweets but children didn't?

Encourage them to explain their answers by asking: Why?

Wrap up

Review the focus word meanings by asking which is the most similar word to each focus word:

- 'moaned': shouted, whispered, whined, sobbed
- 'hard': carefully, weakly, angrily, sneakily
- 'fair': secret, right, kind, wrong

Challenge the children to try to use one of the focus words each day. If the words are displayed on the board they could add a tick next to the word. Which is the word they most commonly use?

Follow-up independent sessions

You will need

- Resource sheet: Role-play for *Good Fun Farm*
- Resource sheet: Animal words

Ask children to take turns to role-play the farmer or his wife. They can ask questions of their own or use those supplied on Resource sheet: Role-play for *Good Fun Farm*. The questions could be cut out, so children take it in turns to pick a question to ask.

Give pairs of children the Resource sheet: Animal words. Tell them the words are to do with the cow, pig or sheep. Ask them to copy the words into the relevant animal shape.

The Stone Cutter

Book Band: Turquoise

A story from Japan that tells a tale of a poor stone cutter who wishes to be a rich man.

Skills focus

- Draw on knowledge of vocabulary to understand texts
- Identify/explain the sequence of events in texts
- Predict what might happen on the basis of what has been read so far
- Read words accurately and fluently

Guided reading session

You will need

- Multiple copies of Collins Big Cat *The Stone Cutter*
- Globe or world map
- Pictures or photographs of Japan
- Resource sheet: 'or' words

Tune in

Begin by finding Japan on a globe or world map. Display some pictures of Japan and discuss what it is like. What do the children know about Japan? Discuss the children's knowledge and/or experiences if relevant.

Explain that they are going to read a story from Japan. Look at the front cover of the book and read the title. Point out the split digraph 'o-e' in stone and the '–er' ending in cutter.

Ask the following questions:

- What do you think a stone cutter does? *(cuts stone that can be used for things or made into things)*
- What do you think the stone cutter is thinking as he looks up at the grand house/palace?

Turn the book over and model reading the blurb using fluency and accuracy.

Ask: Why do you think the word REALLY is in capital letters? *(to emphasise it/ make it stand out)*

Ask children to predict what will happen. Will the poor stone cutter become a rich man? Will he like being a rich man? Does the stone cutter look happy?

Ask: Have you ever wished to be someone else?

Discuss the word 'poor' asking:

- What does it mean? *(not having very much money/a person we feel sorry for)*
- Do you think being a stone cutter is hard work?
- Why do you think he wants to be someone else?

Point out that the 'oor' sound in 'poor' is the same as in 'door'. Use Resource sheet: 'or' words, to explore other trigraphs and digraphs that make the 'oor' sound, for example: 'or', 'ore', 'oor', 'our', 'aw'.

Heads together

Turn to pages 2 and 3. Read the text together, encouraging the children to point at the words and to join in. Discuss what a chisel is (a tool for stone cutting). Ask children to describe the picture: mountains, Japanese hat and clothes, Japanese palace, a rich man walking by. Can children make a 'TACK TOCK' noise?

Read pages 4 and 5 together. Can children point out the speech marks/inverted commas? Read with expression – can children use a voice for the speech? Ask children to describe the man on page 5.

Ask the following questions:

- What is he wearing?
- How does he look?
- Do they think he is happy being a rich man?

What do the children predict will happen next?

Look at pages 6 and 7 together.

Ask the following questions:

- What is an emperor? *(a king or ruler)*
- Why do you think the man wanted to be the emperor? *(because he is important and powerful)*

Ask children to discuss what will happen next in pairs: will the man become the emperor? Will he like being the emperor? Is anything more powerful than an emperor?

Recap strategies to use when reading independently, such as: decoding; identifying high frequency words; checking it makes sense; picture clues; and context.

Ask children to read pages 8 to 21 independently. Listen to children read and support where needed. Can they find out what happened to the stone cutter next?

Wrap up

Turn to pages 22 and 23 and explore the diagram together. Ask children to retell the story to a partner using the diagram as a guide.

Discuss the way the story goes full circle and the man becomes the stone cutter again.

Ask: Do you think this story has a message/moral?

Vocabulary boost session

You will need

- Multiple copies of Collins Big Cat *The Stone Cutter*

Vocabulary table

Focus word	Child-friendly explanation	Example sentence	Tell me...
emperor	An emperor is a king or ruler.	The **emperor** lived in a grand palace.	Tell me if you would like to be an emperor.
powerful	If someone is powerful, they have lots of control and influence over others.	The emperor was the most **powerful** in the land.	Tell me the name of someone who is powerful.
grander	If something is grander, it is most impressive.	The emperor's palace was even **grander** than I imagined.	Tell me what the emperor's palace looks like.

Tune in

Explain that in this lesson the children are going to look in more detail at some of the words that the author has used. Write the three focus words clearly for the children to see. Read the words together. Discuss and explain the child-friendly meaning of each word.

Reread the text, demonstrating fluency and expression. Ask children to listen out for the focus words: 'emperor', pages 6 to 10; 'powerful', page 9; 'grander', page 9.

Heads together

As a group, discuss and record words to describe the emperor.

Ask the following questions:

- What would his clothes feel like?
- What do they look like?

Encourage the children to use adjectives and detailed description. They should verbally form sentences to describe the emperor, for example: The emperor's cloak was long, velvet and blue. The emperor was powerful, grand and majestic.

Wrap up

Recap the three focus words by discussing the questions in the 'Tell me' column of the table above.

Challenge the children to think of a sentence using one of the focus words.

Follow-up independent sessions

You will need

- Resource sheet: 'or' words
- Resource sheet: Flow diagram
- Coloured pencils or pens

Let the children explore the different spellings of the 'or' sound. Children cut out the words from Resource sheet: 'or' words and sort the different spellings.

Ask children to use Resource sheet: Flow diagram, to draw a diagram with labels showing the events of the story.

Harry the Clever Spider

Book Band: Turquoise

A little girl called Clare finds a hairy spider. She wants to keep the spider and names him Harry. But her family aren't so sure, until Harry proves useful.

Skills focus

- Draw on knowledge of vocabulary to understand texts
- Make inferences from texts

- Predict what might happen on the basis of what has been read so far
- Read words accurately and fluently

Guided reading session

You will need

- Multiple copies of Collins Big Cat *Harry the Clever Spider*
- Mini-whiteboards and pens

Tune in

Ask the following questions to begin the lesson:

- Who likes spiders?
- Where might you find a spider?
- What do you know about spiders?
- How many legs do they have?

Introduce the book by exploring the front cover. Model reading the title, using accuracy and fluency.

Ask the following questions:

- Where do you think the story is set?
- Who might the characters be?
- What do you think Harry does that is clever?

Turn the book over to read the blurb on the back cover. Model reading the blurb, using fluency and expression.

Ask the following questions:

- Who do you think Clare is?
- Where do you think Clare found Harry?

Open the book to look at the title page together. Explain that this is called the title page. Reread the title.

Ask the following questions:

- Who is the author? (Julia Jarman)
- Who is the illustrator? (Charlie Fowkes)

Recap strategies to support independent reading.

Turn to page 2 and ask children to work in pairs and skim the page to look for any high frequency words that they recognise (saw, the, on, Saturday, it, was, in, to, up and, went, then, got) and record them on their whiteboards.

Heads together

Read pages 2 and 3 together. Encourage the children to point to the words as you read and join in where they can.

Ask the following questions:

- Why is the word 'SPLOSH' in capital letters? *(for emphasis, to say it loudly)*
- How did Clare feel about the spider? *(she felt sorry for him, he made her laugh)*

Point out the speech marks and ask children to practise rereading the speech using expression.

Continue on to pages 4 and 5 together. Encourage children to point to the words as you read and join in where they can.

Ask the following questions:

- What does Clare think about the spider now? *(impressed, she thinks he is clever)*
- What do you think will happen when Clare shows her family the spider?

Read pages 6 and 7 as a group. Point out the exclamation marks and discuss why the author has used them.

Ask the following questions:

- What do you think Charlie thinks of spiders? *(scared)*
- What words does Charlie use to describe the spider? *(big, horrible, hairy)*
- What do you think will happen next?

Ask children to read pages 6 to 15 with their Reading Partner.

Ask the following questions:

- How is Mum feeling? *(she has toothache)*
- Why does the family need the car keys? *(to go to the dentist)*
- Where did Clare put the spider? *(in a box)*
- What do you think will happen next?
- What could Harry do to impress Mum, Dad and Charlie?

Ask children to read pages 16 to 21 independently. Listen to children read and support where needed.

Wrap up

Challenge the children to find all the words used to describe Harry in the story: big, hairy, horrible, monster, helpful, clever.

Ask the following questions:
- What do you think will happen next in the story?
- Do you think Clare will take Harry the Spider to school on Monday?

Vocabulary boost session

You will need
- Multiple copies of Collins Big Cat *Harry the Clever Spider*

Vocabulary table

Focus word	Child-friendly explanation	Example sentence	Tell me...
enormous	If something is enormous, it is very big.	The **enormous** digger was in the garden.	Tell me another word that means enormous.
mantelpiece	A shelf on top of a fireplace.	I put a vase of flowers on the **mantelpiece**.	Tell me about what people might put on a mantelpiece?
horrible	If something is horrible, then it is not very nice.	The pizza tasted **horrible** cold.	Tell about something you have tasted that was horrible.

Tune in

Explain that in this lesson the children are going to look in more detail at some words linked to the text. Write the three focus words clearly for the children to see. Read the words together. Discuss and explain the child-friendly meaning of each word.

Reread the text.

Ask children to find the words 'big' (pages 6, 7 and 21), 'mantelpiece' (page 12) and 'horrible' (pages 6, 7, 8 and 15) in the text.

Heads together

Ask children to think of as many different words as they can that mean 'big'. Write the children's ideas as a word bank. For example: huge, large, giant, gigantic, massive, enormous, vast.

Play a memory game. Each player has to complete the sentence 'On the mantelpiece, Clare put...' remembering everything that has been put on before. For example, player 1 might say: On the mantelpiece, Clare put a spider. Player 2 would say: On the mantelpiece, Clare put a spider and a...

Wrap up

Recap the three focus words by discussing the questions in the 'Tell me' column of the table above.

Challenge the children to think of a sentence using one of the focus words.

Follow-up independent sessions

You will need
- Resource sheet: Role on the wall: Clare
- Resource sheet: Storyboard
- Paper, coloured pens or pencils

Using Resource sheet: Role on the wall: Clare, the children label the picture with adjectives to describe Clare's character on the inside and her appearance on the outside.

Ask children to complete Resource sheet: Storyboard. They draw pictures and add labels or write sentences.

Ask children to draw a diagram of the setting (house) and label it.

Fly Facts

Book Band: Turquoise

This non-chronological report explores the life of common flies and explains how they can be both dangerous and useful.

Skills focus

- Draw on knowledge of vocabulary to understand texts
- Identify/explain key aspects of fiction and non-fiction texts, e.g. character, events, title
- Identify/explain the sequence of events in texts
- Read words accurately and fluently

Guided reading session

You will need

- Multiple copies of Collins Big Cat *Fly Facts*

Tune in

Introduce the book by asking children to read the title together.

Ask the following questions:

- What kind of book do you think this is? *(information)*
- What makes you think that? *(title, photograph)*
- Do you know what a fly is?
- What do you know about flies?
- What do you want to know about flies?

Before you turn to the title page:

Ask the following questions:

- Can you name the features of an information book? *(contents list, photographs, captions, labels, diagrams, glossary, index)*
- Where in the book can we find the contents list? *(title page)*

Turn to the title page and read the contents aloud, encouraging the children to follow and join in with you. Look together at the words 'fly' and 'flies'. Write them both on the board and check that the children understand that 'flies' is the plural for 'fly'.

Ask: How does the spelling of 'fly' change when it becomes 'flies'.

Heads together

Before you start reading, tell the children that in this lesson you will be focusing on reading fluency (reading ahead to each word so that your reading is smooth and moves quickly) and the life of a fly.

Read page 2 aloud and encourage the children to follow as you read. Model reading smoothly, demonstrating how you read ahead so that you have already thought about the next word as you reach it.

Ask children to read up to page 20 alone. As they read, move around the group, listening to each child. If necessary, support them in reading longer words and observe how fluently they are reading.

Wrap up

Return to the book, praising the children for reading fluently. You may want to ask children to demonstrate how they read a line fluently.

Ask the following questions:

- What did you find out about the life of a fly?
- Is there a part of the book that is about the life of a fly? *(pages 12 to 15)*
- Can you use the book to help you find out what happens after the mother fly lays the eggs? Next? After that?
- In the whole book, what did you find most interesting about flies?
- Was there a part of the book that you didn't like? Why?
- Did you like this book? Why?

Vocabulary boost session

You will need

- Multiple copies of Collins Big Cat *Fly Facts*

Vocabulary table

Focus word	Child-friendly explanation	Example sentence	Tell me...
tiny	Tiny means very, very small.	He had a **tiny** cut on his finger.	Tell me about something that is tiny.
sticky	If something is sticky, it is soft or thick and wet and it sticks to other things.	When the drink spilled, it left a **sticky** mark.	Tell me what things are sticky.
invisible	If something is invisible, it means it cannot be seen, maybe because it is hidden or very small.	The green caterpillar was **invisible** on the green leaf.	Tell me about a time when something has been invisible.

Tune in

Explain to the children that in this lesson they are going to look closely at some of the words the author has used and what those words mean.

Read the book aloud to the children, asking them to follow and join in as you read.

Refer back to each of the focus words within the context of the story, writing up the word, giving a child-friendly explanation and asking children to say the focus word with you. For example: The book tells us that flies have tiny pads on their feet. Tiny means very, very small. Now, say the word with me – 'tiny'.

You may wish to use the examples in the table, above.

Refer to each of the focus words that you have written up and give the children the example sentences. Then ask them to interact with the word meanings by asking the questions in the 'Tell me' column. You may wish to demonstrate by giving some examples of your own.

Ask children to say the words with you once more.

Heads together

Explain to the children that you are going to say some sentences that make sense and some that don't make sense. They have to decide – if it makes sense, they should say 'yes'; if it doesn't make sense, say 'no'. Tell them to listen carefully!

- On my birthday, I brought in a cake. Everyone in the class had a big piece. The cake was tiny. *(no)*
- When the chocolate melted in the sun, it went sticky. *(yes)*
- Everyone could see the spider. It was invisible. *(no)*
- The ant was tiny. *(yes)*
- When they washed and dried the cloth it was sticky. *(no)*
- The germs on a fly's feet are invisible. *(yes)*

Encourage the children to make links to their own lives and experiences to help them.

Wrap up

Review the word meanings by doing the following activity. Turn to page 7.

Ask the following questions:

- It says that the fly has 'tiny' pads on its feet. Can you tell me what 'tiny' means?
- It also says that the pads are covered in 'sticky' hairs. Can you tell me what 'sticky' means?

Turn to page 8 of the book.

Ask: It says that the fly brings 'invisible' germs with it. Can you tell me what 'invisible' means?

Challenge the children to use the words as often as they can, both at school and at home.

Follow-up independent sessions

You will need

- Multiple copies of Collins Big Cat *Fly Facts*
- Resource sheet: Questions for *Fly Facts*

Ask children to work with their Reading Partners and to read the book aloud. Encourage them to practise reading smoothly by reading ahead and getting ready for the next word.

Give children a copy of Resource sheet: Questions for *Fly Facts*. Say that the children are going to be the teacher! They make up some questions to ask their partner about the book.

How to Make Storybooks

Book Band: Turquoise

An instruction text on how to plan, write, edit, illustrate and make your own storybook.

Skills focus

- Draw on knowledge of vocabulary to understand texts
- Identify/explain key aspects of fiction and non-fiction texts, e.g. character, events, title
- Identify/explain the sequence of events in texts
- Read words accurately and fluently

Guided reading session

You will need

- Multiple copies of Collins Big Cat *How to Make Storybooks*

Tune in

Read the title of the book together and ask children if they have come across any other 'How to' books. Discuss the purpose of 'How to' books (they tell you how to make or do something).

Ask: What do we call text that tells us how to do something?

Elicit how it is instructional text. Describe other examples of instructional texts if necessary, such as how to play games and recipe books telling you how to make things like cakes.

Flick through the book and say: I can see an important way in which the text is laid out, which tells me this is definitely a book with instructions in it.

Ask children to flick through the pages and say what tells them this is an instruction book. Draw their attention to the use of numbering and lists, such as on pages 6 and 7. Point out the diagram and labels on page 16. Explain that labels are often used in instruction books.

Ask: What sorts of things do you think you need to do to make a storybook?

Write their suggestions on the board in the order in which the children say them.

Heads together

Read pages 4 to 8 aloud to the children, asking them to follow as you read. Demonstrate how you worked out longer words on page 7. Write 'characters' on the board, then again alongside but showing how it can be split into letter sounds: ch-a-r-a-c-t-er-s. Repeat for 'treasure' t-r-ea-s-ure. Point out any unfamiliar letter–sound correspondences.

Write 'guarding' on the board and ask a volunteer to point to or write the letters that make each sound: gu-ar-d-i-ng. Point out the silent 'u'.

Ask children to reread pages 2–7 with you as a group.

Ask: What is the first step in making a storybook. *(think of a good idea)*

Write 'idea' at the head of a new list. Praise the children if it appears on the class list from the earlier discussion.

Focus on pages 6–7. Ask children to look independently at the pictures and box on the right. Discuss why they are useful. (The pictures give ideas and the box on the right gives examples of what a child has done.)

Ask children to finish reading the book independently in groups, each child taking a turn. Challenge them to find what the stages are in making a storybook.

Move around the groups, checking they recognise how more than one letter makes one sound and that they recognise familiar spellings.

Wrap up

Encourage the group to feed back. **Ask:** What do you have to do after thinking up ideas and characters for the story? *(what happens)*

Add children's feedback to the list on the board. If their suggestions are out of sequence, encourage them to check back to find the correct next step.

Ask the following questions:

- Do you think you could make a storybook using these instructions?
- Do you think the pictures are helpful?

Ask children if they found the meanings of any of the words difficult. Hold a quiz. Turn to a page, read a sentence and ask what one of the words means. For example: ask children to turn to page 17 and read the point 2 text.

Ask: What does 'blurb' mean? *(the writing on the back cover that tells us about the book)*

Turn to the contents and read it together.

Ask: Could we have read this book in any order?

Elicit how it would be more useful to read this book in order as there is a logical sequence. For example say: I can't check my spelling until I've written some words!

Vocabulary boost session

You will need

- Multiple copies of Collins Big Cat *How to Make Storybooks*

Vocabulary table

Focus word	Child-friendly explanation	Example sentence	Tell me...
characters	Characters are the imaginary creatures, animals or people, in a story.	My **favourite** character in Little Red Riding Hood is the grandma!	Tell me about your favourite story characters.
editing	Editing is what an author does to make what they have written better by checking, correcting and improving it.	When **editing** my story, I changed the name of my dragon so that it sounded scary.	Tell me why you think editing a story is important.
dictionary	A dictionary is a book of words and their meanings.	I looked up the word 'treasure' in a **dictionary** to find out what it means.	Tell me about a time you have used a dictionary.

Tune in

Tell the children that after you have read the book to them, you will return to some of the words and examine what they mean. Read the book to the children, asking them to follow the words closely as you read. Reread the sentences that contain the focus words and pause, saying for example: 'Characters' – that's an interesting word that we'll look at again.

After you have read the book, write the focus words on the board. Read the words in their context again and give a child-friendly explanation using everyday language.

Ask children to reread the focus word and then give an example sentence containing the word. Example sentences are given in the table, above, but you could make up your own.

Next, challenge the children with the questions in the 'Tell me' column of the table, above, in order to encourage further interaction with the words. The questions will prompt the children to think more carefully about the word in the context of their own lives. You could support them by giving some examples of your own.

Ask children to say the words with you again.

Heads together

Develop the children's understanding of the focus words by writing them on the board.

Ask the following questions:

- Which word goes with 'meanings'? *(dictionary)*
- Which word goes with 'imaginary'? *(characters)*
- Which word goes with 'checking'? *(editing)*

Discuss the children's answers and talk about what other words could go with each focus word.

Wrap up

Ask the following questions to develop the children's understanding of the focus words:

- Are characters important in stories? Why?
- What might you do when editing?
- Why would you look up a word in a dictionary?

Ask the group to create a 'Writers' word wall', adding the focus and other words on the topic of writing stories. Encourage volunteers to offer definitions to a word of their choice each day.

Follow-up independent sessions

You will need

- Dictionaries
- Resource sheet: Glossary
- Resource sheet: Planning

Point out how the book does not have a glossary. Help the children to use dictionaries to either write simple definitions or discuss definitions in groups. A structure and words to define are supplied on the Resource sheet: Glossary.

Encourage the children to follow the instructions and write their own story. They could use the Resource sheet: Planning, to help structure their initial ideas.

A Visit to the Farm

Book Band: Turquoise

A recount of a residential trip to a farm, written as a letter from Sam to his parents. Find out about feeding the pigs, counting the sheep and milking the cows.

Skills focus

- Draw on knowledge of vocabulary to understand texts
- Identify/explain key aspects of fiction and non-fiction texts, e.g. character, events, title
- Identify/explain the sequence of events in texts
- Check reading makes sense

Guided reading session

You will need

- Multiple copies of Collins Big Cat *A Visit to the Farm*

Tune in

Ask: Have you ever been to a farm?

Discuss the children's experiences of farms if relevant.

Ask the following questions:

- What animals might there be at a farm? *(pigs, sheep, cows, goats, donkeys, chickens, geese, horses, ducks)*
- What do you think it would be like visiting a farm?
- What jobs do farmers do? *(feed the animals, clean the animal sheds, milk the cows, grow crops)*

Introduce the book by looking at the front cover. Read the title.

Ask the following questions:

- What is the photograph of? *(a piglet)*
- What type of book do you think this is? *(non-fiction/information book/a recount)*

Turn the book over and read the blurb. Discuss the picture.

Ask the following questions:

- Who is going to the farm? *(Sam)*
- Who is he going with? *(school)*

Establish that Sam is a boy who is going on a school trip to the farm.

Look at the title page. Discuss who the book is written by *(Michael Morpurgo)* and who took the photographs *(Steve Lumb)*.

Ask: Where can you find the index page? *(at the back of the book)*

Challenge the children to find the index page. Explain that the index page lists key words and the pages that they are on. Read through the list.

Ask the following questions:

- Which is your favourite farm animal and what pages can you find it on?
- On what page can you find out about eggs? *(pages 14 and 15)*

Recap strategies the children can use when reading, such as: decoding, identifying high frequency words, using picture clues and checking it makes sense.

Heads together

Read pages 2 and 3 together. Model reading with expression. Establish that this is a letter from Sam about his residential trip to the farm. Discuss that it is written from Sam's point of view.

Ask the following questions:

- Who is Sam writing to? *(his mum and dad)*
- What does he think of the farm? *(it's magic/he is enjoying it/excited)*
- What words does Sam use to describe the house? *(huge, great)*

Turn to pages 4 and 5.

Ask the following questions:

- What time did the children start work on the farm? *(7:30am)*
- What did they have to wear? *(coats and wellies)*
- Why do you think that they wore *two* pairs of socks? *(because it was cold)*
- What was Sam's first job? *(feeding the pigs)*
- What did Sam think of the pigs? *(noisy and smelly and the little ones were sweet)*
- How old were the piglets? *(three weeks old)*
- Why do you think the word 'smell' is in bold writing? *(to emphasise how smelly it was)*

Ask children to read on independently or in pairs from page 6 to 21. Listen to the children read and support where needed. Can they find out what else Sam did on the farm? What animals did he see? What jobs did he do?

Wrap up

Discuss Sam's time at the farm.

Ask the following questions:

- What animals did Sam see? *(pigs, piglets, sheep, lambs, calves, horses, donkeys, chickens, geese, ducks, cows)*
- What jobs/tasks did he do? *(feeding the pigs, counting the sheep, mucking out, collecting eggs, milking)*

- Do you think he had a good time? *(yes)*

Look at the timetable on page 22.

Ask the following questions:

- What time did Sam have breakfast? *(8:30am)*
- What activity did he do first? *(feeding the pigs)*
- What did he do after teatime? *(milk the cows and clean the dairy)*

Vocabulary boost session

You will need

- Multiple copies of Collins Big Cat *A Visit to the Farm*

- A selection of 'smell pots' (small pots with different things for children to smell)

Vocabulary table

Focus word	Child-friendly explanation	Example sentence	Tell me...
stinkiest	If something is the stinkiest, it is the smelliest.	The cheese was **stinky**.	Tell me what smells you like/dislike.
mucked out	Mucked out the shed means cleared all the poo and dirty straw out of the shed.	I helped my aunty **muck out** the stables.	Tell me what Sam thought about mucking out.
waddle	If you waddle, you rock from side to side as you walk.	The penguins **waddled** to the pool.	Tell me which farm animals were waddling.

Tune in

Explain that in this lesson the children are going to look in more detail at some of the words the author has used. Write the three focus words clearly for the children to see. Read the words together. Discuss and explain the child-friendly meaning of each word.

Reread the text.

Find the focus words in the text ('stinkiest', page 10; 'mucked out', page 10; 'waddle', page 14).

Heads together

Discuss the questions in the 'Tell me' column of the table, above.

Ask children to close their eyes and smell different 'smell pots'. Can they identify the smells? Which one do they think is the stinkiest?

Wrap up

Challenge the children to think of a sentence using one of the focus words.

Ask children if they can waddle like a duck.

Follow-up independent sessions

You will need

- Resource sheet: Animal match
- Resource sheet: Ordering events
- Poster paper and paint

Ask children to match the animals to their offspring using the cards cut from Resource sheet: Animal match.

Ask children to order the events in the text using cards cut from Resource sheet: Ordering events and write a sentence to go with each picture.

Hot seating: ask a volunteer to play the character of Sam. The rest of the group interview 'Sam' about his trip to the farm.

Let the children paint a picture of the farm setting and add labels.

Harry the Clever Spider at School

Book Band: Turquoise

When Harry the spider is taken into school for a minibeasts project, he shows just how clever he is by finding the teacher's glasses.

Skills focus

- Draw on knowledge of vocabulary to understand texts
- Identify/explain the sequence of events in texts
- Make inferences from texts
- Read words accurately and fluently

Guided reading session

You will need

- Multiple copies of Collins Big Cat *Harry the Clever Spider at School*
- Mini-whiteboards and pens
- Resource sheet: Book talk for *Harry the Clever Spider at School*

Tune in

Ask children to read the front and back covers of the book. Encourage them to tell you what they know about the book, for example, it's a story, it's about Harry the spider, it's written by Julia Jarman.

Read pages 2 and 3 aloud to the children, demonstrating how to use the meaning and dialogue to help you to read with expression.

Ask the following questions:

- Which characters have we met so far in the story? *(Clare and Harry)*
- Where do you think the story is happening? *(on the way to school)*

Explain that you would like the children to read the rest of the story and to note down on their whiteboards the names of the other characters and any other places where the story happens.

Heads together

Give the children time to read the rest of the story.

As they read, move around the group, listening to the children's use of expression, the strategies that they use for decoding unfamiliar words and reminding them to note down characters and settings.

Wrap up

Take feedback from the activity, writing up the names of new characters (Joanne, Simon, Miss Bradley) and settings (school) on the board.

Ask: What happened in the story?

Encourage the children to go through the main events checking that they are recounting them in chronological order.

Give the children a copy of Resource sheet: Book talk for *Harry the Clever Spider at School*. Talk through the prompts.

Ask the following questions:

- What did you like about the story?
- Tell me about anything you didn't like.
- Do you have any questions that you'd like to ask the characters?
- Does the story remind you of any others that you have read?

Encourage the children to support their responses with reasons and evidence from the text.

Following the discussion, allow the children time to fill in their ideas on the Resource sheet: Book talk for *Harry the Clever Spider at School*.

Vocabulary boost session

You will need
- Multiple copies of Collins Big Cat *Harry the Clever Spider at School*
- Mini-whiteboards and pens

Vocabulary table

Focus word	Child-friendly explanation	Example sentence	Tell me...
observe	If you observe something, you look at it carefully.	Nicky **observed** the birds on the bird table.	Tell me about something you would like to observe.
upset	If you are upset, you are unhappy about something.	Fran was **upset** when she lost her pen.	Tell me about something that might upset you.
furious	If you are furious, you are very cross.	Sami was **furious** with Billy.	Tell me about something that would make you furious.

Tune in

Explain to the children that you would like them to think about the teacher in the story – Miss Bradley.

Ask: What do you think she is like?

Encourage them to support their observations with reasons and evidence.

Say that you think the author has chosen her words very carefully when she writes about Miss Bradley to help us to get an impression of her.

Turn to pages 6 and 7 and read the text aloud, using an appropriate 'formal' voice for Miss Bradley.

Explain the meaning of the word 'observe', using the information in the table above.

Ask: Why do you think Miss Bradley asked the children to 'observe' rather than using a phrase like 'look at'?

Establish that her way of speaking tells us something about her.

Read aloud to page 18, explaining the meanings of the other focus words ('upset' and 'furious').

Ask the following questions:
- Who was upset? *(Clare and Miss Bradley)*
- Why were they upset? *(Clare was upset because she'd lost Harry: Miss Bradley was upset because she'd lost her glasses)*

- Why was Miss Bradley furious? *(because she'd told Clare to keep Harry inside his box)*

Heads together

Write up the three focus words on the board.

Tell the children about something that you have observed, or would like to observe, giving reasons to support your statement.

Give the children the 'Tell me' prompts from the table above, asking them first to share their ideas and reasons with their Reading Partners and then with the rest of the group.

Encourage the children listening to ask questions about the statements.

Wrap up

Ask children to work with their Reading Partners and to develop three sentences that each contain one of the focus words. They can write these sentences on their mini-whiteboards. Ask children to share their sentences and check that they have used the focus words correctly.

Help the children to choose one of the focus words as their word of the week. Challenge them to use it as often as they can – both at home and at school.

Follow-up independent sessions

You will need
- Multiple copies of Collins Big Cat *Harry the Clever Spider at School*

Ask children to reread the story. They can then work with their Reading Partners and create a story map that shows the main events of the story in order. They can use their story map to retell the story to the rest of the group.

Ask children to use their story maps to retell the story, but this time as if it were Miss Bradley who was telling it. Remind them to think about what she is like as a character and how she might have felt at different points in the story.

Going Fast

Book Band: Turquoise

This non-chronological report looks at some of the fastest animals and machines in the world and explains how their shape helps them to go fast.

Skills focus

- Draw on knowledge of vocabulary to understand texts
- Identify/explain key aspects of fiction and non-fiction texts, e.g. character, events, title
- Make inferences from texts
- Read words accurately and fluently

Guided reading session

You will need

- Multiple copies of Collins Big Cat *Going Fast*

Tune in

Tell the children that they are going to introduce the book themselves. Ask them to read the title, the blurb and the title page on their own and then to prepare to talk about what the book is about.

Give them a minute to do the task and then read the title aloud.

Ask the following questions:

- What kind of book is this?
- How do you know?
- What is it about?

Heads together

Before they start reading, tell the children what you will be focusing on for this session: reading strategies (recognising tricky words, blending phonemes to read longer words, breaking words up, for example, 'some/thing', 'power/ful') and noticing the features of a non-fiction text and how they help the reader.

Explain that the children are going to choose chapters to read today by looking at the contents page. Ask them to turn to the title page and choose a chapter to read. Remind them that they can move on to another chapter if they finish reading the first one.

As they read, move around the group, listening to each child. If necessary, support them in reading longer words and observe how fluently they are reading.

Wrap up

Return to the book, praising children for reading fluently. You may want to ask children to demonstrate how they read a line fluently.

Ask the following questions:

- What features of non-fiction texts did you spot as you read?
- How do they help the reader?

Remind the children to show you what they have found in addition to giving a verbal answer.

Explain that you are now going to ask children some clue questions; they may have to think quite carefully to help them to answer.

Ask the following questions:

- All of the things in the book have a special shape to help them to go fast. Can you explain what that shape is? *(smooth, simple, streamlined)*
- Some animals' or birds' bodies are good for going fast. What is special about their bodies? *(cheetah's small head, long body, powerful legs; falcon can fold its wings; dolphin's pointed snout, they shed their skin)*
- What kind of people do you think the people who drive or ride vehicles that go fast are? What makes you think that?

Vocabulary boost session

You will need

- Multiple copies of Collins Big Cat *Going Fast*

Vocabulary table

Focus word	Child-friendly explanation	Example sentence	Tell me...
fast	If you do something fast, you do it at great speed.	She ran **fast** to win the race.	Tell me about something that is fast.
faster	If something is faster than something else, it is 'more' fast, for example, a car is faster than a bicycle.	Ellie was **faster** than Jude.	Tell me what is faster than a car.
fastest	If something is the fastest, it is the 'most' fast, for example, a rocket is the fastest.	Sana was the **fastest** so she won the race.	Tell me about the fastest thing, animal or person that you know.

Tune in

Explain to the children that in this lesson they are going to look closely at some of the words the author has used and what those words mean.

Read the book aloud to the children, asking them to follow and join in as you read.

Refer back to each of the focus words within the context of the story, writing up the word, giving a child-friendly explanation and asking children to say the focus word with you. For example: The book title is *Going Fast*. If you do something fast, you do it at great speed. Now, say the word with me – 'fast'.

You may wish to use the examples in the table, above.

Refer to each of the focus words that you have written up and give the children the example sentences. Then ask them to interact with the word meanings by asking the questions in the 'Tell me' column. You may wish to demonstrate by giving some examples of your own.

Ask children to say the words with you once more.

Heads together

Explore and develop children's understanding of the focus words by doing the following activity. Tell them

you are going to give them three words. For each word, they are going to decide which is 'fast', 'faster' or 'fastest'. There may be more than one in each set. (Encourage the children to make links to their own lives and experiences to help them.)

- boat, fish, penguin
- elephant, lion, hippopotamus
- cat, dog, rabbit
- rocket, aeroplane, train

Wrap up

Review the word meanings by doing the following activity. This time ask children to come up with their own three things or animals that are 'fast', 'faster' and 'fastest'. For example: My three things are insects; they are spider, fly and butterfly. A spider can be fast, a butterfly can be faster and a fly is the fastest. Give them one minute to think of three things or animals.

After thinking time, ask each child to name their three things or animals and say which is fast, faster and fastest.

Ask: Can you explain the difference between 'fast', 'faster' and 'fastest'?

Follow-up independent sessions

You will need

- Multiple copies of Collins Big Cat *Going Fast*
- Resource sheet: Adding labels
- Coloured pencils or pens

Ask children to work with their Reading Partners and to read the book aloud. They should choose

a chapter that they enjoyed last time, or choose one that they have not read yet. Encourage them to practise reading smoothly by reading ahead and getting ready for the next word.

Hand out copies of Resource sheet: Adding labels. The children read pages 4 and 5 again. They then add labels to a picture of a man riding a bike to show how the bike is built to go fast and the cyclist is helping.

Chewy Hughie

Book Band: Turquoise

This rhyming story is about a dog that can't stop chewing… until he starts to chew something under the bed.

Skills focus

- Draw on knowledge of vocabulary to understand texts
- Make inferences from the text
- Predict what might happen on the basis of what has been read so far
- Read words accurately and fluently

Guided reading session

You will need

- Multiple copies of Collins Big Cat *Chewy Hughie*

Tune in

Look together at the front cover picture. Ask children to look carefully at spellings as you sound out the title. Write the title on the board and underline the letters that make the /ee/ sound at the end (Chewy Hughie). Point out how different spellings have the same sound.

Ask: Do the words share another sound that is spelled differently?

Ask children to read the words slowly. Circle the letters that make the same /oo/ sound (Chewy Hughie)

Read the back cover blurb and point out the rhyming words 'chew' and 'do'. Ask children what might be special about the way this story is written. Elicit that it is a rhyming story.

Reread the blurb.

Ask the following questions:

- Do you think the rhyming story will be funny or sad?
- What do you think Hughie found under the bed?

Heads together

Read page 2 aloud to the children, asking them to follow as you read and to listen for a rhyme. Check that they spot the rhyming words at the end of each sentence ('chew', 'do').

Read pages 3 and 4 aloud to the children, asking them to follow as you read and to listen for a rhyme. Again, check that they spot the rhyming words at the end of each sentence ('bones', 'phones').

Point out the rhyming pattern: the words at the end of each two lines rhyme. Explain that by knowing this we can expect a rhyming word, which helps us to read the end of line words.

Demonstrate by asking them to join in the last word of page 5. Say: When I pause, say the word you think will follow. Read page 5 and pause before 'rolls'.

Read pages 2 to 7, pausing before each second rhyming word to encourage the children to join in.

Ask the following questions:

- What has happened so far?
- What happens when Mum says 'No!'? *(Hughie wags his tail)*
- What does this tell us about Hughie?

Ask children to follow the words carefully as you read the rest of the story.

Pause after page 16.

Ask the following questions:

- Why is Chewy Hughie in trouble? *(He chewed bubble gum.)*
- What do you think will happen next?

Finish reading the poem.

Ask: What sort of poem was it – funny or scary? Why?

Ask children to read the poem with you. Pause before repeated rhymes to see if they continue reading.

Wrap up

Ask: What did Hughie chew at the end? *(bubble gum)*

Encourage the children to explain what happened next (he ended up in a bubble of bubble gum) and finally (the bubble went pop).

Ask: Why did Hughie stop chewing?

Encourage the children to look again at pages 16 to 21. Encourage them to 'jump into the picture' on page 16 and describe how they would feel. Guide the children towards inferring that Hughie had a bad time, which scared him so much that he stopped chewing.

Turn to page 21.

Ask the following questions:

- What has Hughie done? *(dug holes in the garden)*
- What is the family thinking?
- Do you think Hughie cares?

Return to any words the children found difficult and help them sound them out.

Support the children in practising a dramatic reading of the poem. Ask volunteers to act out sections of the poem, while the group reads the words.

Vocabulary boost session

You will need

- Multiple copies of Collins Big Cat *Chewy Hughie*

Vocabulary table

Focus word	Child-friendly explanation	Example sentence	Tell me...
mobile	If something is mobile, it can be moved around – a mobile phone can be carried around in a bag.	The **mobile** library is a van full of books that travels from village to village.	Tell me about things that you have seen that are mobile.
care	If you care about something, you are interested and concerned about it. If you care about a person, you will want them to be okay.	I **care** about my grandma because I love her and want her to be happy.	Tell me about something or someone you care about.
trouble	If someone is in trouble, then they are facing a problem or a danger and aren't happy.	I got into **trouble** for forgetting my books for the lesson.	Tell me about any time you, or a character in a story, have got into trouble.

Tune in

Explain to the children that in this lesson they are going to talk about some of the words the author has used and what those words mean.

Read the book aloud to the children, emphasising the repeated and rhyming words and reading expressively. Focus the children on each focus word within the context of the story. Write the word on the board, give a child-friendly explanation and ask children to read the focus word with you. For example, say: In the story it says that Chewy Hughie does not care that he chews the dirty underwear! That means he isn't interested or concerned about the things he chews. Now, let's read the word together – 'care'.

Suggestions for simple definitions are supplied in the table, above.

Next, encourage the children to focus on each focus word on the board, as you give them an example sentence containing each. Then ask them to answer the question from the 'Tell me' column of the table. This will encourage them to think about the word in the context of their own lives. You could support them by giving your own 'Tell me' answer first.

Ask children to read the words with you again.

Heads together

Ask the following questions to explore and develop the children's understanding of the focus words:

- Which would you describe as mobile – a mountain or a bicycle?
- What might you most care about – a lost pet or a lost book?
- Who might get into trouble – someone in a boat in a storm or someone playing on a sunny beach?

Encourage them to explain their answers.

Wrap up

Review the word meanings by asking children to put their hand up when they hear a word that links with the focus words. Say:

- 'mobile': lamppost, pavement, home
- 'care': concern, anger, funny
- 'trouble': safety, danger, happy

Ask children to choose one of the focus words as their word of the week. Ask them to use the word as often as they can, both at school and at home.

Follow-up independent sessions

You will need

- Resource sheet: Feelings
- Resource sheet: Role-play for *Chewy Hughie*

Ask children to pretend that they are the boy in the story and to draw a face according to how they might feel for each thing that Chewy Hughie chews. The children could discuss their views in small groups before completing the Resource sheet: Feelings.

Ask children to take turns to role-play a talking Chewy Hughie. Provide them with the questions on the Resource sheet: Role-play for *Chewy Hughie*, if necessary.

Africa's Big Three

Book Band: Turquoise

A non-chronological report about elephants, rhinos and hippos; includes spectacular photographs.

Skills focus

- Draw on knowledge of vocabulary to understand texts
- Identify/explain key aspects of fiction and non-fiction texts, e.g. character, events, title
- Identify/explain the sequence of events in texts
- Check reading makes sense

Guided reading session

You will need

- Multiple copies of Collins Big Cat *Africa's Big Three*
- A globe or world map
- Mini-whiteboards and pens

Tune in

Begin by finding Africa on a globe or world map.

Ask: What animals do you think live in Africa?

Explain to the children that they are going to look at a book about elephants, rhinos and hippos. Discuss and record on the board what the children know about the three animals.

Introduce the book by exploring the front cover. Discuss the beautiful photographs.

Ask: What type of book do you think this is? *(non-fiction/information book)*

Turn the book over and read the blurb.

Ask the following questions:

- Can you identify the question words? *(where, what, why)*
- What other question words can you think of? *(how, when, who)*

In pairs, ask children to think of and write a question about one of the animals on their whiteboard. (For example: What do elephants eat? Why do rhinos have a horn?) Save these so that they can check if the book has answered them at the end.

Recap strategies to use when reading, such as: decoding, identifying high frequency words, checking it makes sense and picture clues.

Discuss the features of non-fiction/information texts and create a list, including: headings, photographs, introduction, captions, labels and fact boxes. Challenge the children to look through the book and find each of the features.

Heads together

Look at the contents page together. Read through the headings. Ask children to practise saying 'rhinoceroses' and 'hippopotamuses'. Practise using the contents page.

Ask the following questions:

- On what page can you find out about hippos? *(page 14)*
- What would you find out about on page 4? *(elephants)*

Turn to pages 2 and 3. Model reading the text.

Ask: What features of non-fiction texts are on these pages? *(heading, introduction, photographs, captions)*

Ask the following questions:

- Which animal is the biggest? *(elephant)*
- Which animals live on the banks of rivers? *(hippos)*

Ask children to work in pairs and choose one section to read in detail. Encourage the children to read aloud, pointing to the words and rereading to check it makes sense. Can they find out three facts to report back to the rest of the group?

Wrap up

Give each pair time to feed back what they have found out to the rest of the group.

Turn to pages 20 and 21 and find out how people affect the lives of these animals. Model reading the text.

Ask: Why are people the worst enemies of elephants, rhinos and hippos? *(they hunt them for ivory, meat, oil and horns; using up their land)*

On pages 22 and 23 explore the factfile. Show the children how to read the table.

Ask the following questions:

- How long do white rhinos live? *(30–40 years)*
- How rare are hippos? *(becoming rare)*
- Which live the longest? *(elephants)*

Go back to the questions the children wrote at the start of the session. Did they find the answers?

Vocabulary boost session

You will need

- Multiple copies of Collins Big Cat *Africa's Big Three*
- Timer
- Resource sheet: Sizes

Vocabulary table

Focus word	Child-friendly explanation	Example sentence	Tell me...
biggest	If something is the biggest, it is bigger than the others.	I had the **biggest** ice-cream.	Tell me which is the biggest animal – a kitten, a cat or a tiger?
protect	If you protect something, you are looking after it and stopping it from coming to harm.	A computer tablet cover can **protect** the computer tablet from drops, breakages and spills.	Tell me how you protect yourself from the sun.
rare	If something is rare, it is not very common; there are not very many of them.	Some wild animals are becoming **rare**.	Tell me why elephants, hippos and rhinos are becoming rare.

Tune in

Explain that in this lesson the children are going to look in more detail at some of the words the author has used. Write the three focus words clearly for the children to see. Read the words together. Discuss and explain the child-friendly meaning of each word.

Reread the text.

Challenge the children to find the focus words in the text.

Heads together

Ask children to think of as many words as they can that mean 'big' in one minute, using a timer.

The children use pictures cut from Resource sheet: Sizes and order them from smallest to biggest/largest. Encourage them to use the vocabulary 'bigger' and 'biggest', 'taller' and 'tallest', 'smaller' and 'smallest', 'larger' and 'largest' to describe the pictures and create sentences. For example: The sunflower is taller than the rose.

Wrap up

Recap the three focus words by discussing the questions in the 'Tell me' column of the table, above.

Challenge the children to think of a sentence using one of the focus words.

Follow-up independent sessions

You will need

- A selection of magazines and catalogues, grey fabric, coloured card, felt, glue, scissors, paper, coloured pencils
- Resource sheet: Elephant outline
- Poster paper, coloured pencils or pens
- A selection of books about elephants, rhinos and hippos (stories, poems and non-fiction)

Ask children to create a collage of an elephant. They can use magazines and catalogues to cut out the colour grey, tear the paper into small pieces and stick on to Resource sheet: Elephant outline. Ask children to design a 'Save the elephants' poster. They might also use grey fabric and coloured card or felt.

Using Resource sheet: Elephant outline, the children label the picture with facts about elephants.

Let the children explore a selection of books about elephants, rhinos and hippos (stories, poems and non-fiction).

Going for a Drive

Book Band: Turquoise

Going for a Drive is a collection of poems that take children on a journey from morning to night.

Skills focus

- Draw on knowledge of vocabulary to understand texts
- Identify/explain key aspects of fiction and non-fiction texts, e.g. character, events, title
- Make inferences from texts
- Read words accurately and fluently

Guided reading session

You will need

- Multiple copies of Collins Big Cat *Going for a Drive*

Tune in

Ask children to look at the front cover of the book and to read the title.

Ask the following questions:

- Where do you think the people in the car might be going?
- How do you think they are feeling?

Read the blurb on the back cover aloud, emphasising the rhyme and rhythm.

Ask: What do you notice. *(it rhymes)*

Challenge them to spot the rhyming words. Establish that the book is a collection of poems.

Ask: Where is the contents likely to be in the book? *(near the front)*

Turn to the contents page and elicit that each heading is the title of a poem. Explain that you would like to read the first poem 'Going for a Drive' because it is the title of the book.

Turn to page 3 and read the poem with expression, emphasising the rhythm. Remind the children that they looked at a picture of these people going for a drive on the front cover.

Ask: Does the poem help you to work out how they are feeling? *(They are happy and enjoying themselves.)*

Heads together

Ask each child to choose another poem from the contents page that they would like to read aloud to their partner.

Ask: What do you need to think about when you are reading aloud? *(using expression, speaking clearly)*

Ask children to practise reading their chosen poem quietly. As they read, work around the group, supporting them in reading unfamiliar words and praising the use of expression.

If necessary, demonstrate how to use rhythm and rhyme to help with this.

Wrap up

Give the children the opportunity to read their chosen poem aloud. Encourage Reading Partners to comment positively on what they liked about the reading and to suggest ways in which it could be made even better.

Ask children to explain why they chose their particular poems and what they liked about reading them aloud.

Vocabulary boost session

You will need

- Multiple copies of Collins Big Cat *Going for a Drive*

Vocabulary table

Focus word	Child-friendly explanation	Example sentence	Tell me…
chubby	If someone or something is chubby, it is round and fat.	The little lamb had **chubby** legs.	Tell me about a chubby baby animal you have seen.
merry	If something is merry, it is happy.	The lamb was having a **merry** time jumping in the hay.	Tell me about a time when you have felt merry.
gorgeous	If someone or something is gorgeous, it is beautiful	The little lamb was **gorgeous**.	Tell me why you think something is gorgeous.

Tune in

Explain to the children that you have spotted a poem in the book that has some really interesting words. Remind them that writers choose words very carefully when they write so you'd like the children to look at and think about some of the words in this poem.

Ask children to use the contents page to find the poem 'Caterpillar'.

Read the poem aloud to the children, briefly explaining the meaning of the focus words as you read. You may wish to refer to the information in the table, above, to support this.

Heads together

Write up each of the focus words on the board. Revisit each of the words and support the children in identifying the noun connected with each focus word.

Establish that all of the focus words are adjectives and that they are describing particular nouns.

Take each focus word in turn.

Ask: What other words could the poet have chosen?

List the children's suggestions on the board, alongside the focus words.

Ask: Why do you think she chose these words?

Establish that the focus words are more unusual and sound better than some of the alternatives.

Wrap up

Ask children the 'Tell me' prompts from the table, encouraging them to make connections with the focus words and their own experiences in order to develop understanding of the word meanings.

If necessary, offer some of your own examples to demonstrate the sort of responses you are looking for.

Follow-up independent sessions

You will need

- Multiple copies of Collins Big Cat *Going for a Drive*
- Resource sheet: Poems
- Sticky notes

Ask children to use the contents page to find and read another poem. Give each child a copy of Resource sheet: Poems for them to complete. Ask them to share their chosen poem and their thoughts and pictures on Resource sheet: Poems, with their Reading Partner.

Ask children to work with their Reading Partner and to turn to pages 22 and 23. Explain that these pages show the poems as a journey. Give children sticky notes and ask them to write down the titles of the poems that the sentences on these pages are taken from. They can then place the sticky notes alongside the relevant sentence.

What's that Building?

Book Band: Turquoise

This information book explores some of the world's most amazing buildings, inside and out, with facts about how they are built and what they do.

Skills focus

- Draw on knowledge of vocabulary to understand texts
- Identify/explain key aspects of fiction and non-fiction texts, e.g. character, events, title
- Make inferences from texts
- Read words accurately and fluently

Guided reading session

You will need

- Multiple copies of Collins Big Cat *What's that Building?*

Tune in

Introduce the book by asking children to read the title together.

Ask the following questions:

- What kind of book do you think this is?
- What makes you think that?
- Can you predict what features of a non-fiction book will be in it? *(contents, photographs, labels, glossary, index)*

Read the title again and point to the apostrophe in the word 'What's'.

Ask the following questions:

- What is that?
- What job does it do? *(tells us that a letter is missing from the word 'is' – the word 'is' has been shortened)*

Point to the question mark.

Ask the following questions:

- What is that?
- What job does it do? *(tells the reader that it is a question)*

Turn to the back cover and read the blurb aloud, encouraging the children to join in with you.

Ask: What is the book about?

Heads together

Turn to the title page and read it aloud; encourage the children to follow and join in with you.

Ask the following questions:

- What do you think the building in the picture is for?
- Why do you think it is that shape?

Explain that the children are going to read most of this book together. As they read they are going to think about the use of question marks and apostrophes for missing letters.

Read pages 2 to 5 aloud to the children, asking them to follow as you read and join in. Model strategies for reading longer words and model the use of expression where necessary.

Turn back to page 2.

Ask the following questions:

- Can you point to a question mark?
- Who can point to an apostrophe?
- Can you tell me what the missing letter is?

Continue reading aloud to page 9, with the children following and joining in.

Ask: Were our predictions right (about the palm house)?

Read to page 11, with the children following and joining in.

Ask the following questions:

- Who can point to an apostrophe on page 10?
- Can you tell me what the missing letter is?

Wrap up

Read to page 21, with the children following and joining in.

Ask the following questions:

- In the blurb, it says that the buildings in the book are special. Do you think that they are? Why?
- Which building do you think is the most special? Why?
- What is the most interesting fact that you have learned from reading this book?

Vocabulary boost session

You will need

- Multiple copies of Collins Big Cat *What's that Building?*

Vocabulary table

Focus word	Child-friendly explanation	Example sentence	Tell me…
unusual	Something that is unusual is interesting or different from other things.	The coloured bird they saw was **unusual**.	Tell me about something you have seen that is unusual.
vast	If something is vast it is very, very big. We usually use the word 'vast' to tell us about places.	The football stadium is **vast**.	Tell me about a vast place or building.
bright	If we say a light is 'bright', it means that it is shining strongly and full of light.	She couldn't see because the sunshine was too **bright**.	Tell me the names of some things that are bright.

Tune in

Explain to the children that in this lesson they are going to look closely at some of the words the author has used and what those words mean.

Read the book aloud to the children, asking them to follow and join in as you read.

Refer back to each of the focus words within the context of the story, writing up the word, giving a child-friendly explanation and asking children to say the focus word with you. For example: In the book, it says that some buildings are made of 'unusual' materials. Something that is unusual is interesting or different from other things. Now, say the word with me – 'unusual'.

You may wish to use the examples in the table, above.

Refer to each of the focus words that you have written up and give the children the example sentences. Then ask them to interact with the word meanings by asking the questions in the 'Tell me' column. You may wish to demonstrate by giving some examples of your own.

Ask children to say the words with you once more.

Heads together

Explain to the children that they are going to do a thinking activity (word associations). They are going to come up with words that make us think of and remember what the key words mean.

Take each of the following words in turn and ask children to call out words that pop into their heads when you say them:

- 'unusual' (interesting, strange, different, new to us)
- 'vast' (football pitch, sea, ship, skyscraper)
- 'bright' (light, dazzling, sun, moon, stars)

Encourage children to make links to their own lives and experiences to help them.

Wrap up

Review the word meanings by doing the following activity.

Turn to page 2. Explain it says that some buildings are made of 'unusual' materials. Ask children to talk to their Reading Partner about what 'unusual' means.

Ask: Now, can you tell me what 'unusual' means?

Turn to page 3. Explain it says that some buildings are so 'vast' that workers use scooters to get around. Ask children to talk to their Reading Partner about what 'vast' means.

Ask: Now, can you tell me what 'vast' means?

Turn to page 6. Explain it says the lamp is as 'bright' as a million candles. Ask children to talk to their Reading Partner about what 'bright' means.

Ask: Now, can you tell me what 'bright' means?

Follow-up independent sessions

You will need

- Multiple copies of Collins Big Cat *What's that Building?*
- Resource sheet: Titles and facts

Ask children to work with their Reading Partners and to read the book aloud. They should choose two chapters that they enjoyed last time.

Hand out copies of Resource sheet: Title and facts. The children write a title and an interesting fact about each picture.

The Journey of Humpback Whales

Book Band: Turquoise

An information book on humpback whales and their long journey every two years as they migrate to have babies.

Skills focus

- Draw on knowledge of vocabulary to understand texts
- Identify/explain key aspects of fiction and non-fiction texts, e.g. character, events, title
- Identify/explain the sequence of events in texts
- Check reading makes sense

Guided reading session

You will need

- Multiple copies of Collins Big Cat *The Journey of Humpback Whales*
- Dictionaries

Tune in

Introduce the book by asking children what they think it is about. Suggest that they look at the cover and then flick through the pages.

Encourage the children to look at the words as you read the title aloud to them.

Ask: What sort of book do you think this is and why?

Read the back cover blurb and discuss the type of book it is again. Say: To check the type of book, I'm going to flick through the pages to see what kind of things are in it. I can see maps… what can you see?

If necessary, point out the contents, photographs (not illustrations), labels with pointer rules, captions, fact panels, glossary and index. Check that children link these to it being a fact book.

Heads together

Read pages 2 to 6 aloud to the children, asking them to follow as you read and be alert to information. Model rereading to make sense by saying, for example: Did everyone understand that page? I'll read it again just in case.

Explain to the children that rereading and asking ourselves questions are good ways of checking our understanding.

Reread pages 2 to 6, stopping after each page and asking questions to check that they have understood the main points.

On page 6, demonstrate how we can check our understanding by using the glossary, for example, to find out exactly what barnacles and sea lice are.

Point to the bold type on page 6 and then find and read the definitions on page 20 together.

Demonstrate using a dictionary to look up, for example, 'breaching' on page 6. Compare the dictionary definition with what it says on page 6. Point out how both the glossary and a dictionary can be useful.

Ask children to read the rest of the book in pairs to find out more about the journey and humpback whales. As they read, move around the pairs, asking what they have learned. Encourage them to use the glossary and dictionaries.

Wrap up

Ask children if they found the book interesting.

Ask: Which did you think was the most interesting page? Why?

Ask children if they looked any words up in a dictionary and if they found the glossary useful.

Ask: What new words did you learn? What did they mean?

Focusing on pages 8 and 9, ask children to explain what the map shows. Suggest that they reread the text to check. Point to the red arrow.

Ask the following questions:

- Is this the journey?
- What do the captions show? *(different stages of the journey)*

Ask children to feed back on the stages of the journey, in the correct order if possible.

Ask: How can you check you are correct? *(by rereading)*

Reread the book as a group, pausing to ask what a word means now and then. If they struggle at all, offer a definition in child-friendly language and reread the sentence again.

Vocabulary boost session

You will need
- Multiple copies of Collins Big Cat *The Journey of Humpback Whales*
- Pictures of animals

Vocabulary table

Focus word	Child-friendly explanation	Example sentence	Tell me...
impress	If you impress someone, you do something special to make them think you are amazing.	I want to **impress** my friend by wearing my new jacket.	Tell me about a time when you wanted to impress someone.
protection	Protection is a way of making something extra safe.	I keep my hens locked in a coop at night for **protection** against foxes.	Tell me about something that needs protection.
survive	If animals survive, it means they live, even though they have been in danger.	You will **survive** the cold weather if you wear thick clothes.	Tell me about any animals you think may only just survive sometimes.

Tune in

Tell the children to follow the words in the book as you read it to them. Explain that you will be looking closely at some of the words about the whales.

Next, ask them to read the book with you, letting them take the lead. Stop when they stumble over a word; help them to read it by sounding out the letters. Offer a child-friendly explanation if necessary.

Write the three focus words on the board. Ask children to read them and then look at them again in the context of the book. Explain their meanings using the explanations in the table, above, or your own definitions. Ask children to say the focus words with you afterwards.

For each word, give them an example sentence that incorporates the word. Again, you can use those in the table or make up your own.

Next, challenge them with the 'Tell me' questions in the table, above. Support them by offering your own answer, for example: I think wild elephants need extra protection because too many get killed.

Finally, ask children to say the words with you again.

Heads together

Ask the following questions to explore and develop the children's understanding of the focus words:
- What would you do to impress someone important?
- Would you be surprised if someone offered you extra protection?
- Would you survive a trip through Antarctica or another dangerous place?

Wrap up

Ask the following questions to review the focus word meanings:
- If we say we impress someone, does it mean we make them think we are better or worse?
- If an animal gets extra protection, does it mean that it will be safer or in more danger?
- If a camel survives in a hot desert, does it mean the camel lives or dies?

Display the focus words as part of an animal display. Provide pictures of animals for the children to stick by the relevant word, for example, 'impress' – a peacock displaying its feathers; 'protection' – a lion with its cubs; 'survive' – a lone Arctic hare in the snow.

Follow-up independent sessions

You will need
- Multiple copies of Collins Big Cat *The Journey of Humpback Whales*
- Resource sheet: Words
- Dictionaries
- Resource sheet: Humpback whale factfile

Provide the word cards copied and cut from Resource sheet: Words. Ask children to work in small groups, taking it in turn to pick a card. They must guess its meaning. Another member of the group checks the meaning in the glossary or a dictionary and the group decides if the player was wrong or right.

Give individual children the Resource sheet: Humpback whale factfile. Ask them to read and find information to add to the boxes, draw a picture and add a caption.

The Lost Village of Skara Brae

Book Band: Turquoise

An information book about an ancient village discovered on the Scottish Orkney Islands. The book contains information about how the village remains were discovered and what this tells us about the past.

Skills focus

- Draw on knowledge of vocabulary to understand texts
- Identify/explain key aspects of fiction and non-fiction texts, e.g. character, events, title
- Make inferences from texts
- Read words accurately and fluently

Guided reading session

You will need

- Multiple copies of Collins Big Cat *The Lost Village of Skara Brae*
- Map of the UK
- Resource sheet: Key words

Tune in

Begin by looking at the front cover of the book. Read the title together. Check the children know what a 'village' is.

Ask the following questions:

- Can you describe the picture on the front cover? *(stone wall, water/sea)*
- How do you think a village can be lost?

Turn to the back cover and read the blurb. Model reading with accuracy and expression. **Ask** the following questions:

- What type of book is this? *(a non-fiction/ information book)*
- Where is Scotland?

Look at a map of the UK and find Scotland. Discuss what the children know about Scotland.

Ask: Where can you find the contents page? *(at the front of the book)*

Turn to the contents page. Read through the headings together.

Ask the following questions:

- On what page can you find out about 'The Great Storm of 1850'? *(page 4)*
- What is page 16 about? *(the village today)*
- What is a glossary? *(it tells you what words used in the text mean)*

Challenge children to use the contents page to find the glossary. *(page 20)* Read the words in bold and discuss what they mean. Close the book.

Use Resource sheet: Key words, to match the key words cut from the sheet to the correct meanings, working as a group.

Heads together

Look at pages 2 and 3 together. Model reading the text, demonstrating accuracy and fluency. Show the children that the words in bold (Orkneys, archaeologists, New Stone Age and flint) are in the glossary.

Ask the following questions to check children's understanding:

- What was the village buried under? *(sand and soil)*
- Where was the village found? *(the Orkney Islands)*

Continue through the book together reading pages 4 to 19. Read together, encouraging the children to join in and point to the words. Do they recognise the high frequency words? Can they decode unfamiliar words? Ask questions to check the children's understanding as you progress through the text.

Wrap up

Ask children to discuss what life in Skara Brae would have been like 4,000 years ago. Would it have been hard work? What do they think that they would/ wouldn't have liked?

Discuss whether they would like to be an archaeologist or if they would like to visit Skara Brae now.

Turn to pages 22 and 23 and discuss the timeline. Explain that it shows the events through time in the order that they happened.

Vocabulary boost session

You will need

- Multiple copies of Collins Big Cat *The Lost Village of Skara Brae*

Vocabulary table

Focus word	Child-friendly explanation	Example sentence	Tell me...
archaeologist	An archaeologist is someone who digs up artefacts to learn about the past.	The **archaeologist** found some pieces of pottery.	Tell me what an archaeologist does.
preserved	If something is preserved, it is kept as it is/not destroyed.	The fruit was made into jam to **preserve** it.	Tell me why it is important to preserve things.
village	A small group of houses and facilities. Smaller than a town.	My cousin lives in a **village**.	Tell me how a village is different to a city.

Tune in

Explain that in this lesson the children are going to look in more detail at some of the words the author has used. Write the three focus words clearly for the children to see. Read the words together. Discuss and explain the child-friendly meaning of each word.

Reread the text.

Challenge the children to find the focus words in the text. ('archaeologist', pages 2 and 10; 'preserved', page 12; 'village', in the title)

Heads together

Ask children to work in pairs to write a question that they would ask an archaeologist about their job.

Help the children to design and draw a map of an imaginary village. What would you include in your village?

Wrap up

Recap the three focus words by discussing the questions in the 'Tell me' column of the table, above.

Challenge the children to think of a sentence using one of the focus words.

Follow-up independent sessions

You will need

- Buried items/treasures in a sand tray, magnifying glasses, paint brushes
- Resource sheet: My treasure

Provide buried items/treasures in a sand tray for the children to role-play being an archaeologist. Using paint brushes and magnifying glasses, children see what they can find in the trays. They use Resource sheet: My treasure, to record what they have found.

Brown Bear and Wilbur Wolf

Book Band: Turquoise

When Brown Bear discovers he has lost his sense of smell, Wilbur Wolf steps in to help and they realise that two heads are better than one.

Skills focus

- Draw on knowledge of vocabulary to understand texts
- Identify/explain the sequence of events in texts
- Make inferences from texts
- Read words accurately and fluently

Guided reading session

You will need

- Multiple copies of Collins Big Cat *Brown Bear and Wilbur Wolf*

Tune in

Ask: What are your favourite smells and why?

Share some of your own, giving reasons why you like them.

Ask: What do you think animals use their sense of smell for? *(finding food, finding other animals)*

Show the children the front cover of the book and ask them to read the title.

Ask the following questions:

- Where do you think these animals live? *(mountains, forests)*
- Do you think that they would normally be friends or enemies? *(enemies)*

Ask children to read the blurb on the back cover. Return to the discussion about animals using their sense of smell and make the connection between Brown Bear's situation.

Read page 2 aloud to the children and ask them to identify the verbs that tell them what Brown Bear did when he came out of his den.

Ask children to read pages 4 to 7 aloud to find out what Brown Bear did next.

Take feedback from the reading.

Ask the following questions:

- What is the problem with Brown Bear having lost his sense of smell? *(He can't find any food.)*
- How does it make Brown Bear feel? *(sad)*

Ask children to read Brown Bear's dialogue in a sad voice.

Remind the children that in the blurb it asks if Wilbur Wolf could help.

Ask: How do you think he might help Brown Bear?

Heads together

Ask children to read pages 8 to 21 to find out whether Wilbur Wolf helped Brown Bear and, if so, how.

Remind them to think about how characters might speak when they are reading.

As the children read, work around the group, supporting the children as they come across unfamiliar vocabulary and praising expressive, enthusiastic reading.

Wrap up

Ask children to recount what happened in the story. As they do so, create a story map on the board that shows the main events.

Ask the following questions:

- Why did the animals run away or fly away from Brown Bear? *(They were frightened even though Brown Bear just wanted to be friends.)*
- How do you think Brown Bear feels each time the animals run away? *(He might have felt sad or his feelings might have been hurt.)*
- Can you summarise how Wilbur Wolf helped Brown Bear. *(by sniffing out food)*
- How will Brown Bear help Wilbur Wolf? *(by catching food)*

Work with the children to develop a sentence that summarises the message in the story, for example: Two heads are better than one; friends help each other out.

Use the story map to help the children to retell the story.

Vocabulary boost session

You will need
- Multiple copies of Collins Big Cat *Brown Bear and Wilbur Wolf*
- Resource Sheet: Question cards

Vocabulary table

Focus word	Child friendly explanation	Example sentence	Tell me...
alone	If you are alone, you are on your own.	The bear was all **alone** in the forest.	Tell me how you would feel if you were alone somewhere.
scared	If you are scared, you are afraid of something.	The film we watched last night **scared** me!	Tell me something that would make you scared.
weak	If you are weak, you have no strength.	Naila was feeling **weak** because she was so tired.	Tell me about something that you would find hard if you were feeling weak.

Tune in

Explain to the children that the focus for this lesson is the words that the author of the story has used. Remind the children that authors choose words very carefully when they write and that you would like them to look at the part of the story where Brown Bear and Wilbur Wolf meet.

Read pages 14 to 17 aloud to the children. As you come to the focus words, briefly explain them, using the information in the table, above.

Ask the following questions:
- What do the words tell us about how Brown Bear and Wilbur Wolf are feeling?
- How do the words make us feel about the characters?

Heads together

Ask for a volunteer to be in the 'hot seat' as Brown Bear. Hand out the question cards from Resource sheet: Question cards and give the children a few minutes to think of two or three questions that they can ask Brown Bear.

Repeat the activity with Wilbur Wolf in the hot seat.

Ask children what they think about Brown Bear and Wilbur Wolf.

Ask: Do you think that it was a good thing that they met up?

Wrap up

Use the 'Tell me' prompts from the table, above. Encourage the children to develop their understanding of the meanings of the focus words by making connections with the words and their own experiences.

Follow-up independent sessions

You will need
- Multiple copies of Collins Big Cat *Brown Bear and Wilbur Wolf*
- Resource sheet: Role on the wall: Brown Bear and Wilbur Wolf

Ask children to reread the story and to create their own story maps. They can then use these to retell the story to each other.

Give children the Resource sheet: Role on the wall: Brown Bear and Wilbur Wolf. Ask them to work with their Reading Partners and to write words and phrases on the character outlines that describe the two characters and the appearance of Brown Bear and Wilbur Wolf.

The Big, Bad City

Book Band: Turquoise

In this traditional tale, Little Red Hen is lost in the big, bad city until a smiley stranger offers to help her find her granny's house.

Skills focus

- Draw on knowledge of vocabulary to understand texts
- Make inferences from texts
- Predict what might happen on the basis of what has been read so far
- Read words accurately and fluently

Guided reading session

You will need

- Multiple copies of Collins Big Cat *The Big, Bad City*

Tune in

Introduce the book by asking children to look closely at the front cover.

Ask the following questions:

- What can you see?
- What do you think the characters' names are? *(Fox, Hen)*
- What do you think that they are doing or thinking?

Read the title aloud; ask children to join in.

Ask the following questions:

- What do you think the story is about?
- Do you know any other stories with these characters or the words 'big, bad' in?

Turn to the back cover and read the blurb aloud, encouraging the children to follow and join in with you.

Ask the following questions:

- Do you have any more ideas about what the story might be about?
- What are the characters' names? *(Little Red Hen and Granny)*

Turn to the title page, read the title again and then ask children to point to the part that tells us who wrote and illustrated the book. *(Shoo Rayner)* Read this together.

Heads together

Tell the children that they are going to read the story on their own.

Ask: What strategies can you use to help you if you get stuck on a word? *(read the first sound and then think about what the word might be, look at the pictures and guess what word would make sense, look for parts of the word that you already know)*

Tell the children that when they read, you want them to think about their reading strategies and about using expression, particularly for when characters are speaking. They should also use 'prediction' as they read, that is, thinking about what is happening and what might be about to happen.

Ask children to read pages 2 to 21, on their own. As they read, move around the group, listening to each child while the others read in their heads. Check their reading strategies and listen for use of expression as they read dialogue.

Wrap up

Identify and praise children's use of reading strategies that you observed them using to help with reading longer or difficult words and their use of expression for dialogue.

Tell the children that you're going to ask them about their predictions. Turn to page 3.

Ask the following questions:

- What kind of character did you predict the smiley stranger would be?
- Were you right?
- What kind of character is Mr Fox?
- What makes you think that?

Encourage the children to explain their ideas; they should be inferring as well as using direct information from the text.

Ask the following questions:

- What did you predict would happen to Little Red Hen?
- How did you predict the story would end?
- What kind of character is Little Red Hen?
- What makes you think that?

Vocabulary boost session

You will need

- Multiple copies of Collins Big Cat *The Big, Bad City*

Vocabulary table

Focus word	Child-friendly explanation	Example sentence	Tell me...
sigh	When you sigh, you let out a deep breath. It is a way of showing that you are happy, unhappy or tired.	"What a lovely day," **sighed** Ali.	Tell me about something that makes you sigh.
explain	If you explain something, you talk about it clearly so that others know what you mean.	The teacher **explained** how the chicks hatched.	Tell me about something an adult has explained to you.
chirp	Chirp is the sound that a bird makes; it is usually a short, high-pitched sound.	When the sun came up, the birds started **chirping**.	Tell me about a time you have heard birds chirping.

Tune in

Explain to the children that in this lesson they are going to look closely at some of the words the author has used and what those words mean.

Read the book aloud to the children, modelling how to use the punctuation and dialogue to read aloud with expression.

Refer back to each of the focus words within the context of the story, writing up the word, giving a child-friendly explanation and asking children to say the focus word with you. For example: In the story, Little Red Hen sighs when she can't find Granny's house. When you sigh, you let out a deep breath. It is a way of showing that you are happy, unhappy or tired. Now, say the word with me – 'sigh'.

You may wish to use the examples in the table, above.

Refer to each of the focus words that you have written up and give the children the example sentences. Then ask them to interact with the word meanings by asking the questions in the 'Tell me' column. You may wish to demonstrate by giving some examples of your own.

Ask children to say the words with you once more.

Heads together

Explore and develop the children's understanding of the focus words by doing the following activity.

Tell the children that you will say a word and that they are to tell you which of the three new words it makes them think of: 'sigh', 'explain' or 'chirp'.

- Which word does 'bird' make you think of? (*chirp*) Why?
- Which word does 'breathe out' make you think of? (*sigh*) Why?
- Which word does 'talk clearly' make you think of? (*explain*) Why?

Encourage the children to make links to their own lives and experiences to help them.

Wrap up

Ask the following questions to review the word meanings:

- Can you show me what a sigh might look like?
- When might someone sigh?
- If someone explains something, what do they do?
- Can you show me what a chirp might sound like?
- What animal chirps?

Ask children to choose one of the focus words as their word of the week. Challenge them to use the words as often as they can, both at school and at home.

Follow-up independent sessions

You will need

- Multiple copies of Collins Big Cat *The Big, Bad City*
- Resource sheet: Story map for *The Big, Bad City*

Ask children to work with their Reading Partners and to read the book aloud. Remind them to use expression when the characters are speaking.

Give children a copy of Resource sheet: Story map for *The Big, Bad City* and challenge them to draw a story map of the book. They then retell the story to their partner.

Homes Sweet Homes

Book Band: Turquoise

A collection of poems, including shape poems, about animals' contrasting homes or habitats.

Skills focus

- Draw on knowledge of vocabulary to understand texts
- Make inferences from texts
- Check reading makes sense

Guided reading session

You will need

- Multiple copies of Collins Big Cat *Homes Sweet Homes*

Tune in

Read the title aloud to the children.

Ask: Have you ever heard a common saying that is similar to this?

If necessary, tell them about the saying 'Home Sweet Home'.

Ask the following questions:

- What is it saying about someone's home?
- How do you feel when you get home?
- What animals can you see on the front cover? *(owl, badger, hedgehog, birds, squirrels)*
- What do you think that they have got to do with the title?

Read the back cover blurb together. Ensure the children understand the meanings of 'habitats' and 'contrasting'. If necessary, give a child-friendly definition, for example, a habitat is where an animal lives, so it is a sort of 'home'; contrasting means completely different, like hot and cold are contrasting temperatures.

Challenge the children to think of any contrasting habitats animals live in, for example, underground, in the sea.

Ask: What makes poems different to any other text?

List their ideas on the board and elicit how poems often rhyme and the lines are set out in special ways.

Reread the blurb.

Ask: What do you think some of the poems will be about?

Encourage specific ideas.

Heads together

Read page 3 aloud to the children, asking them to follow as you read. Read it again with the children joining in.

Ask: What is the verse saying? Focus on the words in the bigger font for a clue.

Elicit how it is saying that whatever you want can be a home. Point out how the last two lines give the main point and the lines above give examples of different homes (web, shell, hole, sea, tree).

Read page 4. Point to the contrasting words: 'busiest' and 'on your own'.

Ask: Do you think this poet likes her home? Why?

Read page 6 with the children. Point out how the poem title and shape of the poem tell us straight away that it is about a worm.

Ask: What is the poem saying about the worm? *(that it might get squashed if it leaves its home underground)*

Ask children to work in pairs and choose two poems from the contents page to read and work out what they are mainly about and what are the most important words.

Move around the pairs, listening to each child. Check that they reread lines that they are unsure of and notice the form of the poem such as whether it is in verses or is a shape poem. If there are verses, say: What is the main point in this verse?

Wrap up

Encourage volunteer pairs to read their chosen poems to the group and then explain what they were about. Encourage them to work through each verse if necessary.

Ask children to feed back on what they think the poem or verse is mainly about. Encourage them to point to words or lines to back up their views.

Read all the poems aloud with the children, while they follow the words closely. Encourage the children to join in with the poems that they are most familiar with.

Ask children which poem they enjoyed most and why. Open their views up to a group debate so that children can exchange and back up their views.

Ask: Do you think the poet likes animals? Why?

Vocabulary boost session

You will need

- Multiple copies of Collins Big Cat *Homes Sweet Homes*

Vocabulary table

Focus word	Child-friendly explanation	Example sentence	Tell me…
squished	If you squished something, you would have squeezed it flat.	I **squished** a ball of clay into a flat pancake shape.	Tell me about something you have squished.
skimmed	If you skimmed something, you would move across its surface, hardly touching it.	I **skimmed** the cream off the top of the milk.	Tell me about anything you have seen skimming across a surface.
miniature	When something is a miniature of something else, it is the same but very tiny.	I sailed a **miniature** boat in my bath.	Tell me about a miniature thing you have seen.

Tune in

Tell the children that they are going to look carefully at some of the words the poet has used in the book and what those words mean.

Read the book aloud to the children, emphasising the rhythm and rhymes in each poem.

Write the focus words on the board and read them to the children. Point out the past-tense endings in 'squished' and 'skimmed'.

Point to each of the focus words in the poems and read the line or verse in which the focus word appears.

Give an explanation of the word using words that are familiar to the children or use the explanation in the table, above. Ask children to repeat the word.

Give the children example sentences for each focus word, again using those in the table, above, if necessary.

Encourage them to think of the word meanings in the context of their own lives by asking them questions from the 'Tell me' column. You could support them by giving some example answers of your own first.

Ask children to read the focus words with you again.

Heads together

Ask the following questions to explore and develop the children's understanding of the focus words:

- Do you think you could squish a rock? Why?
- Could someone have skimmed a pond without getting wet? Why?
- Would I be able to fit a miniature elephant in my pocket? Why?

Wrap up

Ask the following questions to review the word meanings:

- If I say I squished something, would it now be flat or fat?
- Do you think a dolphin could have skimmed across the sea?
- If I had a miniature house, would it be big enough to put dolls in or not?

Ask children to think of a sentence each day that contains one of the words. They could be displayed and read by the class every day.

Follow-up independent sessions

You will need

- Poster paper, coloured pencils or pens
- Resource sheet: Book talk for *Homes Sweet Homes*

Ask children to draw an animal in its own habitat (home). They should think of words that they might include in a poem about the animal and its home.

Encourage them to find rhyming pairs of words if they can. Ask them to write them around their picture. The children could use their work towards writing an illustrated poem of their own.

Give pairs of children Resource sheet: Book talk for *Homes Sweet Homes*. Ask them to read through the poems aloud again and decide which is their favourite. Ask them to give a 1 to 5 score for the main ideas, words and layout.

From Tree to Book

Book Band: Turquoise

This information book shows how books are made, from turning trees into paper, through the printing process and on to the warehouse where the books are stored.

Skills focus

- Draw on knowledge of vocabulary to understand texts
- Identify/explain key aspects of fiction and non-fiction texts, e.g. character, events, title
- Identify/explain the sequence of events in texts
- Read words accurately and fluently

Guided reading session

You will need

- Multiple copies of Collins Big Cat *From Tree to Book*

Tune in

Tell the children that they are going to introduce the book themselves. Ask them to read the title, the blurb and the title page on their own and so that they learn enough to be able to talk about what the book is about. Give them a minute to do the task and then read the title aloud.

Ask the following questions:

- What kind of book is this? *(information)*
- How do you know? *(photographs, title, about real things)*
- What is it about? *(how a book is made)*

Turn to pages 22 and 23. Explain that you are going to read about the whole journey from tree to book first. Read aloud, encouraging the children to follow and join in. Check the children's understanding of key words: 'felled', 'printer' and 'warehouse'.

Heads together

Tell the children that they are going to read the book on their own.

Ask: What strategies can you use to help you if you get stuck on a word? *(read the first sound and then think about what the word might be; leave the word and come back to it when you have read the rest of the sentence; look out for words you already know)*

Tell the children that when they read, you want them to think about their reading strategies and to read smoothly, that is, looking ahead to the next word and being ready to read it so that you read smoothly.

Ask children to read pages 2 to 20 on their own. As they read, move around the group, listening to each child while the others read in their heads. Check their reading strategies and listen for reading fluency as they read.

Wrap up

Return to the book, praising children for using their reading strategies and for reading fluently. You may want to ask children to demonstrate how they read a line fluently.

Ask the following questions:

- In the book, there are three 'did you know?' boxes. Can you find one and tell me why the author has put these in? *(to make it more interesting, to make the information stand out, to encourage the reader to read more)*
- Why are some of the words in the book written in bold font? *(glossary words)*
- Can you find the glossary?
- The chapters in the book are written in a special order. Why? *(to organise the information, it tells us about the journey from tree to book)*

Vocabulary boost session

You will need

- Multiple copies of Collins Big Cat *From Tree to Book*

Vocabulary table

Focus word	Child-friendly explanation	Example sentence	Tell me...
factory	A factory is a very big building with machines where they make things like sweets or paper.	A lorry carried the boxes of pens from the **factory** to the shop.	Tell me what you think might be made in a factory.
machine	A machine uses electricity or an engine to do or make things. A washing machine washes clothes.	I used a sewing **machine** to mend the zip on my trousers.	Tell me what machines you might see at home or at school.
warehouse	A warehouse is a very large building for storing or looking after things.	The tins of baked beans were stored in the **warehouse** before they were taken to the supermarket.	Tell me what things you think might be stored in a warehouse.

Tune in

Explain to the children that in this lesson they are going to look closely at some of the words the author has used and what those words mean.

Read the book aloud to the children, asking them to follow and join in as you read.

Refer back to each of the focus words within the context of the story, writing up the word, giving a child-friendly explanation and asking children to say the focus word with you. For example: The book tells us that wood is taken to a factory. A factory is a very big building with machines where they make things like sweets and paper. Now, say the word with me – 'factory'.

You may wish to use the examples in the table, above.

Refer to each of the focus words that you have written up and give the children the example sentences. Then ask them to interact with the word meanings by asking the questions in the 'Tell me' column. You may wish to demonstrate by giving some examples of your own.

Ask children to say the words with you once more.

Heads together

Explore and develop the children's understanding of the focus words by playing the 'yes/no' game.

Tell the group that you have some sentences that make sense and some that don't make sense. They must decide – if it makes sense, say 'yes'; if it doesn't make sense, say 'no'.

- The factory made the sea. *(no)*
- I use a machine to help me wash the plates. *(yes)*
- The warehouse was smaller than my classroom. *(no)*
- We watched the biscuits being made at the factory. *(yes)*
- We got in the machine to have our bath. *(no)*
- The new school chairs were stored in a warehouse. *(yes)*

Encourage the children to make links to their own lives and experiences to help them.

Wrap up

Review the word meanings by doing the following activity. Turn to page 4.

Ask: It says that the wood is taken to a factory. Can you tell me what a factory is?

Turn to page 5.

Ask: It says that the wood is put into a machine. Can you tell me what a machine is?

Turn to page 18.

Ask: It says that a warehouse can store millions of books. Can you tell me what a warehouse is?

Challenge children to use the words as often as they can, both at school and at home.

Follow-up independent sessions

You will need

- Multiple copies of Collins Big Cat *From Tree to Book*
- Resource sheet: Questions for *From Tree to Book*

Ask children to work with their Reading Partners and to read the book aloud. Encourage them to practise reading smoothly by reading ahead and getting ready for the next word.

Give children Resource sheet: Questions for *From Tree to Book*. Say that they are going to be the teacher! They should make up some questions to ask their partner about the book.

Landmarks of the World

Book Band: Turquoise

This information book looks at man-made landmarks all over the world and explores what makes them so special.

Skills focus

- Draw on knowledge of vocabulary to understand texts
- Identify/explain key aspects of fiction and non-fiction texts, e.g. character, events, title
- Make inferences from texts
- Read words accurately and fluently

Guided reading session

You will need

- Multiple copies of Collins Big Cat *Landmarks of the World*
- Globe or world map

Tune in

Introduce the book by asking children to look closely at the front cover and then read the title together.

Ask: Do you know what a landmark is?

Discuss the children's ideas. Explain that the book is about landmarks of the world.

Ask: Where do you think it means when it says the 'world'?

Turn to the back cover and read the blurb aloud; encourage the children to follow and join in with you.

Ask the following questions:

- What kind of book is this? *(information)*
- How do you know? *(title, photographs, about real things)*

Heads together

Turn to the title page. Before you read it, explain to the children that each chapter in the book is about a part of the world. Those parts have names.

Ask: What type of letter do we always use at the beginning of a name? *(capital letter)*

Locate the places on the globe or map.

Read the contents aloud; encourage the children to follow and join in with you. Model the use of reading strategies to read long or difficult words.

Explain that the children are going to read most of this book together. The children are going to choose which chapters to read. Ask them to look at the contents page and choose a chapter.

Read it aloud to the children, asking them to follow as you read and join in. Model strategies for reading long or difficult words. When you have read it, ask an open-ended question, such as:

- Do you think people like the landmark? Why?
- Why do you think this landmark is so famous?

Wrap up

Go through the same process for more chapters, reading with the children joining in, modelling reading strategies and asking open-ended questions.

Vocabulary boost session

You will need

- Multiple copies of Collins Big Cat *Landmarks of the World*

Vocabulary table

Focus word	Child-friendly explanation	Example sentence	Tell me...
visit	If you visit somewhere, you go to it and spend time there. If you visit someone, you go to see them and spend time with them.	Yesterday we **visited** the zoo.	Tell me about a place you have visited.
guard	If you guard something, you stand near to it to watch it and keep it safe.	Soldiers **guard** Buckingham Palace.	Tell me about something that needs guarding.
reach	If you can reach something, you can touch it by stretching out your arm or leg.	"I can't **reach** the biscuits," Hassan moaned.	Tell me what things you have to reach for.

Tune in

Explain to the children that in this lesson they are going to look closely at some of the words the author has used and what those words mean.

Read the book aloud to the children, asking them to follow and join in as you read.

Refer back to each of the focus words within the context of the story, writing up the word, giving a child-friendly explanation and asking children to say the focus word with you. For example: In the book, it says 'let's visit some of' the landmarks. If you visit somewhere, you go to it and spend time there. Now, say the word with me – 'visit'.

You may wish to use the examples in the table, above.

Refer to each of the focus words that you have written up and give the children the example sentences. Then ask them to interact with the word meanings by asking the questions in the 'Tell me' column. You may wish to demonstrate by giving some examples of your own.

Ask children to say the words with you once more.

Heads together

Explore and develop the children's understanding of the focus words by doing the following activity. Tell the group that you're going to play 'Have you ever...?' You will ask a question and then each person in the group has to answer with 'Yes, I have...' and then say a bit more about it. For example: Have you ever visited someone? Yes, I have visited my grandma. We went to her house and she had made a cake.

Encourage the children to make links to their own lives and experiences to help them and to make up their answers too.

Ask the following questions:

- Have you ever visited someone?
- Have you ever visited a place?
- Have you ever guarded something?
- Have you ever reached for something?

Wrap up

Ask the following questions to review the word meanings:

- What's the word that means to stand near to something to watch it and keep it safe?
- What's the word that means to go to somewhere or someone and spend time there or with them?
- What's the word that means to touch it by stretching out your arm or leg?

Challenge the children to use the words as often as they can, both at school and at home.

Follow-up independent sessions

You will need

- Multiple copies of Collins Big Cat *Landmarks of the World*
- Resource sheet: Landmark advert
- Resource sheet: Glossary words for *Landmarks of the World*

Ask children to work with their Reading Partners and to read the book aloud. Encourage them to choose chapters that they are interested in or those that they have not read yet.

Give children Resource sheet: Landmark advert. Ask them to use the book to help them to write an advert for a famous landmark.

Give the children Resource sheet: Glossary words for *Landmarks of the World*. They find the word in the book and write what page it is on.

Child's name: _____ Date: _____ Assessed by: _____

Guided Reading Assessment Record Sheet   Year 1

'Working at the Expected Standard'

Assessment criteria	Date evidenced			Notes
Listen to and discuss a wide range of poems, stories and non-fiction at a level beyond which they can read independently				
Link what they read or hear to their own experiences				
Retell stories, considering their particular characteristics				
Recognise and join in with predictable phrases				
Appreciate and recite rhymes and poems				
Discuss word meanings, linking new meanings to those already known				
Understand books by drawing on what they already know/on background information and vocabulary provided by the teacher				
Check that text makes sense and correct inaccurate reading				
Discuss the significance of the title and events				
Make inferences on the basis of what is being said and done				
Predict what might happen on the basis of what has been read so far				
Participate in discussion about what is read to them, taking turns and listening to what others say				
Explain clearly their understanding of what is read to them				

Child's name: _____ Date: _____ Assessed by: _____

Top Dinosaurs

Book Band: Blue

Text type: Non-fiction – An information book

Does the child...						
Draw on information from the illustrations	Use letter sounds and blend to word build	Use knowledge of high frequency words	Break down large words into syllables	Listen to what they are reading to hear if it makes sense, self-correcting if necessary	Go back and reread to self-correct (a word or sentence)	Read to the end of a sentence to solve a new or unknown word

Questions (Literal/Inferential)

1. (L) Explain what a contents page is.

2. (L) Page 5 reads 'These dinosaurs were very scary.' What does the word 'scary' mean?

   funny   frightening

3. (L) Do you think the Tyrannosaurus rex was friendly?

4. (L) Which two words describe the Brachiosaurus?

   tall and heavy   kind and tiny

5. (L) Name the dinosaur that had a very small brain.

Child's name: _____ Date: _____ Assessed by: _____

Percy and the Badger

Book Band: Blue

Text type: Fiction – A story with a familiar setting

Does the child...						
Draw on information from the illustrations	Use letter sounds and blend to word build	Use knowledge of high frequency words	Break down large words into syllables	Listen to what they are reading to hear if it makes sense, self-correcting if necessary	Go back and reread to self-correct (a word or sentence)	Read to the end of a sentence to solve a new or unknown word

Questions (Literal/Inferential)

1. Ⓛ Where is the story set?

    the beach   the park

2. Ⓛ For question 2, use the cards cut from **Assessment Resource sheet 1**. Ask the children to put the pictures in the order they happen in the story.

3. Ⓛ Which word does the author use to describe the sound of the badger falling in the water? (page 10)

    Bang!   Splash!

4. Ⓛ Look at page 12. What does Percy think of the badger falling in the bath?

    He thinks it is funny.   He is very cross.

5. Ⓘ Do you think the badger will stay clean now?

Child's name: _____ Date: _____ Assessed by: _____

What's Underground?

Book Band: Blue

Text type: Non-fiction – A non-chronological report

Does the child...						
Draw on information from the illustrations	Use letter sounds and blend to word build	Use knowledge of high frequency words	Break down large words into syllables	Listen to what they are reading to hear if it makes sense, self-correcting if necessary	Go back and reread to self-correct (a word or sentence)	Read to the end of a sentence to solve a new or unknown word

Questions (Literal/Inferential)

1. (L) Look at the contents page. On which page can you find out about plants?

2. (L) Look at page 6. What do the wires carry to our homes?

3. (I) Look at page 13. How do you think the people feel when they find treasure?

4. (I) Look at page 13. What else do you think the people might dig up or find?

5. (L) What word means the same as 'amazing'?

    difficult   dark   brilliant

Child's name: _____   Date: _____   Assessed by: _____

Harry's Garden

Book Band: Blue

Text type: Non-fiction – An instruction text

Does the child...						
Draw on information from the illustrations	Use letter sounds and blend to word build	Use knowledge of high frequency words	Break down large words into syllables	Listen to what they are reading to hear if it makes sense, self-correcting if necessary	Go back and reread to self-correct (a word or sentence)	Read to the end of a sentence to solve a new or unknown word

Questions (Literal/Inferential)

1. (L) If you are gentle, are you:

careful?   rough?   firm?

2. (L) Which of these is an instruction?

I used an old wheelbarrow.   Put some little stones in the bottom.   Where do you want to put the plants?

3. (L) Name two things you need to make your own garden.

4. (L) What order do you put these things in the wheelbarrow?

bark chipping

little stones

plants

soil

5. (L) What do you think will happen to Harry's plants if he does not water them?

Child's name: _____ Date: _____ Assessed by: _____

Going to the Zoo

Book Band: Blue

Text type: Fiction – A poem

Does the child...						
Draw on information from the illustrations	Use letter sounds and blend to word build	Use knowledge of high frequency words	Break down large words into syllables	Listen to what they are reading to hear if it makes sense, self-correcting if necessary	Go back and reread to self-correct (a word or sentence)	Read to the end of a sentence to solve a new or unknown word

Questions (Literal/Inferential)

1. (L) Match the animals with what they are doing at the zoo.

   parrots   munching crunchy crisps

   chimpanzees   eating carrots

   penguins   eating peas

   tigers   skiing on the water

2. (I) Would you like to go to the zoo in the story? Why or why not?

3. (L) Number these animals in the order that the boy sees them at the zoo.

      giraffes

      parrots

      kangaroos

      lions

      bears

4. (L) Bears like to hide in their lairs. Which word do you think has a similar meaning to 'lairs'?

   cages   hiding places   beds

5. (I) Do you think the family will want to go to the zoo again? Explain your answer.

Child's name: _____ Date: _____ Assessed by: _____

Animals in Hiding

Book Band: Blue

Text type: Non-fiction – An information book

Does the child...						
Draw on information from the illustrations	Use letter sounds and blend to word build	Use knowledge of high frequency words	Break down large words into syllables	Listen to what they are reading to hear if it makes sense, self-correcting if necessary	Go back and reread to self-correct (a word or sentence)	Read to the end of a sentence to solve a new or unknown word

Questions (Literal/Inferential)

1. Ⓛ Finish this sentence: Animals use _ to hide.

2. Ⓛ What is the name of the list that tells us what is in the book?

3. Ⓛ Number these headings in the order that they come in the book.

> What is camouflage?
>
> Colour change!
>
> Camouflage in the sea
>
> Camouflage in grass

4. Ⓘ In the book, some animals use camouflage to hunt and some use it to hide. Which do you think is better, to use it to hunt or use it to hide?

5. Ⓛ What is the best camouflage of all?

Child's name: _____ Date: _____ Assessed by: _____

Fishy Friend

Book Band: Blue

Text type: Fiction – A poem

Does the child...						
Draw on information from the illustrations	Use letter sounds and blend to word build	Use knowledge of high frequency words	Break down large words into syllables	Listen to what they are reading to hear if it makes sense, self-correcting if necessary	Go back and reread to self-correct (a word or sentence)	Read to the end of a sentence to solve a new or unknown word

Questions (Literal/Inferential)

1. (L) What does the word 'mate' mean?

2. (L) Name a word from the book that rhymes with 'beans'.

3. (L) How do we know that this text is a poem?

   There are pictures   It is about a crab.   Some words rhyme.
   and words.

4. (L) Which came first?

   Dad dug a moat.

   Sam fetched water.

   Mum built a sandcastle.

   A crab pinched Sam's toe.

5. (L) Was Harry pleased to find the crab in his bag?

Child's name: _____ Date: _____ Assessed by: _____

Mojo and Weeza and the New Hat

Book Band: Blue

Text type: Fiction – A fantasy story

Does the child...						
Draw on information from the illustrations	Use letter sounds and blend to word build	Use knowledge of high frequency words	Break down large words into syllables	Listen to what they are reading to hear if it makes sense, self-correcting if necessary	Go back and reread to self-correct (a word or sentence)	Read to the end of a sentence to solve a new or unknown word

Questions (Literal/Inferential)

1. (L) Who are the characters in the story?

2. (L) Why did Mojo and Weeza look very smart when the story starts?

3. (L) At the end of the story, where did they find Weeza's hat?

4. (I) Do you think Weeza was sad about losing his hat?

5. (I) What do you think happened when Mojo and Weeza went home?

Child's name: _____ Date: _____ Assessed by: _____

The Magic Pen

Book Band: Green

Text type: Fiction – A fantasy story

Does the child...						
Draw on information from the illustrations	Use letter sounds and blend to word build	Use knowledge of high frequency words	Break down large words into syllables	Listen to what they are reading to hear if it makes sense, self-correcting if necessary	Go back and reread to self-correct (a word or sentence)	Read to the end of a sentence to solve a new or unknown word

Questions (Literal/Inferential)

1. Ⓛ Who is the main character in *The Magic Pen*?

The mouse   Mr Big   The shopkeeper

2. Ⓛ 'His house was big, his car was big and his cat was big.' Which word could you use instead of 'big' without changing the meaning?

small   large   grumpy

3. Ⓛ Why did Mr Big make his own ink for the big pen?

The man in the shop forgot the ink.   He wanted blue ink.   He thought it would be fun.

4. Ⓘ How do you think Mr Big felt when he opened the door and saw Mrs Big?

5. Ⓘ What do you think Mr Big might write next with the magic pen and why?

Child's name: _____ Date: _____ Assessed by: _____

Worm Looks for Lunch

Book Band: Green

Text type: Fiction – A playscript

Does the child...						
Draw on information from the illustrations	Use letter sounds and blend to word build	Use knowledge of high frequency words	Break down large words into syllables	Listen to what they are reading to hear if it makes sense, self-correcting if necessary	Go back and reread to self-correct (a word or sentence)	Read to the end of a sentence to solve a new or unknown word

Questions (Literal/Inferential)

1. (L) Worm says "I think I'll try some grass." What is 'I'll' short for?

2. (L) Why didn't Worm like grass?

3. (L) Why was Worm very scared when he met Bird?

4. (L) Number the creatures that Worm met in the same order as in the story.

    Rabbit

    Bird

    Deer

    Beetle

5. (L) What does Worm like eating at the end of the story?

Child's name: _____   Date: _____   Assessed by: _____

A Day at the Eden Project

Book Band: Green

Text type: Non-fiction – A recount of a visit

Does the child...						
Draw on information from the illustrations	Use letter sounds and blend to word build	Use knowledge of high frequency words	Break down large words into syllables	Listen to what they are reading to hear if it makes sense, self-correcting if necessary	Go back and reread to self-correct (a word or sentence)	Read to the end of a sentence to solve a new or unknown word

Questions (Literal/Inferential)

1. Ⓛ Use the contents page to find out which page is about 'oranges and lemons'.

2. Ⓛ What were the giant greenhouses called?

3. Ⓛ In which biome did the girls see bananas growing?

   the Mediterranean Biome   the Tropical Biome

4. Ⓛ Did the girls enjoy their visit to the Eden Project?

5. Ⓘ Do you think the girls will go back to the Eden Project?

Child's name: _____ Date: _____ Assessed by: _____

Nick Butterworth: Making Books

Book Band: Green

Text type: Non-fiction – A recount

Does the child...						
Draw on information from the illustrations	Use letter sounds and blend to word build	Use knowledge of high frequency words	Break down large words into syllables	Listen to what they are reading to hear if it makes sense, self-correcting if necessary	Go back and reread to self-correct (a word or sentence)	Read to the end of a sentence to solve a new or unknown word

Questions (Literal/Inferential)

1. Ⓛ Finish this sentence: Nick Butterworth is an author and _____.

2. Ⓛ What type of book is this – a story or an information book?

3. Ⓛ Number these in the order that they come in the book.

      about Percy the Park Keeper

      about Nick working at home

      about Nick's wife and children

      about Nick drawing animals

4. Ⓘ Where do you think Nick gets ideas for his stories from?

5. Ⓘ Do you think Nick likes working with children?

Child's name: _____ Date: _____ Assessed by: _____

Ella the Superstar

Book Band: Green

Text type: Fiction – A story with a familiar setting

Does the child...						
Draw on information from the illustrations	Use letter sounds and blend to word build	Use knowledge of high frequency words	Break down large words into syllables	Listen to what they are reading to hear if it makes sense, self-correcting if necessary	Go back and reread to self-correct (a word or sentence)	Read to the end of a sentence to solve a new or unknown word

Questions (Literal/Inferential)

1. Ⓛ In the sentence 'A policeman marched over' which word could you use to replace 'marched' without changing the meaning?

   walked   leaped   fell

2. Ⓛ How did Ella get rich?

3. Ⓛ How many people did Ella scare in the park?

4. Ⓘ How do you think the policeman will feel when he sees the newspaper on page 22?

5. Ⓘ What do you think Ella will do next?

Child's name: _____ Date: _____ Assessed by: _____

Scary Hair

Book Band: Green

Text type: Fiction – A simple story

Does the child...						
Draw on information from the illustrations	Use letter sounds and blend to word build	Use knowledge of high frequency words	Break down large words into syllables	Listen to what they are reading to hear if it makes sense, self-correcting if necessary	Go back and reread to self-correct (a word or sentence)	Read to the end of a sentence to solve a new or unknown word

Questions (Literal/Inferential)

1. (L) Who is the main character in the story?

2. (L) Finish this sentence: Rex didn't want to eat animals. He wanted to give them _____ _____.

3. (L) How did Rex help Pong?

4. (I) How do you think Rex's dad felt at the end of the story?

5. (I) What do you think happened next to Rex?

Child's name: _____ Date: _____ Assessed by: _____

I've Just Had a Bright Idea!

Book Band: Green

Text type: Non-fiction – An information book

Does the child...						
Draw on information from the illustrations	Use letter sounds and blend to word build	Use knowledge of high frequency words	Break down large words into syllables	Listen to what they are reading to hear if it makes sense, self-correcting if necessary	Go back and reread to self-correct (a word or sentence)	Read to the end of a sentence to solve a new or unknown word

Questions (Literal/Inferential)

1. (L) Look at page 3 and find this sentence: 'Sometimes inventors see something strange, which gives them an idea.' What do you think the word 'strange' means in this sentence?

    funny   plants   unusual

2. (L) Zips were invented before bicycles. True or false?

3. (L) Look at page 10. Tick two ways that are shown to keep your jacket closed.

    toggles   glue   Velcro   buttons

4. (I) Look at pages 14 and 15. Why do you think people thought refrigerators were a bright idea when they were invented in 1834?

5. (I) Look at pages 16 and 17. Why do you think the heading 'A moving idea' has been used?

Child's name: _____   Date: _____   Assessed by: _____

Seahorses

Book Band: Green

Text type: Non-fiction – An information book

Does the child...						
Draw on information from the illustrations	Use letter sounds and blend to word build	Use knowledge of high frequency words	Break down large words into syllables	Listen to what they are reading to hear if it makes sense, self-correcting if necessary	Go back and reread to self-correct (a word or sentence)	Read to the end of a sentence to solve a new or unknown word

Questions (Literal/Inferential)

1. (L) Male seahorses have a pouch. Which word is similar to 'pouch'?

   balloon   pocket   nest

2. (L) What does the male seahorse have that no other male animal has?

3. (L) What do seahorses spend most of the day doing?

4. (L) Order these stages in the life cycle of a seahorse.

   The male pushes the babies out.

   The adult seahorses find a mate.

   The female puts her eggs in the male's pouch.

   The seahorses join tails.

5. (L) Are seahorses bigger than some shrimps?

Child's name: _____ Date: _____ Assessed by: _____

Arthur's Fantastic Party

Book Band: Orange

Text type: Fiction – A humorous story

Does the child...						
Draw on information from the illustrations	Use letter sounds and blend to word build	Use knowledge of high frequency words	Break down large words into syllables	Listen to what they are reading to hear if it makes sense, self-correcting if necessary	Go back and reread to self-correct (a word or sentence)	Read to the end of a sentence to solve a new or unknown word

Questions (Literal/Inferential)

1. (L) What kind of party did Arthur want?

2. (L) What did the pigs say they loved that made them fantastic?

3. (L) Finish this sentence

    Flora told the three pigs, who told the _____, who

    told the _____.

4. (I) What other games do you think that they played at Arthur's party?

5. (I) At the end of the story, how do you think Arthur felt?

Child's name: _____ Date: _____ Assessed by: _____

How to Make Pop-up Cards

Book Band: Orange

Text type: Non-fiction – An information text

Does the child...						
Draw on information from the illustrations	Use letter sounds and blend to word build	Use knowledge of high frequency words	Break down large words into syllables	Listen to what they are reading to hear if it makes sense, self-correcting if necessary	Go back and reread to self-correct (a word or sentence)	Read to the end of a sentence to solve a new or unknown word

Questions (Literal/Inferential)

1. Ⓛ Put the events in order.

    making the spring

    making the frame

    finishing the card

2. Ⓛ Name two things that you will need to make a pop-up card.

3. Ⓛ On page 7, the instruction is 'Use felt pens to write a greeting'. What is a greeting?

    a story   a short message   a number

4. Ⓛ Explain what the pebble is for.

5. Ⓛ What will happen when someone opens the pop-up card?

Child's name: _____ Date: _____ Assessed by: _____

Fire! Fire!

Book Band: Orange

Text type: Non-fiction – An information book

Does the child...						
Draw on information from the illustrations	Use letter sounds and blend to word build	Use knowledge of high frequency words	Break down large words into syllables	Listen to what they are reading to hear if it makes sense, self-correcting if necessary	Go back and reread to self-correct (a word or sentence)	Read to the end of a sentence to solve a new or unknown word

Questions (Literal/Inferential)

1. Ⓛ Find and copy the words that fit into this sentence:

    Fire keeps us _____ and gives us _____.

2. Ⓛ What is the word that means 'a list of what is in the book'?

3. Ⓛ Number these in the order that they come in the book:

    Introduction

    Forest fires

    Glossary

    People who fight fires

4. Ⓛ Find and copy the words that mean small boats that are ridden like motorbikes:

    _____   _____

5. Ⓛ Giant airships, robots and fast fire-cars aren't used to put out fires because…

    they aren't   they won't work   they haven't been   they don't
    good enough   invented yet   need them

Child's name: _____   Date: _____   Assessed by: _____

A Letter to New Zealand

Book Band: Orange

Text type: Non-fiction – A recount/explanation text

Does the child...						
Draw on information from the illustrations	Use letter sounds and blend to word build	Use knowledge of high frequency words	Break down large words into syllables	Listen to what they are reading to hear if it makes sense, self-correcting if necessary	Go back and reread to self-correct (a word or sentence)	Read to the end of a sentence to solve a new or unknown word

Questions (Literal/Inferential)

1. (L) Who is sending a letter?

2. (L) How does Tama know the letter is from Jack before he opens it?

3. (L) Which word means the same as 'puts'?

   organises   pops   turns

4. (L) Did the letter take more than a day to get there?

5. (L) Put these sentences in order to show the order of the letter's journey.

   The post goes onto the planes.

   Airmail letters are put into bags

   The letter goes to a sorting office near Tama's home.

   Jack posts the letter.

Child's name: _____ Date: _____ Assessed by: _____

First Day

Book Band: Orange

Text type: Fiction – A humorous story with a familiar setting

Does the child...						
Draw on information from the illustrations	Use letter sounds and blend to word build	Use knowledge of high frequency words	Break down large words into syllables	Listen to what they are reading to hear if it makes sense, self-correcting if necessary	Go back and reread to self-correct (a word or sentence)	Read to the end of a sentence to solve a new or unknown word

Questions (Literal/Inferential)

1. (L) Who is the main character in this story?

2. (L) What does the word 'nervous' mean?

3. (L) What did the cook do wrong on his first day?

4. (I) Describe how Flynn is feeling on page 21 and why.

5. (I) Do you think Flynn will enjoy his first day at school?

Child's name: _____ Date: _____ Assessed by: _____

What is CGI?

Book Band: Orange

Text type: Non-fiction – An information book

Does the child...						
Draw on information from the illustrations	Use letter sounds and blend to word build	Use knowledge of high frequency words	Break down large words into syllables	Listen to what they are reading to hear if it makes sense, self-correcting if necessary	Go back and reread to self-correct (a word or sentence)	Read to the end of a sentence to solve a new or unknown word

Questions (Literal/Inferential)

1. (L) What does CGI stand for?

2. (L) Using the contents page, tell me what I will find out about on page 8.

3. (L) Does Jon prefer creating images on:

   the computer?   with pencil and paper?

4. (L) Put the events in order.

   Add a background.

   Start with a block of cubes.

   Add texture.

5. (I) Look at the picture on pages 16 and 17. What do you think might happen next with the shark and diver?

Child's name: _____   Date: _____   Assessed by: _____

Clementine's Smile

Book Band: Orange

Text type: Fiction – A poem

Does the child...						
Draw on information from the illustrations	Use letter sounds and blend to word build	Use knowledge of high frequency words	Break down large words into syllables	Listen to what they are reading to hear if it makes sense, self-correcting if necessary	Go back and reread to self-correct (a word or sentence)	Read to the end of a sentence to solve a new or unknown word

Questions (Literal/Inferential)

1. (L) Find this sentence on page 3: 'It's like a party every day.'

   What do you think this sentence means?

   They get presents every day.   They have fun every day.   They have lots to eat every day.

2. (L) Where does Clementine have a pain?

   in her nose   in her back   in her tooth   in her toes

3. (I) Why do you think Clementine hid when her mum was taking her to the dentist?

4. (L) Put the events in order.

   Mum phones the dentist.

   Clementine happily cleans her teeth.

   Clementine has a pain in her tooth.

   Mum rescues the dentist from Clementine's jaws.

   Clementine sits in the dentist's chair.

5. (I) At the end of the story it says that Clementine has a smile that fills the room. What do you think this means?

Child's name: _____ Date: _____ Assessed by: _____

Turtle's Party in the Clouds

Book Band: Orange

Text type: Fiction – A traditional tale

Does the child...						
Draw on information from the illustrations	Use letter sounds and blend to word build	Use knowledge of high frequency words	Break down large words into syllables	Listen to what they are reading to hear if it makes sense, self-correcting if necessary	Go back and reread to self-correct (a word or sentence)	Read to the end of a sentence to solve a new or unknown word

Questions (Literal/Inferential)

1. (L) What did Turtle want to do?

2. (L) How did Turtle get to the party?

3. (L) In the story Turtle sobbed. Which word means the same as 'sobbed'?

   sighed   bounced   cried

4. (I) Do you think the forest animals were kind to Turtle at the end?

5. (L) Number the sentences below to show the order they happen in the story.

   Turtle's shell smashed.

   The animals stuck the pieces together.

   Turtle got into the guitar.

   Turtle fell out of the guitar.

Child's name: _____ Date: _____ Assessed by: _____

The Bogeyman

Book Band: Turquoise

Text type: Fiction – A story with a familiar setting

Does the child...						
Draw on information from the illustrations	Use letter sounds and blend to word build	Use knowledge of high frequency words	Break down large words into syllables	Listen to what they are reading to hear if it makes sense, self-correcting if necessary	Go back and reread to self-correct (a word or sentence)	Read to the end of a sentence to solve a new or unknown word

Questions (Literal/Inferential)

1. (L) Who is the main character in this story?

2. (L) Why is Harry afraid to step on the cracks in the pavement?

3. (L) Explain why Harry leapt into his seat on page 7?

4. (L) Name two other words that mean afraid.

5. (I) Do you think Harry will stand on the cracks in the pavement now?

Child's name: _____ Date: _____ Assessed by: _____

Castles

Book Band: Turquoise

Text type: Non-fiction – A report and explanation text

Does the child...						
Draw on information from the illustrations	Use letter sounds and blend to word build	Use knowledge of high frequency words	Break down large words into syllables	Listen to what they are reading to hear if it makes sense, self-correcting if necessary	Go back and reread to self-correct (a word or sentence)	Read to the end of a sentence to solve a new or unknown word

Questions (Literal/Inferential)

1. (L) Look at page 16. What was a 'garderobe'?

2. (L) Look at page 16. Which two non-fiction features can you see?

   photograph   heading   labels   bullet points

3. (L) Look at page 18. When was the great hall used for feasts?

   during attack   during peaceful times

4. (I) What do you think it would have been like to use the garderobe?

   comfortable   cold and smelly

5. (I) Do you think castles will continue to be used?

Child's name: _____ Date: _____ Assessed by: _____

A Visit to the Farm

Book Band: Turquoise

Text type: Non-fiction – A recount of a visit

Does the child...						
Draw on information from the illustrations	Use letter sounds and blend to word build	Use knowledge of high frequency words	Break down large words into syllables	Listen to what they are reading to hear if it makes sense, self-correcting if necessary	Go back and reread to self-correct (a word or sentence)	Read to the end of a sentence to solve a new or unknown word

Questions (Literal/Inferential)

1. (L) Who did Sam write his letter to?

2. (L) What was Sam's first task on the farm?

    painting a picture　　　　　　　mucking out　　　　　　　feeding the pigs

3. (L) Do you think Sam liked the sheep?

4. (L) Which three words does Sam use to describe the new-born lamb?

5. (I) Do you think Sam would like to go farming again?

A Visit to the Farm

Child's name: _____   Date: _____   Assessed by: _____

Going for a Drive

Book Band: Turquoise

Text type: Fiction – A poetry book

Does the child…						
Draw on information from the illustrations	Use letter sounds and blend to word build	Use knowledge of high frequency words	Break down large words into syllables	Listen to what they are reading to hear if it makes sense, self-correcting if necessary	Go back and reread to self-correct (a word or sentence)	Read to the end of a sentence to solve a new or unknown word

Questions (Literal/Inferential)

1. (L) In the poem 'Talking' on page 9, who is the narrator of the poem?

Mummy   a child   a friend

2. (L) In the poem 'Talking' on page 9, it says that when Mummy and her friend talk 'it drives me round the bend'.

What do you think this means?

It makes me run round the corner.   It makes me get in a car.   It makes me go crazy.

3. (L) In the poem 'Summer Haiku' on page 13, what do you think is being described in the last line?

4. (L) On which page is the poem 'Caterpillar'?

5. (L) Number these events from the poem 'Caterpillar' in the right order.

Caterpillar spins a cocoon.

Caterpillar eats a leaf.

The butterfly warms its wings.

The cocoon opens.

Caterpillar spends time in the cocoon.

A butterfly comes out of the cocoon.

Child's name: _____ Date: _____ Assessed by: _____

The Journey of Humpback Whales

Book Band: Turquoise

Text type: Non-fiction – An information book

Does the child...						
Draw on information from the illustrations	Use letter sounds and blend to word build	Use knowledge of high frequency words	Break down large words into syllables	Listen to what they are reading to hear if it makes sense, self-correcting if necessary	Go back and reread to self-correct (a word or sentence)	Read to the end of a sentence to solve a new or unknown word

Questions (Literal/Inferential)

1. (L) Why are humpback whales known as 'acrobats of the sea'?

2. (L) What does the bold font mean?

3. (L) What sort of picture is used to show the route of the journey?

4. (L) Number the stages in the life cycle, as followed in the book.

       They go back to Antarctica.

       The females mate.

       They go to Tonga.

       The calves are born.

5. (L) Is it true that a newborn humpback whale is bigger than an adult human?

Child's name: _____ Date: _____ Assessed by: _____

The Big, Bad City

Book Band: Turquoise

Text type: Fiction – A traditional tale

Does the child...						
Draw on information from the illustrations	Use letter sounds and blend to word build	Use knowledge of high frequency words	Break down large words into syllables	Listen to what they are reading to hear if it makes sense, self-correcting if necessary	Go back and reread to self-correct (a word or sentence)	Read to the end of a sentence to solve a new or unknown word

Questions (Literal/Inferential)

1. (L) In the story, what kind of stranger does it say asked Little Red Hen whether she needed help?

2. (L) Where is the setting for the story?

3. (L) Where did Little Red Hen and Mr Fox go after the park?

4. (I) What do you think Mr Fox thought when he heard someone singing in the tunnel?

5. (I) At the end of the story, when Little Red Hen gets to Granny, what do you think she tells Granny about her journey?

Child's name: _____ Date: _____ Assessed by: _____

Homes Sweet Homes

Book Band: Turquoise

Text type: Fiction – A poetry collection

Does the child...						
Draw on information from the illustrations	Use letter sounds and blend to word build	Use knowledge of high frequency words	Break down large words into syllables	Listen to what they are reading to hear if it makes sense, self-correcting if necessary	Go back and reread to self-correct (a word or sentence)	Read to the end of a sentence to solve a new or unknown word

Questions (Literal/Inferential)

1. (L) In 'Tree House', what is 'There's' short for?

2. (L) In 'Tree House', how many pairs of rhyming words are there?

3. (L) Which poems are 'shape poems'?

4. (L) Number the events in the same order as in 'The Pond'.

       skimmed the water

       caught a tadpole

       cupped their hands

       found the pond

5. (L) In 'Worm!' does the poet want to squish the worm?

Child's name: _____ Date: _____ Assessed by: _____

From Tree to Book

Book Band: Turquoise

Text type: Non-fiction – An information book

Does the child...						
Draw on information from the illustrations	Use letter sounds and blend to word build	Use knowledge of high frequency words	Break down large words into syllables	Listen to what they are reading to hear if it makes sense, self-correcting if necessary	Go back and reread to self-correct (a word or sentence)	Read to the end of a sentence to solve a new or unknown word

Questions (Literal/Inferential)

1. (L) Find and copy the words that fit into this sentence:

   Most _____ comes from trees grown in sustainable _____.

2. (L) Some of the words in the book are written in bold font. Explain why.

3. (L) Number these in the order that they come in the book:

   At the printer

   Contents

   Where do books come from?

   Glossary

4. (L) Find and copy the meaning of the word 'pulp'.

5. (L) The book started life as a tree. What other things that we read do you think started life as a tree?

Answers

Top Dinosaurs
Book Band: Blue

1. It lists the headings in the books and which page they are on.
2. frightening
3. no
4. tall and heavy
5. Stegosaurus

Percy and the Badger
Book Band: Blue

1. the park
2. b, c, d, a
3. Splash!
4. He thinks it is funny.
5. Yes or no. The children may be able to give a reason. For example: Yes, because he doesn't want another bath. No, because he lives underground and it is muddy.

What's Underground?
Book Band: Blue

1. page 9
2. electricity
3. For example: pleased/excited/happy
4. Accept any reasonable answers: bits of pottery, jewellery, bones and so on.
5. brilliant

Harry's Garden
Book Band: Blue

1. careful
2. Put some little stones in the bottom.
3. Any two from: wheelbarrow, spade, stones, soil, water/can, plants, gloves, trowel, bark chippings
4. little stones
   soil
   plants
   bark chippings
5. They will die

Going to the Zoo
Book Band: Blue

1. parrots/eating carrots; chimpanzees/eating peas; penguins/skiing on the water; tigers/munching crunchy crisps
2. Accept any answer that involves a reasonable response with reasons.
3. Number these animals in the order that the boy sees them at the zoo.
   giraffes 2
   parrots 1
   kangaroos 3
   lions 5
   bears 4
4. hiding places
5. Accept any reasonable answer.

Animals in Hiding
Book Band: Blue

1. camouflage
2. Contents
3. What is camouflage? 1
   Colour change! 4
   Camouflage in the sea 2
   Camouflage in grass 3
4. Accept any reasonable answer.
5. colour change

Fishy Friend
Book Band: Blue

1. friend
2. jeans
3. Some words rhyme.
4. Mum built a sandcastle.
5. Yes, because Sam shared his baked beans with the crab.

Mojo and Weeza and the New Hat
Book Band: Blue

1. Mojo and Weeza
2. Mojo had new shoes and Weeza had a new hat.
3. in the mud
4. Accept any reasonable answer.
5. Accept any reasonable prediction.

The Magic Pen
Book Band: Green

1. Mr Big
2. large
3. The man in the shop forgot the ink.
4. Accept any answer that implies he was happy or pleasantly surprised.
5. children's own ideas

Worm Looks for Lunch
Book Band: Green

1. I will
2. It was too chewy.
3. Worm was very scared when he met Bird because Bird says he likes eating worms.
4. Rabbit 1
   Bird 4
   Deer 2
   Beetle 3
5. He likes eating earth.

A Day at the Eden Project
Book Band: Green

1. page 14
2. Biomes
3. the Tropical Biome
4. Yes, they are smiling and having fun. They are interested in the biomes.
5. Yes I think they will visit again, because it says they can't wait to come back.

Nick Butterworth: Making Books
Book Band: Green

1. illustrator
2. information
3. about Percy the Park Keeper 2
   about Nick working at home 4
   about Nick's wife and children 1
   about Nick drawing animals 3
4. Accept any reasonable answer.
5. Accept any reasonable answer.

Ella the Superstar
Book Band: Green

1. walked
2. She had her own TV show, was in the newspapers and wrote a book.
3. Three – the lady, the policeman and the man walking his dog.
4. Accept any answer that suggests he would not be happy/not pleased including grumpy, cross, embarrassed, silly, and mad.
5. Accept any suggestions of special talents, for example, play football, cooking.

Scary Hair
Book Band: Green

1. Rex
2. dinosaur haircuts
3. He gave Pong a wash and dry; stopped him from smelling.
4. Accept any reasonable answer.
5. Accept any reasonable prediction.

I've Just Had a Bright Idea!
Book Band: Green

1. unusual
2. false
3. toggles and buttons
4. They were easier to use/more convenient than other ways of keeping food cold.
5. The pages are all about different ways of moving.

Seahorses
Book Band: Green

1. pocket

2. babies

3. eating

4. The adult seahorses find a mate.
   The seahorses join tails.
   The female puts her eggs in the male's pouch.
   The male pushes the babies out.

5. Yes, because seahorses eat thousands of shrimps every day.

Arthur's Fantastic Party
Book Band: Orange

1. fantastic

2. mud

3. Flora told the three pigs, who told the wolf, who told the bears.

4. Accept any reasonable answer.

5. Accept any reasonable answer.

How to Make Pop-up Cards
Book Band: Orange

1. making the frame, making the spring, finishing the card

2. Any two of the following: a pair of scissors, some thin card, a pencil, strips of coloured paper, a ruler, a large pebble, photographs or pictures, a glue stick, a stapler or some felt-tipped pens.

3. a short message

4. to hold the spring down while the glue dries

5. They will be surprised and/or the picture will pop out.

Fire! Fire!
Book Band: Orange

1. Fire keeps us warm and gives us light.

2. contents or index

3. Introduction 1
   Forest fires 3
   Glossary 4
   People who fight fires 2

4. jet skis

5. they haven't been invented yet

A Letter to New Zealand
Book Band: Orange

1. Jack

2. The airmail letter, stamp and postmark tells him it is from Jack.

3. pops

4. Yes, because just the plane journey takes about 24 hours.

5. Jack posts the letter.
   Airmail letters are put into bags.
   The post goes onto the planes.
   The letter goes to a sorting office near Tama's home.

First Day
Book Band: Orange

1. A schoolboy called Flynn.

2. Accept any answer that implies worried or anxious.

3. He put jam in the sausage rolls.

4. Accept any answer that implies he is shocked/ horrified because he is in his pyjamas.

5. Accept any reasonable answer (based on personal experiences of school or the book) and a reason.

What is CGI?
Book Band: Orange

1. computer-generated images

2. texture

3. the computer

4. Add a background. 3
   Start with a block of cubes. 1
   Add texture. 2

5. Accept any answer that is based on the picture, for example: the diver will swim away very fast; the shark will chase the diver; the shark might eat the diver!

Clementine's Smile
Book Band: Orange

1. They have fun every day.
2. in her tooth
3. She didn't want to go./She was afraid of the dentist.
4. Mum phones the dentist. 2
   Clementine happily cleans her teeth. 5
   Clementine has a pain in her tooth. 1
   Mum rescues the dentist from Clementine's jaws. 4
   Clementine sits in the dentist's chair. 3
5. She is very happy./She has a big smile.

Turtle's Party in the Clouds
Book Band: Orange

1. go to a party
2. Turtle climbed inside Vulture's guitar.
3. cried
4. They were kind because they dragged the pieces of Turtle's shell to him and stuck them together.
5. Turtle's shell smashed. 3
   The animals stuck the pieces together. 4
   Turtle got into the guitar. 1
   Turtle fell out of the guitar. 2

The Bogeyman
Book Band: Turquoise

1. A boy called Harry.
2. Because Carrie told him the Bogeyman comes to get you.
3. To avoid the cracks in the floor/so the Bogeyman didn't get him.
4. Accept any two words that mean afraid, for example: frightened, fear of, scared, worried, terrified, troubled.
5. Yes, because he knows the Bogeyman isn't real and there is nothing to be frightened of.

Castles
Book Band: Turquoise

1. toilet/lavatory
2. heading
   labels
3. during peaceful times
4. cold and smelly
5. Accept an answer with a reason, for example: Yes, people like to visit them./No, they are not needed anymore.

A Visit to the Farm
Book Band: Turquoise

1. His mum and dad.
2. feeding the pigs
3. Yes, he thinks they are funny.
4. slimy, steaming, beautiful
5. Yes, because he is really enjoying it.

Going for a Drive
Book Band: Turquoise

1. a child
2. It makes me go crazy.
3. The sun shining on the sea.
4. page 16
5. Caterpillar spins a cocoon. 2
   Caterpillar eats a leaf. 1
   The butterfly warms its wings. 6
   The cocoon opens. 4
   Caterpillar spends time in the cocoon. 3
   A butterfly comes out of the cocoon. 5

The Journey of Humpback Whales
Book Band: Turquoise

1. Because they leap like acrobats out of the sea.
2. You can find the meaning of the words in the glossary.
3. a map
4. They go back to Antarctica. 4
   The females mate. 1
   They go to Tonga. 2
   The calves are born. 3
5. Yes, it is 5 metres long and an adult human is under 2 metres.

The Big, Bad City
Book Band: Turquoise

1. smiley

2. city

3. crossed a bridge/motorway/tunnel

4. Accept any reasonable answer that suggests negativity, for example: Oh no, I thought we'd be alone./That's awful singing.

5. Accept any reasonable answer.

Homes Sweet Homes
Book Band: Turquoise

1. There is

2. Two (tree/three; tall/all)

3. 'Worm!'; 'The Baobab'; 'The Weather Tree'

4. skimmed the water 3
   caught a tadpole 4
   cupped their hands 2
   found the pond 1

5. No

From Tree to Book
Book Band: Turquoise

1. Most paper comes from trees grown in sustainable forests.

2. They are glossary words.

3. At the printer 3
   Contents 1
   Where do books come from? 2
   Glossary 4

4. a soft, wet material

5. For example: newspaper, comic, magazine, leaflet.